OCT   2009

WILLIE'S BOYS

WILLIE'S BOYS

The 1948 Birmingham Black Barons, the Last
Negro League World Series, and the
Making of a Baseball Legend

JOHN KLIMA

WILEY

John Wiley & Sons, Inc.

Copyright © 2009 by John Klima. All rights reserved

Published by John Wiley & Sons, Inc., Hoboken, New Jersey
Published simultaneously in Canada

Photo credits: pages 30, 32, 39, 44, 57, 60, 61, 69, 86, 92, 103, 114, 128, 182, 195, 223, 249, 255 from the T. H. Hayes Collection, Memphis and Shelby County Reading Room, Memphis Public Library and Information Center; page 49 from the Birmingham Public Library Archives; pages 97, 247, 257, 261, 276 from the author's collection; page 110 from the Bill Greason Collection.

For general information about our other products and services, please contact our Customer Care Department within the United States at (800) 762-2974, outside the United States at (317) 572-3993 or fax (317) 572-4002.

Wiley also publishes its books in a variety of electronic formats. Some content that appears in print may not be available in electronic books. For more information about Wiley products, visit our web site at www.wiley.com.

Library of Congress Cataloging-in-Publication Data:

Klima, John, date.
  Willie's boys: the 1948 Birmingham Black Barons, the last Negro League world series, and the making of a baseball legend / John Klima.
        p. cm.
  Includes index.
  ISBN 978-0-470-40013-5 (cloth)
1. Birmingham Black Barons (Baseball team)—History. 2. Negro Leagues—History.
3. Mays, Willie, 1931– 4. Baseball—Alabama—Birmingham—History. I. Title.
  GV875.B57K55 2009
  766.357'6409761781—dc22

                                                              2009006815

To Piper Davis, who earned this dedication because he was the kind of man who would have never asked for the recognition he deserves, and to Chris Fullerton, who might never again have wanted to play ball with the Yankees

I would pitch a lot of slow stuff to Mays, particularly when he is anxious to hit. The slow curve he "slobbers" all over the place. You might occasionally get the fastball by him but I would worry about it a bit. I would try to make him hit the breaking stuff and particularly the changes. This does not mean at all that he will never hit the changes. The fellow is simply too good a hitter.

—Branch Rickey's scouting report on Willie Mays, 1955

If given the chance, I feel certain with all my heart that I could make the grade. My comparatively short baseball career has been a successful one. My last year in high school, I led the league in strikeouts and was the league's only undefeated pitcher. Of course scouts weren't looking for colored players.

—Willie Green, written to
scout Charles "Pop" Kelchner, May 8, 1951

Willie Mays has just hit his five hundred and twenty-second home run. He has gone past me and he's pushing. And I say to him, "Go get 'em, Willie!"

—Ted Williams, 1969

Make the bones walk around.

—Bobby Veale, 2008

CONTENTS

ACKNOWLEDGMENTS

Though he may never read this, the first thank-you should go to the understanding Arkansas state trooper who decided not to give me a speeding ticket when he pulled me over on the race from Kansas City to Memphis. I owe a similar debt to the Alabama state troopers who stopped me when I got lost in the middle of the night amid the trees and the back roads outside Birmingham. When I explained that I was trying to retrace the road on which Charlie Rudd's Black Barons' bus once pulled Willie Mays and Piper Davis back home, the state troopers were more amused than threatened.

Writing a historical narrative like *Willie's Boys* was entirely about traveling new roads in terms of research; I gathered both narrative and historical perspectives. The men of the Negro Leagues remain largely lost to time, and it was my sincerest hope to illuminate their way of life, as well as their happiness, hopes, and dreams. Because no white kid from California could possibly do that alone, I had much help along the road, starting with Willie Mays.

Though Willie was completing his own memoir, he took a few moments over the phone to help me retrace some of those long-forgotten bus rides in the 1948 Negro American League when he was only seventeen. Most of the details he provided were small but helpful; in reconstructing this lost world, no pottery shard was meaningless. Mays offered a high compliment that I shall not soon forget. "You know more about this than I do," he said.

I would not have earned that compliment had it not been for Bill Greason, Jimmy Zapp, and Artie Wilson, who at the time of the manuscript's completion were, along with Mays, the last surviving players from the 1948 Birmingham Black Barons. I will retain fond memories of interviewing Reverend Greason, the right-handed preacher, in his church in Birmingham. Jimmy Zapp, Willie's buddy, hosted me in his home along the banks of the Cumberland River in Nashville, where we listened to Duke Ellington, had a beer and a bowl of ice cream, and talked baseball. Artie Wilson and his son, Artie Jr., contributed meaningful quotes and clarifications. Sammy C. Williams, who passed away shortly after our brief interview, reminded me of Piper Davis's smooth ways.

I circled the streets of downtown Birmingham to find Piper's daughter, Faye, who received me unannounced at her office and helped illuminate her father's wonderful personality. And on the highway out of Birmingham, perched up on a little hill where the birds sing and the kittens roam, is Bobby Veale, whose invaluable contributions were matched by his amusement at a foolish kid wearing shorts in the woods during mosquito season.

At the Birmingham Public Library, archivist Jim Baggett lit the candle in my coal miner's helmet. He dusted off a shoebox full of oral history interview tapes conducted a dozen years earlier by Birmingham reporter Ben Cook, and the stories of former Black Barons such as Wiley Griggs, an infielder on the 1948 team, sprung to life. Jim led me to the library's clip files and, of course, the *Birmingham World* microfilm, where I set a speed record rolling through the 1948 film in the one afternoon afforded to me.

Jim's friend the late Chris Fullerton was the real expert on Birmingham's Industrial League and the role of the Black Barons in society. His thesis and subsequent book, *Every Other Sunday*, is a must-read for those who want to taste the liquor at Bob's Savoy with the coal miners and the pipe fitters and the ballplayers. It is my hope that this book is a worthy companion to Chris's work. Thanks also to David Brewer of the Friends of Rickwood Field for providing early advice. Also at the Birmingham Public Library Central Branch, thanks to Linda McFarland.

Through Chris's work and Jim's direction, I discovered the personal papers of Black Barons owner Tom Hayes in the T. H. Hayes Collection at the Memphis Public Library's Memphis and Shelby County Room. Thanks to archivist Wayne Dowdy for his gracious release of invaluable documents and photographs, as well as to his assistant Andy Carter. Thanks to the staff at the Spencer Research Library of the University of Kansas for their gracious release of the T. R. Baird Collection. Thanks to Mr. Baird for being so blunt in his letters, and to archivist Tim Rives, who deserves all the credit for shining the light on Baird's ceremonial wardrobe.

Along the library trail, thanks to Library of Congress archivist David Kelly, and to Bill Deane, my hired gun at the Baseball Hall of Fame's Giamatti Research Center. Rod Nelson, the best baseball research manager in the business, provided me with countless valuable leads. Among them were Peter Gorton, whose thoughtful research on John Donaldson's career will hopefully lead to Donaldson's induction into the Hall of Fame, where he rightfully belongs. I hope the same will one day be true for former scout Pop Kelchner. His patron saint, Ron Smiley, led me to Bob Scranton, the former manager of Rickwood Field, who can tell you how much a hot dog cost at the park in 1948.

Several other members of the Society for American Baseball Research (SABR) made valuable contributions to the research of *Willie's Boys*. Lee Lowenfish did library time for me in New York City. J. D. Mah's vast knowledge of the Canadian minor leagues helped me track the 1948 Black Barons. Jim Sandoval's precious collection of the *Sporting News* guides was called on often. The SABR minor league, scouting, and ballpark databases, which are maintained by devoted researchers, were valuable resources.

The late Jules Tygiel fielded my questions, and I hope this book is a worthy successor to his classic *Baseball's Great Experiment: Jackie Robinson and His Legacy*. Theodore Rosengarten conducted the best interview anybody ever did with Piper Davis and was gracious with his memories. Thanks also to Lester Rodney, John Paul Hill, Brent Kelley, and Raymond Doswell for fielding various questions.

A special thank-you to writer Arnold Hano and his ever-patient wife, Bonnie, who allowed me to crawl through their attic and storage spaces to find Arnold's forty-year-old notes about Mays, Willie McCovey, Bob Gibson, and Alex Pompez.

Among baseball men, I am deeply grateful to scouts George Genovese, George Digby, Al LaMacchia, Jim Marshall, and Bob Zuk. Just as Ted Williams once had to urge the Baseball Hall of Fame to accept Negro League players, I hope that one day an advocate will propel the Hall of Fame to honor amateur talent scouts. When the day comes, I hope Genovese, Zuk, and Digby are among the first to be honored.

Thank you to baseball men Bill Wight, Lenny Merullo, Paul Pettit, Jerry Stephenson, Roland Hemond, Harry Minor, Dario Lodigiani, Spider Jorgensen, Gary Hughes, Eddie Bockman, Tommy Butler, John Young, Lou Johnson, Andy Porter, Lenny Yochim, Mike Scioscia, Joe Torre, Torii Hunter, and Dusty Baker for their time, interviews, and suggestions.

Thank you to Glenn Stout and David Maraniss, who chose my story "Deal of the Century" to appear in *The Best American Sports Writing 2007* and thus helped launch my book career. Thanks to both gentlemen for reading the manuscript.

Thank you to Dennis Gilbert, whose Professional Baseball Scouts Foundation honored Willie Mays and the 1948 Black Barons in 2006; that event served as the genesis for this project. Thanks to Lisa Jackson, who saw Willie with his boys and remembered, "He looked like he was thirteen again." Thanks to Willie for choosing to honor his former teammates. Willie, you led me to Piper Davis.

Former minor league catcher Charles Staniland is my Piper, and like Piper, the numbers he put up with the bat—126 career home runs— prove he belonged in the big leagues, too. Thanks to two educators, Coach Dick Billingsley and Dr. J. S. "Noble" Eisenlauer, for helping shape my body, mind, and future.

Professionally, literary agent Scott Waxman scouted me out of the slush e-mail and gave me my agent, Farley Chase. Farley helped me shape a winning proposal out of a thousand ideas with editorial savvy, direction, patience, and commitment that I deeply appreciate.

Thank you to my editor at Wiley, Hana Lane, whose sharp pencil and wise suggestions helped me find my story without losing my voice.

Thank you to Jennifer. I don't suppose any woman enters into a relationship with the expectation that she will one day be able to correctly rattle off the names of the teams of the 1948 Negro American League. For reading every word, dealing with every mistake, listening to every thought of mine for hours on end, finding books and libraries from one end of the country to another, fixing microfilm machines, digging with me and discovering things I needed (like my car keys), making suggestions that are seen in this narrative, and helping support me every day so I could find time to research and write, I owe you a hockey game.

"THE BEST BASEBALL PLAYER I'VE EVER SEEN"

The boy's throwing arm dangled loosely at his right side like a coiled whip hanging off a nail. His glove hand hovered slightly above his left knee as though he was balancing himself, but in truth his glove wasn't touching his leg at all. His body swayed with every pitch, as if the wind whipping through center field was elbowing him in the ribs, but Carl Hubbell understood what the boy was doing. He watched the boy position himself with every pitch, balancing himself on the toes of his spikes, his thoughtful stance giving away his true opinion of each batter's abilities. Hubbell noticed how the boy liked to play extremely shallow in center field, which in the cavernous Polo Grounds was like walking the plank. Hubbell had been told about the kid, but his name was not one Hubbell was familiar with. Hubbell had a score sheet in his hands with the names of the Birmingham Black Barons and the host New York Cubans printed on it. He glanced down at his score sheet again. The center fielder wore No. 8. He was eighteen years old. His name was Willie Mays.

Hubbell didn't often come to Negro American League games at the Polo Grounds, although it was his home ballpark. He gained lasting fame here as the pitcher nicknamed "the Meal Ticket," becoming the best left-hander of his decade; in the gutter days of the Great Depression, the fans who could scrounge a nickel always knew they could count on him. Hubbell was now the Giants' talent czar, the head scout who was also in charge of the team's vast minor league system. He had heard stories about Mays, and especially about his throwing arm. Hubbell's informant was a man named Alex Pompez, the owner of the New York Cubans, who had begged Hubbell to be here today to see the center fielder for himself.

Finally, a ball was struck well into left-center field, providing the first chance to watch Mays. The ball landed safely for a base hit, a double in most circumstances. Mays's toes turned so quickly that his cleats severed the grass blades beneath him, and he reached the ball on the first bounce, speared it with his bare hand, and uncoiled the whip. His throw to second base was made off-balance, but arrived with such velocity that Hubbell noticed the second baseman lift his glove to meet the ball, not because Mays missed the target, but because he threw so hard that the ball was still rising. The throw was enough for the trepid base runner to hurry back to first base, like a mouse running for a hole.

Hubbell turned to Pompez, which alone was more of a response than he usually conveyed. Years of pitching in the big leagues had taught Hubbell to conceal his emotions, an advantageous ability for a scout. But Pompez could read a man too. He knew Hubbell was astounded.

There were other plays Mays made in the outfield that day, running catches to his left or his right or behind him, throws made from the warning track to the infield that never clipped the grass. Mays was fast and instinctive, possessing talents that could not be taught, and Hubbell could tell that the teenager took great pride in playing defense. Mays had all the tools he needed to be a dominating center fielder; the hands, the arm, the speed, the reflexes, the hunches, and the hunger. Hubbell was nearly sold right there, but he wanted to see if Mays could hit.

When he came to bat, Mays rubbed dirt in his hands and wasted no time getting ready. Some players went through intricate dalliances with the batter's box, fidgeting with the hat and the hands, scraping at the dirt, posing as though the pitcher was holding the mirror. Hubbell hated guys like that. When he was pitching, he had a hotly competitive streak, and because he couldn't throw hard enough to shove it down someone's throat, he swerved his slicing screwball. Mays, too, had that combative presence when he hit, and Hubbell liked it. What he wanted to see most of all was home run power. Contact was nice, but Hubbell hoped that this kid was not just a slap artist and a great defender. He prayed the prayer of the scout: Dear sweet Jesus, please don't let this guy be horseshit.

And when Mays swung the bat, the heavens opened, or at least that was how Hubbell described his feelings when he witnessed Mays hit for the first time. Hubbell had faced fast bats and great hitters, most famously when he struck out Babe Ruth, Lou Gehrig, and three others consecutively in the 1934 All-Star Game, but they were not capable of moving their bats the way this teenager was. Mays took no projection skills. Hubbell didn't have to guess. He knew some teams would look at Mays and decide two things. One, he is black. Two, he is raw. Hubbell knew that both words meant the same thing. To call him raw because he was young was no different than saying he couldn't play because he was black. It would be their loss, Hubbell decided. Raw was not a bad thing. To him, raw meant talent that should not be touched.

Mays hit a home run that day in June 1949, and Pompez kept edging looks in Hubbell's direction. Hubbell wanted Mays for the New York Giants and he knew he needed help. White scouts in Negro baseball were travelers in a foreign land, and though Hubbell knew about Pompez's background, he never asked. The Giants didn't care that Pompez had once been a numbers king in Harlem, that he had survived a war with Dutch Schultz, or that eight months in a Mexican prison cell had scared him straight. They just didn't want to advertise it. Pompez would be Hubbell's middleman to Mays. Pompez understood and wanted to help. He saw very little difference between scouting players and running the Spanish Lottery. It was all about control of the winning number, so of course Pompez would help Hubbell win the lottery and cover his tracks. That was the Harlem way.

And years later, after the deal had been done and the myth about an accidental discovery had been told, Hubbell would relive that day in the Polo Grounds when the Giants truly discovered the talent, the power, and the voice of Willie Mays. "Gentlemen," he'd say regally, "that was the day I saw the best goddamn baseball player I have ever seen in my life."

TRAPPED IN THE HOT BOX

To convey all the struggles, pangs of inner pain, and disgust tempered by wonderful moments that stayed with them for as long as their memories would allow, Negro League baseball players had their own language. They spoke of heartbreak and happiness and described the mythology that was as real as the times in which they played. They communicated with a clever application of black baseball slang to white baseball lingo, forming a bond that was their own and was passed down to younger players. Through time, their talk became as distinctive as the players themselves, and to play ball with them, you had to speak the language.

This coded speech was coated in pride and created a bond that connected players. It was spoken only by the black ballplayer, learned on the field and on the bus, handed down as one of the secrets of survival. To the young boy playing on an Alabama coal miner's sandlot or a wire mill's factory team, hidden by trees and time in villages that could scarcely be found on a map then or now, understanding this language was the currency needed to escape.

A catcher was never called the catcher. Instead, some long-ago baseball man decided that the field was analogous to a pig. He reasoned that the man behind home plate had to squat in the dirt for a living and destroy his fingers and knees to harness the horsehide, wearing only a flimsy chest protector, a rusty mask, and an archaic glove that made a sound like a drunk's head hitting the barroom floor when the ball came to rest. The position seemed to be the field's rear end, so the catcher came to be called the "pigtail."

The catcher's glove, for some uncertain reason, was known as a "pud," perhaps to mimic the sound of the ball colliding within it, or to borrow from the boxing term for a fighter. The nicknames were always the subject of jokes among catchers, who accepted humor but also reveled in becoming skilled technicians.

If a pigtail could get the ball, universally called the "pill," out of his pud in a hurry, spring to his feet, crack his arm like a whip, and drill a runner trying to steal second base, it could be said that he had an "awful" arm. The term came from "awful good," the description of exceptional skill. A player might be an "awful" hitter, which really meant he was better than you. Of Willie Mays, one could say, "Mays had an awful arm," and everyone knew what it meant.

Profanity had a comfortable seat on the bus, as did the lures of the road, where a trip was called a "jump," a naked white girl a "light," and a naked black girl a "shade." And were a player to brag about bagging a light or a shade, or even having a light and a shade at once, he would most certainly be called a "peppery" player, for this achievement would definitely make him brag. A peppery pigtail would talk a lot behind the plate while punching his pud with his throwing hand, just waiting to "shoot" you out.

After a player with an "awful" arm shot the ball across to a fielder, it would be "waiting on him," meaning the fielder would be ready to tag the runner out because he would have already received a terrific throw, often from an outfielder. In the spring of 1948, many black ballplayers felt they would be thrown out by white baseball long before they had the chance to show what they could do. White folks' ball was an unlikely destination for most black players, who were not sure how, why, or whether they would ever be allowed to pass from their dying league to one that never wanted them at all.

The term "white folks' ball" was coined by Piper Davis, who in 1948 was beginning his first season as the player-manager for the Birmingham Black Barons. Piper crafted phrases before he knew what he was doing. It was a quirky part of his personality. His own nickname, Piper, came from his hometown, a coal-mining village that the cartographers never knew existed, about forty miles southwest of Birmingham. Piper already understood how difficult it was to get out of a delicate jam, because he had been born in one. There was a term for that in black baseball too: "the hot box." Since the moment Piper found out that he was "awful" in his own right, baseball had been his escape, and he had already run a long way. To know Piper, a distinct mind and baseball practitioner, you had to know his roots.

When Lorenzo "Piper" Davis was growing up, Highway 59 was a dirt road wiggling past Fairfield and Bessemer. A traveler on the highway had to break left to find Piper, the town where Lorenzo grew up. The Talladega Forest surrounded the road, the thickness of the trees reminding the traveler of his remote location. The elms stood guard around the fertile mountain where coal miners lived and died by one belief: once you went in, you never came out.

The miners called the little villages that had sprung up around the mountain "camps." They provided low-cost housing for workers in the form of two-room plywood shacks coated in bland white paint with a potbellied stove in the kitchen; the homes were illuminated at night by candles and lanterns. There were a schoolhouse and a church, and life revolved around the mines and the horrible working hours and conditions. Below Bessemer, where the ore turned into rich coal veins deep inside the man-eating mountain, a path connected the camps into a constellation. It led through places called Dogwood, Blocton,

Marvel, and Kolina, and at the tail end came Piper. Like the pigtail on a baseball field, Piper was a gritty, dirty place where fear was part of the family. Here, young Lorenzo learned that he did not want to live his father's life. "My daddy was a coal miner his whole life, forty-some-odd years," he said. "He worked five days a week, but during the Depression he would work seven days. He'd get home, sleep, and go right back to work."

Lorenzo did his walking in bare feet and later cardboard shoes. The proud owner of one pair of overalls, he was too sheltered and naive to understand that he lived in poverty. What he did comprehend was that his father did not wish this life upon his son. The old man wasn't a baseball player, but he had the spirit of one. Like a minor leaguer on the back of a bus, he liked to play his guitar at Saturday night fish fries. His wife ruled the house and made him surrender his guitar to go with her to church on Sunday mornings. He never asked Lorenzo to give up his homemade bats and balls because he knew how much his son loved to play, no bother if it was with the sons of the white miners.

Lorenzo was the only child of John Wesley Davis and Georgia Cox. Born July 3, 1917, he resolved early on to become more than a coal miner. Growing up at the foot of the mountain, he soon realized there was only one way in and out. There was an escape from this way of life, one that possessed a language he did not yet speak. At night he would lie in bed and tune in the family radio to the minor league baseball games that were played at Rickwood Field in Birmingham. The local team was called the Birmingham Barons; they were in the Southern Association of what he would later call white folks' ball. Lorenzo learned all the teams in the league: the Chattanooga Lookouts, Memphis Chickasaws, New Orleans Pelicans, Little Rock Travelers, Atlanta Crackers, Nashville Volunteers, and Mobile Bears. His story-teller was the radio man for the Barons, Bull Connor, who in years to come would become the most powerful lawman in Birmingham. Lorenzo learned that professional baseball was a place for white boys only. He fell asleep, but he was brave enough to dream.

Piper, like every other coal-mining camp, had its own baseball team. Here Lorenzo got his first lesson in the game's Darwinian ways.

He would never be a pitcher because the boy with the best arm in Piper, Nat Pollard, was throwing bullets. Years spent chucking lumps of coal had strengthened Nat's arm to the point where it matched his surly disposition.

There were two teams in town: the First Nine (an adult team) and the Second Nine (a youth team). Lorenzo played for the Second Nine. When he wasn't playing for them, he was the batboy for the First Nine. Ever since he had started swatting rocks with a stick when he was a child, he believed he could hit a baseball, so by the time he was fourteen he was itching to play for the First Nine. His frame was growing, and his lanky arms and legs had yet to fill out, but he already realized baseball was the way out of coal mining. He never gave a second thought to the idea that he was nobody. No white scout would ever come to Piper, a town they didn't know existed, to see a player they didn't know existed. So Lorenzo came to them.

Baseball was serious business for coal miners, true recreation played with hard-nosed vigor and vulgarity. Baseball gave the miners the will to live. When their dreary jobs were done for the week, they could release their tension with bats and balls. For the average miner, the game was his way to forget about the mountain. For the better-than-average ball-player, baseball allowed him to make a few more dollars from the First Nine, and he might also get a slightly better camp job than a less talented ballplayer. For the most gifted ballplayers, those who were good enough to dream, it might mean a chance to play in the Negro Leagues.

The Birmingham Black Barons had been based in Birmingham since 1920 and played at Rickwood Field on Sundays in the summer when the white Barons were out of town. They barnstormed anywhere for a ball game and often played coal-mining teams. These games were also scouting expeditions. Lorenzo knew the Black Barons took players from the company teams. Here he learned the next rule of baseball: somebody will always try to steal your best player.

Lorenzo had three role models to emulate. One was pitcher Harry Salmon, who had toiled in the coal mines from the time he was eight, long before child welfare laws. One of the original Black Barons, Salmon pitched successfully for the team until 1932. In 1926, he pitched against Leroy "Satchel" Paige, a lanky smartass from Mobile, and beat him, 2–1. When Paige came to the Black Barons in 1927, Salmon "showed him some things." Salmon's best days were nearly done. Paige's were ahead of him. Lorenzo knew exactly who Paige was. "The only hero I looked up to," he said, "was Satchel Paige."

Another role model, the strongest boy to ever come out of the Birmingham coal mines, was a slugger named Mule Suttles, who got his nickname because he was as strong as the miner's sidekick, the mule. He played for the coal-mining teams before joining the Black Barons in 1923, and stayed only three years before spending his prime in St. Louis, establishing a pattern. The Black Barons rarely kept their best players, and consequently, they rarely won in the 1920s and 1930s, when they were routinely worked over by pitchers Smokey Joe Williams and Bullet Joe Rogan of the famous, influential, and wealthy Kansas City Monarchs. Northern players hated Birmingham discrimination, which was more extreme than discrimination in the northern states. Lorenzo saw Suttles barnstorming through Alabama in the late 1930s. "Suttles was soft but strong, could no longer hit a good drop ball, but Lord have mercy if you threw it where he could reach it." Like Harry Salmon and Mule Suttles, Lorenzo hoped to become the mountain's offspring.

The Tennessee Coal and Iron Company (TCI), the region's most powerful natural resource company, owned Piper and sponsored the teams. The baseball team was the only place a black man's talent would be respected. When the First Nine's first baseman was injured, the manager looked for Lorenzo, who was shagging foul balls and lining up the bats. For decades, he remembered the manager's words, which began his baseball career: "Put in that little boy." Lorenzo was pleased. "I've played First Nine ever since," he said later in his career.

Lorenzo wasn't just playing. He was plotting escape. The camp's school went no further than the ninth grade, at which point it was assumed that schoolboys were old enough to descend into the mountain. Professor Osborn, Lorenzo's teacher, saw that he was smarter than a coal miner. Now he had two tickets out of camp.

The answer was to attend Interurban Heights, commonly called Fairfield High, which was located in Fairfield, about thirty miles away. Lorenzo left Piper in 1933 at age sixteen. His mother, Georgia, might not have agreed to it, but she had four brothers in Fairfield who worked in the steel mill. Better yet, it was a steel mill with a baseball team. Lorenzo's father, John, didn't hold his son back. He looked on approvingly as Lorenzo escaped the destiny the mountain said he was born for. He would always be a coal miner's son, but he would never become a full-time coal miner.

Lorenzo was a born athlete and soon learned his abilities offered the opportunity to attain prestige and an income his father had never dreamed of. Fairfield High had a basketball team. The kids couldn't remember his name, but they knew he could play basketball. The story became one of his favorites. He was on the bench with his team losing. The kids began chanting, "We want Piper! We want Piper!" Lorenzo got in, won the game, and nobody ever called him Lorenzo again. In the crowd that night, he noticed a pretty young thing named Laura. Piper never forgot her name, and she never forgot to come to his games. Soon, they were sweethearts.

Fairfield High also had a baseball team, and every now and then Piper would play the pigtail. His body was better suited for an infielder, but he was savvy enough to realize that if he could play many positions, he would give himself more than one way to stick. That was the lesson of being a coal miner's son: the more ways you can dig yourself out of that mountain, the better your odds.

Piper played shortstop and second base, first base and third base, grazed in the outfield, put on the pud and played the pigtail. During these years, he played with a center fielder who was, the locals believed, as gifted a player as had ever come along. The boy could run, and when he pursued the ball in the outfield, his hat had a strange tendency to fly off his head. There was an awkwardness to the way he played, perhaps because his body jerked instinctively according to his reactions. He didn't look like a natural, yet he did everything effortlessly. They said he was as quick as a cat, and so the nickname "Cat" fused to him like grime on a miner. His real name was Willie Mays. No one thought to call him Senior until years later, but Cat Mays was only a footnote next to Piper Davis at the time. Piper became a star, and his reputation spread into Birmingham. He became the most famous athlete from Fairfield High until its three-sport star Willie Howard Mays.

Fairfield High was an industrial school, which prided itself in preparing young black adults for service occupations. Piper wanted no part of this, and he developed the fierce resistance that during his baseball career would be his best friend and his worst enemy. He was already thinking about playing baseball in the Negro Leagues. After he finished twelfth grade, he wrote to the Philadelphia Stars asking for a tryout. The team wrote him back and told him he could pay his way to work out with the team in Mississippi, but made no promises. Piper's father said no, proving that protective baseball parents have always existed, and Piper learned another valuable lesson: never play for free.

Basketball offered another possibility. He received a partial basketball scholarship to Alabama State College. The money helped, but it wasn't enough. His father took out a loan to pay the remainder of Piper's tuition, but money was always tight and coming up with it became more difficult when the coal miners went on strike. When the next tuition payment came due, Piper knew his father would have to borrow more money on top of the wages he was already losing. He couldn't stand the thought of asking his father to descend into the mines any longer than he had to, so he dropped out of college and went home to Piper. Insistent upon making his own money, he asked his father to get him a job in the mines. For a very brief period, Piper Davis had to give the mountain the satisfaction.

Jeremiah Nelson, a pitcher Piper played with on the camp team, was also a coal miner's son. When Piper came to work with his father, he heard Jeremiah was working in the same shaft. Piper knew at least one person could understand how much he would rather be playing baseball. He felt scared and out of place. On his first day of work, his father led him into a shaft and told him to stay in his sight. "I could stand with a three-foot shovel on the top of my head and I couldn't touch the top," Piper said. "But on the other end I was on my knees shoveling coal over here to my daddy, so my daddy could load it in the car."

Jeremiah Nelson was loading a car down the line, shoveling the coal from his mule's pack into his electric car. The primitive vehicles were run by one man on top of the line who made the steel cars move by sparking two wires together. The cars moved at only one speed, fast, and they were deadly if a man was caught in their path. Jeremiah Nelson made the mistake of stepping on the empty line, his only light provided by the lamp on his hard hat. A speeding cart knocked him on his back and severed him at the waist.

When Piper heard about the accident, he told his father he didn't want to go back to the mine. He would find another way to escape. John Davis didn't argue with his son. He always sensed his boy was born for more than this. Piper went home and took his bath. Then he went to the pay office to quit. The man told him he couldn't pay him without a reason for why he was resigning. "Just put in there, 'Afraid of mines,'" Piper said. The clerk replied, "That's a good enough reason."

One day in the mines was one too many. Out of money for college tuition, out of escape routes from the mining camp, Piper had gotten lucky and he knew it. Just as his father had to climb up the hill to come home from camp, Piper had to walk down into the valley to leave. He was not afraid to leave the mountain to play baseball for a living. It was a fair trade to him: leave one mountain to climb another.

The coal-mining camps and steel mills in Birmingham had gained a national reputation for being as fertile a ground for baseball players as they were for coal. The Birmingham Black Barons were born of coal miners. No state produced more Negro League ballplayers than Alabama.

One of those player-managers was Charlie Mason, who some called a black Babe Ruth. He had enormous feet that hinted at the physicality he had shown in the 1920s with the Bacharach Giants, then a top-level Negro League team from Atlantic City. Those were grand days and they had given Mason two nicknames: "Suitcase" and "Corporal." There were stories about how he got both, but nobody was as tall or as wide as Charlie Mason so nobody got the story.

When Mason brought his barnstorming team up the mountain to play the First Nine, aware that the mining camps always produced talented ballplayers to sign, he had his first look at Piper and knew a good ballplayer when he dug one out of the earth. He offered Piper a chance to join his travel ball team. He didn't tell him that barnstorming was such a difficult life that it often destroyed young kids who followed the money. They discovered that racism in other parts of the country was just as cruel as in the South, and because white people paid to watch black barnstorming teams, they felt they had the right to hurl as many insults as they pleased.

Mason's rookies weren't used to playing every day. Some struggled with homesickness. Still others had never left the small enclaves they were born in and became terrified of other parts of the country. Everything was unpredictable, from housing conditions to where the next meal would come from. But as far as Negro baseball went, travel ball was the minor leagues.

Teams like Charlie Mason's traveling kids formed the backbone of the Negro baseball economy. Travel team managers like Mason, many of whom had top-level Negro League playing experience, would sign unknown commodities from unknown places. They would eventually sell their most talented players to the top-level travel teams that had loose affiliations with the Negro League teams. Black baseball lacked the organizational structure of white baseball, but like white baseball, it did have its own feeder system of scouting and player development.

Piper couldn't afford not to go with Mason, even though he didn't have any cash. But he knew where his mother saved the family's money, so he pulled ten dollars out of the envelope Georgia hid in the pantry. When she came home, she found him packing her nice suitcase. Piper said he was leaving home to play baseball with Charlie Mason and his team called the Omaha Tigers. Georgia didn't know how far away Omaha was. He told her it was about nine hundred miles. It must have felt like the length of the universe. Georgia still called Piper her baby and told him to wait. She went to the pantry and pulled out another hidden envelope, one that Piper didn't know about. She hid her sorrow and feared to see him go, but put her son's future above her motherly needs and gave him another ten dollars.

"You always keep your train fare back home," she said.

"I sure will," Piper said.

Charlie Mason was an infielder's delight—the target you could not miss. Piper was eighteen when he joined Mason's team in the summer of 1936, and the bouncy bus ride out of Piper, past Birmingham, and out of Alabama took him across state lines for the first time in his life. The team trained in Memphis—everyone ran but Mason—and each ballplayer had to make the team every day to stay. Baseball wasn't coal mining, but Negro League barnstorming had its own perils. If you didn't make the team, you were left for dead.

Piper could play the infield, play in the outfield, or even play the pigtail if needed, he told Mason, but he would need to borrow a pud. Mason didn't need an eighteen-year-old kid telling him how to scout. It didn't work that way in the Negro Leagues, whether on a barnstorming team or the greatest team in the land, the Kansas City Monarchs. The kid ballplayer had no rights. If he was mentored, it was not because they thought the kid was a joy to be around. It was because they thought he could play and would help them make money.

Piper's pay would be $91 a month if he made the team. He knew he wasn't good enough to take the starting catcher's job away, but he thought he was better than the shortstop Mason was playing. Mason sent him to the outfield and immediately recognized that he could catch the ball. In the meantime, the starting shortstop, gifted though he may have been, spent his salary in the saloons. "Looks like I'm going to have to bring you to the infield, because this boy is in bad shape," Piper remembered Mason telling him. The shortstop got so drunk that he came down with alcohol poisoning. The team left Memphis for Omaha with the kid curled up in the back of the bus, groaning and vomiting. When they arrived, Mason called a doctor and sent the shortstop to the hospital. Four days later, he died, and Piper Davis played his first ball game as a rookie-level professional Negro League ballplayer.

He quickly learned that baseball was a difficult life. Finding a black-only hotel was a tricky proposition, so the team usually slept on the bus. One night, Mason made a deal to house his players in a place that actually had mattresses on the cots. He didn't tell them that the beds were in an empty jailhouse. In other towns, they slept in housing built for Negro Pullman porters. Piper collapsed into bed and didn't ask any questions. Things were segregated back home too, but at least it was obvious. Southern racism was overt. Northern racism was not. Outside of the Deep South, Piper was learning that all bets were off.

And he suspected Charlie Mason wasn't honest with the gate money. He looked around at the lifestyle. The team bus was a coal mine on wheels. "Too much traveling and not enough money," Piper explained. "Besides, they didn't finish paying us what little we were supposed to get. We just traveled, traveled. Started in Omaha, played on up to North Dakota, then went across almost to Spokane, then we came on back down through Idaho, Kansas, and places like that. Played white teams along the way, played black teams, barnstorming with local clubs."

When the summer was over, coming home never looked so good. Piper saw the mountain, and he knew his daddy was in there somewhere. He went to live in Fairfield with his mother's family because he knew he could get work and play on a company baseball team. He was officially a ringer now, and after the horrid summer through Indian country, he was pleased to be home. Tennessee Coal and Iron was always hiring for one project or another, so Piper got a job with a construction crew building a tin mill in Fairfield, which in time would house a company team where two men named Mays shared the field.

It was Piper's first taste of the Industrial League baseball that Birmingham was known for. The Industrial League was intense, organized, and competitive. The teams were feeding grounds for the big Negro League franchises. Industrial League baseball was a place where a black man could be respected for his work. TCI had a team, as did companies called Schloss Furnace, Westfield Sheetmill, Perfection Mattress, and Ensley. But the biggest rivals in the Industrial League's manufacturing division were Stockham, a steel mill, and ACIPCO (the American Cast Iron Pipe Company), the New York Yankees of the Industrial League.

Steelworkers were better paid than coal miners and thought to be more skilled. They were one notch above the lowly miners in black society. Ballplayers crawled over one another to get a job with ACIPCO, which would be comparatively easier than coal mining and would allow them to play ball on nights and weekends. The best players frequently wound up playing for the Birmingham Black Barons, but sometimes they stayed with ACIPCO instead. There was no travel and much stability, security, and celebrity. But there was cash under the table and nobody thought twice about playing elsewhere under an assumed name. There was also a limit as to how far a player could go. Piper was more ambitious than that, long before he went to his first shift as a construction worker. When the tin mill was completed and TCI cut the employees, one of Piper's local teammates from the Omaha club told him that a mixed team from Yakima, Washington, was recruiting ball-players. Following the money, he again packed his mother's suitcase.

The Yakima Browns were a sad place for Willie Foster to end his pitching career. He had been one of the greatest left-handed pitchers in Negro League history, and to the young kids on the Yakima bus he would have been a household name for his years of service with such glamorous teams as the Chicago American Giants, Homestead Grays, and Kansas City Monarchs. In 1925 he had pitched for the Black Barons as a prelude to his greatest days with the American Giants when he won twenty-six consecutive games in 1926, and in the Negro National League playoffs he pitched both games of a double-header, beating the Kansas City Monarchs and their dominant ace, Bullet Joe Rogan, in each to win the championship.

Young Buck O'Neil came across Foster and never forgot how imposing he was. Toward the end of his life, Buck wrote scouting reports on a select few black ballplayers whom he felt were among the best he had ever seen. He did so simply for posterity. In the terse and technical terms of a scout wiring a Western Union telegram, Buck described how great Foster had been, abbreviating "FB" for fastball and "CB" for curveball. At the end of his report, he named the left-handed pitcher Foster reminded him of, which alone should stand testament to how good Piper Davis's second manager had once been: "Willie Foster—LHP–6-3, 205—Front Line Starter—Hard sinking FB and over the top CB—Both pitches strike out pitches—Spotted all his pitches well—Koufax reminded me of Foster."

At age nineteen, Piper Davis reminded Willie Foster of how he liked to see baseball played. Piper was young and strong and could play multiple positions. His body stood up to the rigors. As a young man, he was already developing a baseball mind. That's when he began creating words to match the game's idiosyncratic language, a practice he carried on throughout his life. He emulated Foster. In turn, Foster took the time to talk with him. He taught him that the Negro League was a man's league, a place where childhood ended and boys who played scared did not last. In time, Willie told him, it would be his turn to hand down what he was taught. That's the way black ballplayers did it, Willie preached. If they didn't take care of one another, nobody else would.

Among the lessons was that black baseball was different from white folks' ball. Nine innings of Negro League baseball looked nothing like nine innings of big league ball. Black baseball was in a constant state of movement. It was a game of strong arms and swift legs and great natural athletes. Once you got a great athlete who could hit, Willie explained, you had yourself a memorable ballplayer.

Instead of living the celebrity life of a well-paid major league ace pitcher, Willie Foster was leading a bunch of teenagers around the country to play pass-the-hat games, hoping each time his arm would hold up. He didn't throw hard anymore, but his curveball was nobody's business, and if he threw a fastball behind someone's ear, he meant to. Willie Foster didn't miss, but he couldn't control his era.

Willie's team met up with the House of David in Michigan, the traveling Jewish team famous for its players' long beards, and began playing town by town back to Indian country. For a week or two, the Browns played the House of David until the teams split off in different directions. It was the start of another long summer. In Montana, the games were rained out for an entire week, an incredibly difficult ordeal for players who fed themselves based on receiving a percentage of gate money. Piper and the other players couldn't collect their seventy-five cents' daily meal money. Out of options, the team ate on credit at a hotel. When the Yakima Browns couldn't pay their room bills, the hotel took their bags.

The players got sneaky. They smuggled their luggage out the window and loaded the bus. When a woman who ran a boarding house a few miles away caught them red-handed, she hopped on board the bus and led them to her town. The Browns got enough good weather to play a game and pay her back. Willie Foster, star of years gone by, surely tossed a few curveballs to make sure his boys could eat, but when the money stopped coming, he went home to Mississippi. The greatest black left-handed pitcher of the 1920s didn't need anybody to tell him what to do next. He went back to college, finished his education, and became the dean of men and baseball coach at Alcorn State University, where he remained until his death in 1960.

When the bus reached St. Louis, Piper followed Foster's lead and jumped the team. "This is far enough for me," he said. The 1937 Yakima Browns disbanded. Piper went home. Georgia had been wise to make sure he always kept his train fare back. When he came back to Fairfield, the first thing he did was find Laura. They were married in 1938, had two children, and remained together for the rest of his life.

The second thing he did was get a job at ACIPCO. At nineteen, Piper was underage for the steel mill, but lying about basic information never stopped anyone from playing baseball in Birmingham. Piper used his father's name. He began playing for the pipe shop company team in 1939, and for the next four years he was never on the road. This was a welcome change after two barnstorming summers. Piper thought this was better than travel ball. The pipe shop's ballplayers were local celebrities, and ACIPCO spoiled them because they believed it was the ultimate source of corporate propaganda. A winning baseball team created company pride, which of course led to higher productivity, the lifeblood of a town that called itself the Pittsburgh of the South and drew its name from the iron capital of Great Britain.

Black players got everything the white players did, and this alone was a unique privilege in times of segregation and depression. It was so good that some men never wanted to set foot in the Negro Leagues. Cat Mays, who probably never played in the Negro Leagues except for weekend cups of coffee with the Black Barons in the 1930s under an assumed name, spent his career in the Industrial League, chasing fly balls when Willie Mays was born in 1931.

"They'd buy you everything—balls, bats, uniforms," Piper said. "They give you a trip and pay all your traveling; didn't have to worry. It was a better deal than signing with a traveling club. That's why I stayed."

The Negro League code persisted in the Industrial League. It was a base runner's God-given right to slide spikes-up, aiming for the knees. The second basemen and shortstops learned to jump higher. The inner half of home plate belonged to pitchers, and if the batter crowded the neighborhood, he would be evicted with a fastball aimed precisely at his head. If the runner hit safely, he would try to take the next base every single time, so the outfielders learned to get rid of the ball in a hurry, and to throw strongly and accurately to the correct bag. Black baseball was built around pressuring the other team into a mistake and, when one occurred, maximizing its destructive capability with sheer athletic skill and speed, like wolves tearing apart meat.

"I can name a whole lotta top ballplayers who played in the majors and up in Triple-A, in, as we say, 'white folks' ball,'" Piper said. "Yes sir, a lotta them came outta here. A lotta them came out of Birmingham every year and played in the Negro League. Most of them were born a few miles away from here."

Most of Birmingham's best Industrial League players got a taste of Negro League home cooking, because the companies were willing to share their ballplayers up until April 15, the start of the Industrial League season. That meant the Black Barons could steal a ballplayer for a weekend, pay him fifty dollars under the table, and play him for a few days. Most Industrial League stars ate at the Black Baron supper table and had it both ways—a taste of Negro League baseball against some of the big teams that came in, and a comparatively safe and easy job back home paired with Industrial League ball games.

In 1942, ACIPCO had its best team. Piper played second base alongside shortstop Artie Wilson. Together, Piper and Wilson made for an "awful" double-play combination. Herman Bell was the pigtail, light with the bat and quick with his arm. Ed Steele was the star outfielder, a classic right fielder who could hit the long ball and make throws that would be waiting on you. The ACIPCO nine went 49–1 and won the company's tenth Industrial League championship, receiving national recognition in the *Chicago Defender*. Wilson hit .476, Steele batted .472, and Piper hit .390 and led his club with 14 home runs. Nat Pollard grew into a dominating pitcher who went 20–1, struck out 173 batters, and pitched 12 shutouts.

Piper joined the Black Barons in 1942, and Wilson, Steele, Bell, and Pollard soon followed. They would play together on the 1948 team and become like older brothers to young Willie Mays. They watched as Jackie Robinson entered the major leagues in 1947, and though he never had shared the Birmingham experience, they hoped his escape would help facilitate their own. They respected Robinson, but there was a difference: Jackie had never worked in a mill or a mountain.

But by the end of the 1947 season, Birmingham's sons felt as though they were trapped in a coal mine. Robinson's entry did not easily open the door to the major leagues. In some ways, it had made moving forward more difficult. White folks' ball wasn't waiting on Negro League players. To complicate matters, black crowds in many cities were flocking to major league games, meaning attendance was dropping at the Negro League games—a certain death knell for players who were earning their keep based on gate receipts. In the pages of the *Birmingham World*, the city's black newspaper, the exploits of Robinson, Roy Campanella, and Don Newcombe hundreds of miles away were gaining more coverage than the local Black Barons. They had been stars for years, and now they were suddenly becoming extinct.

The stories of how white folks' ball treated black ballplayers circulated through the Negro Leagues. Frustrated black players felt they weren't given a fair chance. They believed they were being held to impossible standards. The Black Barons believed white scouts wouldn't dare journey to segregated Rickwood Field to scout a player their team would never let them sign in the first place. Bull Connor, who had once lulled Piper to sleep, now saw to it that rigid segregation was enforced inside Rickwood Field. The Black Barons came to believe that southern blacks were held in higher disdain than their northern counterparts, and even worse, they had reason to suspect that northern Negro League teams disparaged the Black Barons as nothing but uncouth coal miners and steelworkers who couldn't play and would only cause trouble. All around Birmingham, black baseball's proud, unifying tradition seemed to be decomposing.

Piper's experiences told him something was wrong. In 1945, when Branch Rickey had dispatched scouts throughout the Negro Leagues searching for a player to break the color line, the black press mentioned Piper as a legitimate candidate. The Dodger scout assigned to the South, Wid Matthews, grew up in Raleigh, Illinois, the son of a tobacco worker. There were signs throughout his career that he didn't care for black players. Matthews most likely dismissed Piper with the tag of "too old," a polite baseball term accepted by Dodger scout Clyde Sukeforth in assessing Davis.

Piper was just twenty-eight years old when he was deemed to be past his prime, only two years older than Jackie Robinson and the same age Robinson was when he came to Brooklyn in 1947. Yet Piper was deemed to be ancient, an excuse used to justify a reason for exclusion, although he had similar qualifications to Robinson, Rickey's foregone conclusion. Rickey, after all, had heard of UCLA's Jackie Robinson. He had never heard of Birmingham's Piper Davis.

Like Robinson, Piper was college-educated, albeit for only one year. He was one of the few Negro League stars, along with Robinson, Larry Doby, Joe Black, and Monte Irvin, to have collegiate experience. Like Robinson, Doby, Black, and Irvin, Piper was a multisport athlete. Like Robinson, he showed leadership abilities. Like Robinson, Piper was a married man who did not drink or smoke. He refused to swear and actively avoided nightlife and trouble. Piper was so boring on the road that he roomed with his suitcase. No one in Negro baseball questioned Piper Davis's character.

And like Robinson, Piper had a ferocious temper and was not afraid to show it. But where Robinson's temper served him, Piper's helped deny him. The scouts heard stories of fights early in his career, and, years later, other black players believed the white scouts held it against him. The qualities that endeared him to black players made Piper less desirable to white scouts. His greatest asset was passion, the characteristic that white folks' ball used to reject him. It was hard to discern if Piper Davis, a dark-skinned black man tinted the color of milk chocolate, a shade darker than Robinson, was simply too black for white folks' ball. Even though Piper was considered one of the best in the Negro Leagues, Dodger scout Wid Matthews believed Piper had character flaws and decided that he couldn't play. That snub followed him and made it easier for other teams to reject him, since many scouts ran in packs, trusting others so they would never be wrong themselves. In hindsight, perhaps the Dodger scout's branding of Piper with a reputation less than what he had already proven on the field demonstrates only their inadequate information gathering and talent evaluation of black players and Rickey's insistence that no man be better than his.

Piper absorbed the painful rejection and wondered how he would climb out of the mountain again. He rarely spoke about the time in 1947 when the St. Louis Browns had taken a thirty-day option on him and dispatched a scout to follow him in what Piper believed to be nothing more than a perfunctory task. The option permitted the Browns a thirty-day exclusive window to sign Piper if they wanted him. To join the worst team in white folks' ball, the Browns offered $500 to go to Triple-A, a $300 pay cut from what Black Barons owner Tom Hayes was paying. The money was an insult to both Piper and Hayes. It would not be the last time a major league team tried to lowball Tom Hayes and take his property away from him without fair compensation.

In 1948, Piper wondered whether he was on his daddy's path all over again, caught in a world he could not escape. So, as he had done then, he would use the language to help devise a new route. White folks' ball wasn't hiring but a few, and Piper and the remaining players sensed they were trapped in a "hot box."

One of the few terms shared by Negro and white folks' ball, the hot box was in its literal sense a rundown play, commonly called a "pickle," in which a base runner was trapped between two infielders who chased him back and forth until he was tagged out. Black baseball was full of fast runners, but seldom had a player been seen who could race his way out of the hot box.

The hot box was also the Civil War all over again, with masters and slaves, generals and soldiers. It was fought on letterhead and with typewriters, between scouts and team owners, front office people of both races, between promoters and players. It was a war of attrition for the sake of gaining a beneficial position when it was over. Piper was wise enough to realize that the end of the Negro Leagues was near. Jackie Robinson had fought one battle in 1947, but integration was not over. A guerrilla war was raging below the surface of major league baseball. It was North versus South, Yankees versus Giants, light-skinned blacks versus dark-skinned blacks, and the Kansas City Monarchs, its white owner, and his black "Board of Strategy" muscling their way over the Birmingham Black Barons, those coal-mining rubes from the South. The Birmingham Black Barons of 1948 felt trapped with nobody in white folks' ball waiting on them. The Kansas City Monarchs weren't either. They had their own players to help, the color of the uniform mattered more to the Monarchs than the color of the skin, and a black Monarch was superior to a Black Baron.

But during the 1948 season, when the Black Barons battled the Monarchs for the Negro American League pennant one last time, the Birmingham boys learned that the hot box had a hole in it. Maybe they couldn't squeeze through it, but someone else could.

Everything was cyclical in Birmingham, where families and generations were bound together like the carts that sawed poor Jeremiah Nelson in half. Cat Mays's boy would prove it was possible. Hope, more than coal, iron, or steel, was Birmingham's most precious commodity.

Sixty years later, Black Baron outfielder Jimmy Zapp got excited describing what it meant to see a ballplayer escape the hot box.

Zapp's health had battered him in recent years, but describing Mays was medicine. "Every ballplayer who get in don't get out of the hot box," Zapp said. "But Mays would run and run and run and run and run. His hat would be flyin' off his head. They'd never get him. I swear, no matter how hard they tried. Just couldn't nab him." It took a player who couldn't be trapped to escape the hot box, but Willie Mays did not do this alone. He needed the help of the 1948 Birmingham Black Barons, and most of all the coal miner's son, Piper Davis, the iron ore of Willie Mays's baseball existence.

2

NEGRO AVENUE

Bob Williams, a light-skinned businessman gifted with northern tastes and southern charms, arrived from New York in the 1930s with a drink shaker and a dream. He set up shop on Fourth Avenue, Birmingham's largest run of black businesses, which the locals had christened Negro Avenue. Fourth Avenue housed barbecue stands, butcher shops, soda shops, pool halls, barber and beauty shops. The Carter Theater showed first-run Hollywood movies when the white theaters were finished with the reels. Negro Avenue was Birmingham's Harlem, where cats strutted and gals followed, and hostility turned to hospitality. Bob's Savoy was the premier joint in the neighborhood.

Bob borrowed the nickname from the famous Savoy Ballroom in New York City, priced his drinks for the lower class and his dinners for the upper class, and cashed in on creating a place free from the city's toxic feelings. Bob's was a little bit of everything, from pool hall to gin mill to dining club to a place to pick up girls. He had a taste for baseball, ran his own basketball team, and paid Piper to play on the side.

Cat Mays could be found on the first floor of Bob's on occasion. Birmingham was still a small town, and though Cat would never dare allow then eleven-year-old Willie into the place, there is little doubt that he began to circulate his son's name among the baseball crowd. One way or another, Cat was the kind of father who would see to it that Willie Mays made it into the ears of Birmingham's black sporting community.

Baseball was an ever-present part of black life in Birmingham, and Bob's Savoy was the center of black life in downtown Birmingham, a place where music played and gin flowed, in every way an exact replica of the caste system that existed within Birmingham's black populace. On the first floor was the bar, where the coal miners and steelworkers jammed the walls on Saturday nights, drinking and carousing and feeling free to let it out. You could only dress up a blue-collar worker so much, and if somehow his clothing wouldn't give him away, his black-lung cough, his burn scars, or his fragmented speech would.

Upstairs, however, a different and more upscale world existed. Bob had been wise when he built his place. The bottom was for the bottom, the top was for the top, but the point was that he had been smart enough to cater to all his customers. The Savoy dinner club was upstairs, and of course Bob claimed it was the best restaurant in town. When the famous big bands toured the South, upstairs at Bob's was always booked. Count Basie one o'clock jumped in the joint. Cab Calloway hi-di-hoed and sang about the lady with the fan.

Duke Ellington always had the coolest move, though. His band carried the largest book, Duke's dictionary of his own compositions that multiplied as effortlessly as the guys got loaded. While playing the smoky notes of Harlem ancestry, Duke would tell the band to turn to the page where they kept his 1926 composition "Birmingham Breakdown." It was perfect Ellington: frenzied chaos orchestrated to the last movement. When he was older, Ellington still loved that song and said that a version of it was his favorite recording from his early years.

Ellington played Piper Davis's town. The war years created stress and jobs and found the segregation cauldron boiling. It was difficult for blacks to move freely inside Birmingham without fear. Bus drivers and streetcar conductors wore pistols. Bull Connor hated the influx of new blacks who came to Birmingham to find jobs in the wartime steel industry. He saw his town being taken away and feared race riots. He believed that a legal separation of the races was in order, one that would infuse all aspects of Birmingham society with a rigid divide. "Stations, depots, carriers, busses, and street cars . . . are crowded to capacity; sidewalks are congested, stores and elevators are filled with people," he complained to the *Birmingham News*, the city's white newspaper.

Blacks were angered and whites were agitated. It was a two-way street with blood on the sidewalk. In 1942, while Piper was playing for ACIPCO, a black man argued with a white bus driver over three cents' change. The argument turned into shouting. The driver won when he kicked the passenger off the bus. As the passenger stepped off, the driver pulled his revolver, emptied six shots into the man's back, and drove away.

Black steelworkers felt white unions were trying to break their backs. A steelworker named Clarence Dean, who had begun working in the steel mills when he was eighteen, believed he deserved a promotion to become the man who poured the molten steel rather than guided it. The job was as close to hell as you could get outside of a coal mine, the difference between working in 100-degree heat and 150-degree heat. When he asked his supervisor, Dean said he was told, "We ain't going to give niggers no white folks' jobs."

Negro League baseball players knew how he felt. The buzz in the early 1940s was that white folks' ball would not be able to ignore black ballplayers much longer. What would happen after the war? Nobody knew what the future held, but ballplayers understood that it would be different. They wondered if white folks' ball would give black players jobs. They could worry or they could drink, and most chose the latter. Bob was grateful for their habits. He allowed the team bus to pick them up in front of the Savoy when the team was home. In many ways, the road from Birmingham to white folks' ball ran directly through the Cotton Club of Birmingham. Ellington might break out his "Daybreak Express," and soon the bus would pick up Piper Davis.

Piper had already been offered a chance to play for the Black Barons in 1940. Candy Jim Taylor, who started a team in 1904 called the Birmingham Giants, the city's first all-Negro nine, was managing the Black Barons. Upstairs at Bob's was made for guys like Candy Jim, a Negro League legend from one of the game's most distinguished families. He had done it all in black baseball, and he knew the steel mills were the purest source of fresh talent. He had learned Piper's name and come to see him play at ACIPCO, where Piper was making $3.32 a day. Aside from playing weekend games for the Black Barons for extra cash, Piper didn't want to play on the road again. Candy Jim tried to get him anyhow.

"What are you paying, Uncle Jim?" Piper asked.

The answer was, no more than $175 a month.

"Oh, nooooo, nooooooo, no way!" Piper said.

In 1942, the great success of the 39–1 championship team raised Piper's rates. He, Artie Wilson, and Ed Steele were the stars of that team, but Piper had already played some travel ball, so interest in him spiked. In 1941, Taylor had been replaced as Black Barons manager by a younger man, Winfield Welch.

Winfield Scott Welch was born in Napoleonville, Florida, in 1899; he described himself as "colored of French descent." He got his start in colored baseball close to home with the New Orleans Black Pelicans in the 1920s and then as the player-manager of the Shreveport Acme Giants, a minor league travel team that had a loose affiliation with the Kansas City Monarchs. What that really meant was that the Monarchs would take his best players away for a pittance and tell Welch that he should consider himself lucky. Welch, however, always remembered who spiffed him and who stiffed him.

Welch was smooth and resourceful. While he played and managed in Shreveport, he was also the head bellman at the city's biggest white hotel. He padded his pockets with tips, and when the time was right, he would slip a player he wanted a few extra dollars to join his team. A man's money is only as good as his mind, but Welch proved that he knew what he was looking at. Among the first players he signed for Shreveport was a line-drive-hitting first baseman from Sarasota. Welch knew the kid would never hit for power, but recognized the boy had instincts, intellect, and a savvy for hustle. The player was Buck O'Neil.

Welch was forty-two when he was hired to manage the Black Barons in 1941. By then he had established himself as a well-known Negro League talent hunter and climbed through the ranks of the lowly percentage teams to the top-money Negro League clubs. Birmingham was his first big job. When Black Barons owner Tom Hayes hired Welch in March 1941, the *Chicago Defender* heralded Welch as "one of the best trainers of young players in the business and is credited with having started many of the young stars on the road to fame."

Tom Hayes (second from left) and his wife, Helen (far right), were among the most educated and successful owners in Negro baseball. Hayes was a tough negotiator, but he was loyal to players who were loyal to him. He wanted respect from white teams that wished to buy his players.

Welch wanted the Birmingham job because he knew his geography. The Industrial League teams were ripe for the picking, the perfect place for him to build his own club and beat the Monarchs. Though Welch was smart enough to never say it in print, he couldn't have been pleased that the mighty Kansas City Monarchs kept poaching his prime players. O'Neil was a classic example. Welch gave him his start and fended off overtures. The Monarchs got dirty and showed how they too could be cutthroat. Kansas City owner J. L. Wilkerson arranged for the Memphis Red Sox, the other southern team in the Negro American League, to purchase O'Neil from Shreveport. Welch didn't bat an eye, but only later did he realize he had been fooled. As soon as Wilkerson had first base open, he pulled O'Neil from Memphis and started him on his legendary career with the Monarchs. Welch never got a dime for filling Buck's pockets with quarters. "Winfield Welch never did know how I came to be picked up by the Red Sox," O'Neil wrote in his autobiography, *I Was Right on Time*. "He just thought they had scouted me and liked me."

Welch's business acumen harkened back to his days hustling tips, and he aspired to buy his own team. His New York sporting ties were already firm and he served as business manager and bench coach of the Harlem Globetrotters, the famous traveling basketball team that at the time played for money first, wins second, and laughs third. By the time he came to Birmingham, he was working for promoter Abe Saperstein, who was an occasional business partner of Alex Pompez. Saperstein could make anything happen with a telephone call. He was one of the top sports promoters in the country and was responsible for booking the Black Barons' travel in the war years, scheduling the team in venues it couldn't otherwise play, and finding creative ways to avoid wartime fuel restrictions.

Welch wanted to be the manager to make winners of the Black Barons, who had never won a championship. The Birmingham players were beloved in their neighborhoods, where the comfortable factory jobs made them as strong as steel. When there was enough money in playing for the Black Barons to jump from ACIPCO, the players became the gods of Negro Avenue, and inside Bob's they never drank

The odd couple: Sports promoter Abe Saperstein (left), best known as the promoter of the Harlem Globetrotters basketball team, scouted Negro League ballplayers for the Cleveland Indians. His sporting ties in New York helped guide Tom Hayes (right) into white baseball, territory in which Hayes walked warily.

downstairs. The Black Barons were Birmingham boys all the way, thought by outsiders to be rowdy and cocky.

Tom Hayes, the Black Barons' new owner, an insurance man and mortician based in Memphis, hired Welch to change his team's fortunes. Welch found the talent he needed in the Industrial League to help Birmingham finish in second place in the 1941 Negro American League. The team Welch assembled cemented his baseball reputation in Birmingham and proved him worthy of operating upstairs. Outfielder Lyman Bostock Sr., pitcher Dan Bankhead, and second baseman Tommy Sampson showed they were among the league's top talent, but the Kansas City Monarchs, as usual, finished first.

The Black Barons were gaining momentum in 1942, and so was Welch. He was chosen to manage the West team in the annual East-West All-Star Game at Chicago's Comiskey Park. The game drew 48,000 fans and several scouts. Welch called it the greatest moment of his baseball career. He penciled in a rich lineup that included Cool Papa Bell batting leadoff. But even in his finest moment, Welch was surrounded by the Monarchs. The West team should have been called the Kansas City Monarchs and a few other guys. Two of Welch's finds, Buck O'Neil at first base and Willard Brown in left field, were in the lineup. The Monarch battery of pitcher Hilton Smith and catcher Joe Greene started. Ted Strong, who played for Welch with the Globetrotters, played right field. Bell, who joined the Monarchs in 1948, was almost finished. The greatest Monarch of them all, Satchel Paige, entered a tied game and blew it. He gave up three runs and Welch's West team lost, 5–2. When Welch came back to Birmingham to finish the season, the Black Barons again finished in second place to the Kansas City Monarchs.

Two years without a championship was gnawing at Welch. He knew Tom Hayes's patience would expire, so he asked him if he could spend money to sign the Industrial League's top talent. Hayes worried about hiring too many industrial league players, but Welch knew he would love Piper Davis.

Piper was already playing exhibition games for Welch on the side at the end of 1942. He noticed that Welch had been gradually increasing his pay up to $15 for a double-header. Piper knew exactly what Welch was doing. "He was baiting me up real good," Piper said.

In the fall of 1942, Welch found Piper upstairs in Bob's Savoy one night and began dangling offers of playing for the Black Barons full-time starting in 1943. The money beat the mill. Welch was offering $300 a month and $2 a day in meal money, plus a handsome signing bonus. It was the final ticket out of hard labor. Piper Davis would come to the Birmingham Black Barons and the Negro American League for the 1943 season. While Welch was finishing the details, Bob Williams approached him. "He can play basketball, too," Piper remembered Williams telling Welch.

Welch called Saperstein, who was thrilled to discover a two-sport athlete. He told Welch to pay Piper $350 a month. And so for the next three years Piper Davis was a full-time athlete, playing basketball in the winter and baseball in the summer. He played until the winter of 1945, when, as he recalled decades later to young two-sport star Bo Jackson, his legs began shaking while he was sitting still. During that time he developed a close friendship with Welch. Maybe Cat Mays was downstairs the night Piper made the deal. If he was, he didn't know that the first seeds of his son's career had been planted.

Every fall in his offices at 192 North Clark in Chicago, Abe Saperstein prepared a press release detailing the dominance of his Harlem Globetrotters. To promote the start of the 1943 season, Saperstein gleefully pounded his fingers on his typewriter and informed the world that since the team's inception in 1927, the famous Globetrotters had won 2,352 games and lost only 181.

The road grind was brutal. The Globetrotters played 120 games in 150 days across North America. They played college teams and semipro teams, local ringers, and guys who should have never been wearing shorts. They played black teams and white teams, and in the war years commonly drew as many as four thousand fans per night. Welch was in his mid-forties and would still dress for games, complete with the team's familiar knee-high white socks roped in red and blue stripes. The Globetrotters cashed in on patriotism, always by Saperstein's design. Saperstein was a short, fat man and he probably couldn't run the length of the court without gasping for breath, but he knew how to make money. Six years before the formation of the National Basketball Association, the Globetrotters were annually among the best teams in the United States.

The gimmicks were corny but paid cash, and Piper dreamed of sending his children to college, so he would spin a basketball on each index finger simultaneously. He took part in the antics that included kicking the ball through the hoop and calling it football. The Globetrotters hid the ball under their shirts and dribbled between their legs.

Saperstein had a solid rule: Never run up the score. To the black press, the Globetrotters were true artists: "It's a smart collection of cagers, aptly absorbing the tricks of showmanship and the clever style of play responsible for the Trotters' continued leadership in the favor of fans," the *Chicago Defender* wrote in 1942.

But the Globetrotters were perceived differently in the white media. Upon their arrival for a date at the Shrine Auditorium in 1943, the *Los Angeles Times* called the Globetrotters' game "African voodoo, as applied to basketball," and "masters of monkeyshine." The *Times* finally conceded that the team could "display a rare brand of straight basketball when the occasion requires," but upon promoting the Trotters' return engagement at the Shrine two years later wrote, "If you want to see basketball played in a manner to make Doctor Naismith turn over in his grave, drop in at the Shrine Auditorium Thursday night. The Doctor, you know, originated basketball—but not with baseball, football and 'black magic' included."

In the era when basketball was played below the rim, Piper enjoyed its machinations, the flow of men running in rhythm and the feeling of safety and fun that it created. A well-run basketball team eliminated uncertainty. He had the ability to visualize plays and his athleticism allowed his visions to materialize. A no-look pass to create a teammate's shot from the perimeter or his slashing through the lane to receive such a pass was not a mistake or a mirage, but the culmination of anticipation. Piper understood the moving parts of the world around him and he played his games to match his mind. When the shots fell, when the crowd approved and he was a man first and a black second, he wiped away the perspiration and took delight in the inspiration of his ever-forward-moving mind.

Welch appreciated Piper's mind as a baseball player. To say Piper had modest skills is probably an understatement; to say he had electrifying tools would probably be an overstatement. He had mind and instincts, a gift for interpreting the world around him, the creative abilities that had merged with his athletic skill to allow him to play his way out of the coal mines, and the desire to help those he cared about escape. The world of big-time Negro baseball did not overwhelm Piper.

His summers traveling the country playing baseball, especially with Willie Foster, resonated. Piper had already seen much of the world and, unlike some of his peers, could easily communicate with whites and try to maneuver his way around segregation the best he could. Fragmented records indicate that he batted .386 as Welch's shortstop in 1943. His legs weren't as springy and fresh as they had been before the winter on the road with the Globetrotters, but they were good enough. "I would get a week off between each sport," Piper said.

In the summer of 1943, Piper was twenty-six years old, but if you had asked him he would have shaved a few years off. He thought he was going to play first base, but Welch had Birmingham native Lyman Bostock. Piper wondered about playing third, but Welch had traded for Johnny Britton. Welch told Piper he would play shortstop.

"Man, I haven't played shortstop for years," Piper complained.

"Well, you're going to play today," Welch said.

The move worked and Birmingham's wait for a winner ended in 1943 when Welch and Piper led the Black Barons to the Negro American League championship and took satisfaction in beating the Chicago American Giants in the five-game playoff series. It was the first time a Black Barons team had won a Negro American League pennant, and it began the team's most successful five years. Awaiting the Black Barons in the 1943 Negro World Series were the powerful Homestead Grays. Cool Papa Bell hit leadoff. Shortstop Sammy Bankhead, one of five brothers who had played in the Industrial League, hit second. First baseman Buck Leonard hit third, catcher Josh Gibson fourth. Dave Hoskins, destined for the Cleveland Indians, played right field. The Black Barons, as usual, were underdogs, but pushed the Grays to the full seven games before losing.

The Industrial League began losing its grip when integration became the issue. Any company with a government contract—which meant every factory in Birmingham during World War II—was required to integrate the workforce. Factories discontinued baseball teams rather than integrate. The Fair Employment Practices Committee (FEPC), established at the behest of black civil rights activists, was a near-fatal strike to the Industrial League. A flood of ballplayers became receptive before the 1944 season, and Piper knew a ballplayer who would improve the Black Barons.

"I know a shortstop that can beat me playing shortstop—Artie Wilson," he told Welch. Welch trusted Piper so much that he didn't even ask to see Artie play.

"You think you can get him to leave home?" he asked.

"Sure I can get him," Piper said.

It didn't take much convincing.

"Did you get all your money?" Artie asked Piper.

"Yeah," Piper said. "I got it and more."

"I'll go," Artie said.

The first thing most people noticed about Artie Wilson was that he was missing the tip of his thumb on his right hand. When he played baseball, he was nimble and rangy and glided through the infield dirt. Artie followed the money as surely as he watched a grounder into his glove. He could transfer the ball to his throwing hand so quickly that it looked like he never touched it. "As soon as he got to the ball it was gone," said Jim Marshall, a first baseman who played with Artie a few years later. Artie batted left-handed and never hit home runs, so he used his speed. He sprayed the ball to right field so he was almost impossible to throw out. "The sonofagun could run like hell," said infielder George Genovese, who played against him. "When I played shortstop and he came to the plate, I moved so close to the third baseman that we could hold hands."

Artie was twenty-three in 1943, but his thumb had been gone since 1939, when he was a teenager. Accidents were so common in the factories that he rarely gave it a second thought. Working long hours caught up to him, creating an injury that became his signature. He was underage to be running a saw, but as Wilson recalled, "They didn't care nothin' about that." It was the same as Harry Salmon working in the coal mines at age eight. Work was work.

"I was cleaning up the machine shop," Wilson said. "I happened to be standing close by a machine and then a long piece of iron got hooked and was vibrating in the saw. I tried to grab it but I didn't know what happened. I ran across to the warehouse station and I needed someone to turn off that machine. I didn't know my thumb was [gone] until I pulled the glove off. I pulled out my thumb, which got caught up in that glove."

Wilson went to the infirmary and had his thumb sewn up. He didn't miss a single game or a day of work, but when the white folks' ball scouts saw him, they would always note him as the player with the thumb mysteriously severed off his throwing hand. Sometimes Artie's thumb made it difficult for him to get the grip he wanted, but like Piper, he was determined to play his way out of Birmingham. He would hit a home run if he had to, even though he joked that "if I ever hit a ball out of the ballpark, I'll stop and kiss first base, second base, and third base."

When the veteran Black Barons first saw Artie in 1944, they greeted him with the usual hazing that accompanied breaking into the black big leagues. Artie, as a rookie, would shower last. Veteran players noticed his confidence and guarded their turf. They told him he wasn't as good as he thought he was. They told him the Negro American League was better than the Industrial League. When Welch informed Artie that he was going to be the starting shortstop in 1944, Artie replied with a businesslike "I intend to be."

Some of the older Black Barons laughed at his poise, so Artie took it a step further. He told them he would not only start, but he would play in the East-West game. They told him he was being too ambitious for a rookie. "So what?" Artie said.

"I wish I knew what it was," he said. "I guess I had something inside. I never got nervous. It didn't make a difference if there were 50,000 people in the stands or ten people. I didn't care if it was a right-hander or a left-hander pitching. I believed I could hit. I'd always been that way, even in grade school. I always had it. I wish I could open it up and see it."

You could always see the muscular arms on outfielder Ed Steele, the next player Piper sought. Back in the Industrial League, Steele had picked up the timeless nickname "Stainless." It replaced his real first name, and it held better than his birthdate, which, at 1915, was two years earlier than Piper's. Nobody ever called him Ed and nobody ever

Birmingham Industrial League stars: The feeding system to the Negro Leagues and, later, the first wave of black players in major league baseball was in Birmingham, where factory teams ACIPCO and Stockham provided top competition. In this photo, taken circa 1942, are future Black Barons shortstop Artie Wilson (bottom row, second from left), future major leaguer Sam Hairston (bottom, second from right), and future Black Barons outfielder Ed Steele (top row, second from right). No state produced more Negro League players than Alabama.

called him old. Piper told Welch he would be an ideal right fielder. Steele's Industrial League past was evident the moment he removed his shirt. But, hard as his chest and arms were, his personality was genial and soft. Like Piper, he already played occasionally for the Black Barons before the offer to join the team full-time arrived in 1944. Steele could throw and he could hit for power. He couldn't run very well, but if you put him in the middle of the order and left him alone, you could watch the home runs add up.

Together, Piper, Artie, and Stainless made the 1944 Black Barons fly. They played like veterans and again captured the Negro American League pennant, winning both halves of the season with little resistance because the Kansas City Monarchs, with several starters drafted into military service, were not competitive. Birmingham might have had its best chance to win the Negro League World Series that year, but bad luck intervened. Tommy Sampson and four starters were involved in a head-on car crash twenty miles outside of Birmingham while returning from Louisville a week before the start of the series.

Sampson took the worst of it, breaking his leg, fracturing his hip, and suffering cuts on his hands and face. He was in the hospital for thirteen weeks. Johnny Britton cut up his hands and knees. A backup outfielder, Leandy Young, chipped a bone in his leg. Artie Wilson walked away with a sprained wrist. The Grays walked over the Black Barons, winning the series in five games.

That accident helped shape the Black Barons for the next few years. With Sampson out of the lineup, Piper played second base for the first time with the team. Sampson's leg didn't heal in time for him to start the 1945 season and the Barons sorely missed his bat. The Cleveland Buckeyes, led by their fleet center fielder Sam Jethroe, won the Negro American League and swept the Grays in the World Series. Jethroe was the latest in a long line of standout black center fielders, a lineage that began with Oscar Charleston, continued with Cool Papa Bell and Willard Brown, and was three years away from including young Willie Mays, who in 1945 was in seventh grade and making a name for himself on the sandlots around Birmingham. Willie could be found playing alongside Cat in the outfield for TCI's mill team. He sometimes played first base in games with his daddy.

While Mays grinned, Piper's temper was starting to get him in trouble, a characteristic that hindered his escape from the hot box. In a game in Cleveland in July, he argued a close call with umpire Jimmy Thompson, a wartime replacement. Infuriated by the rookie arbiter's close call, Piper was accused of striking the 135-pound Thompson.

When word of the altercation reached Negro American League president J. B. Martin, he made an example of Piper. At a time when integration rumors were rampant, Martin fined Piper his monthly salary of $50 and banned him from playing in the East-West All-Star Game, for which he would have been the starting second baseman for the West. That was an incident that undoubtedly hurt Piper's chances of escaping the hot box, for how many white folks' ball teams would sign a player who had struck an umpire?

Piper was suspended indefinitely for the remainder of season. Without him, the Black Barons had no chance. "Davis's fine and suspension was only the beginning of breaking up the thing which kills the future of Negro baseball," Martin stated in a letter delivered to all Negro League club owners. "I am extremely sorry to have to deny Davis's services to the West team and to hurt Birmingham's chances of winning the second half."

The Black Barons wondered if it was fair. They asked if the same punishment would have been administered had it been a Kansas City Monarchs player involved. They wondered if the incident would have been reported. Martin was closer to Monarchs owner Tom Baird than he was to Black Barons owner Tom Hayes, writing to Baird in 1955 that "I think Tom Baird has done more for Negro baseball that any person living."

Piper's hard-nosed style surfaced again in 1946. In a game against the Atlanta Black Crackers, Henry Barnes, an aging former Black Baron whose chances of escaping the hot box were gone, was catching with Piper on third base in a close game. Artie Wilson was the batter. In typical Artie style, he slashed the ball to the left side, where the shortstop fielded and threw to the plate. Piper, who had dashed from third base upon contact, homed in on Barnes. The throw was high and Piper saw his opportunity, his lead elbow flying directly at Barnes's chest. He barreled into the vulnerable man's rib cage, the winner of a horrendous collision, taking out the pigtail as though he had pulled a ladder out from under a house painter. Barnes collapsed in pain and Piper scored. "I know he didn't mean to hurt me," Barnes said. "But his elbow broke three or four ribs. I stayed in the hospital for two weeks and it slowed down my throwing after that. I could throw you out now, but my throwing wasn't strong enough for the majors."

In 1947, while Jackie Robinson was proving that a black player could escape the hot box and succeed in the majors, the Black Barons were again beaten in the regular season by Cleveland, which lost to the New York Cubans in the Negro World Series. Alex Pompez, the Cubans' proud owner, boasted it was the best team he had ever had. Pompez believed team-leading Orestes Minoso was one of the best center fielders that Negro League baseball had ever produced. Little did Pompez know, he was still one summer away from seeing the best center fielder Negro League baseball would ever produce.

On the other side of the hot box, the St. Louis Browns looked like the worst team in white folks' ball. Atrocious attendance accompanied its dismal talent level, bottoming out when only 478 fans attended a Monday afternoon game in July. Owner Bill DeWitt purchased two Kansas City Monarchs players, Willard Brown and Hank Thompson. Owner Tom Baird paid for the men's transportation and advocated their success.

The Browns sent both players directly to the majors, where they struggled to adjust to the pitching and were treated poorly by their white teammates. The Browns took a thirty-day option on Piper, which alone offended him. He resented the idea that he wasn't good enough to play on the worst team in white folks' ball. While Brown and Thompson struggled, the Browns dispatched scout Jack Fournier to follow Piper. Fournier, if he was true to his assignment, would have seen Piper go 2-for-3 at the East-West All-Star Game at Comiskey Park. Piper did it all that day. He doubled, stole a base, scored, and turned a double play with Artie Wilson. "If we decide to sign Davis, we'll send a worthwhile check to Tom Hayes Jr.," DeWitt said. A week after the game, the Browns released Brown and Thompson. Both players went back to the Monarchs, taken care of by Baird, who showed no interest in advocating Birmingham's favorite son. Brown and Thompson began sharing their experiences with black players. Soon, young Willie Mays could hear their story as well. The day Thompson and Brown were released, the Browns canceled their option on Piper. Fournier, a former big league first baseman from the 1920s who had once been arrested for his part in a barroom brawl, had long since gone home. "We are still looking every day for players who will strengthen our team and don't care whether they are white, black or green," DeWitt said.

Piper knew that it had been a matter of black, white, and green. While DeWitt was willing to compensate Hayes, he was not willing to give him enough to give Piper a share of the sales price. Piper knew he couldn't escape this hot box. DeWitt didn't understand how black players did business. So Piper stayed with the Black Barons, and though he rarely spoke about it, he had been bitterly disappointed. He knew he was better than what the Browns wanted to give him credit for. To his credit, he blocked out the distractions and finished the season with a .360 batting average. But in the back of his mind he had to ask himself the question: Was he ever going to get a chance to play in the majors? Or would he, like Willie Foster before him, be doomed to a life on the bus and the back roads of the Deep South? As Foster had once told him, his time to make sure a player could escape the hot box would one day arrive. That day was coming quickly.

Tom Hayes couldn't win soon enough and he knew that he couldn't win without Piper. He didn't want to sell his best players for a pittance. Integration was nice, but black teams needed good players to make money. Hayes, like many black owners, resented white teams that tried to steal players for below market value. He had the perfect incentive to prove how valuable Piper was to him. Hayes had been at odds with Sampson, who resumed playing second base in 1946. Piper moved back to first base and it was evident that Hayes liked him more than he liked Sampson. When Birmingham native Lyman Bostock came out of the service, Sampson wanted to play him at first base. Piper would have been the odd man out of the infield. Hayes wanted Piper playing every day, so much so that he told Sampson that Bostock couldn't hit. Sampson knew that wasn't right, and Bostock was sold to Chicago. Hayes protected the players who were loyal to him and disposed of those he viewed as mercurial.

At the end of the 1947 season, Sampson and Hayes fought for the last time. On a road trip to Knoxville, Sampson's appendix burst, and he had emergency surgery. He missed the next several games, and when he returned to Birmingham to collect his paycheck, he found that

Piper Davis's "good look": One of the best Negro League ballplayers of the 1940s, Piper Davis was a two-sport star, playing both for the Birmingham Black Barons and for the Harlem Globetrotters basketball team.

Hayes had deducted $125 for games missed. That was life in the Negro Leagues. Sampson told Hayes he could have the job back.

Between jobs, Sampson scrounged together a travel team that would play for percentages. He took Barnes with him to catch and immediately began scouring Birmingham for new talent. For years, Sampson claimed that it was he and Barnes, not Piper Davis, who discovered Mays playing sandlot ball for a team called the Fairfield Stars, TCI's mill team. "Listen, I found that guy, and do you know, I got no credit for it," Sampson said. He might have been to Mays what Charlie Mason had been to Piper in 1936—his first owner. Sampson said he bought Mays spikes and took him to play against the Newark Eagles in Macon, Georgia, a team that included Leon Day and Monte Irvin, Mays's future teammate with the New York Giants.

After Mays played impressively, pitcher Butch Huber tried to grab him for the Eagles, which became the first of many teams, black and white, to try to steal Willie Mays. "He is reported to have declined a $300 offer from the Newark Eagles," the *World* reported. All it took was a little creativity. Butch Huber was also John Shuber, former Black Barons pitcher. Mays remembered a player named Jack Hardy trying to recruit him. He was also Paul Hardy, a catcher who played several seasons for Alex Pompez. Names changed as easily as the seasons in Birmingham, where older players created aliases to play for Negro League teams without losing Industrial League jobs and younger players falsified names to earn experience. Phony names were endless and mimicked the practices freed slaves used to avoid detection. When he was underage, Irvin played for the Eagles under the alias Jimmy Nelson. He wasn't the only standout player to hide. Pitcher Chet Brewer began playing for pay in high school. "I would slip off and pitch for pro and semi-pro teams under an assumed name," he said. The better the player, the more aliases he was likely to use. No matter what name Mays was playing under, Sampson wouldn't let Newark take him. "I said, 'I couldn't let you have that kid,'" Sampson said. "I just picked him up."

There's a good chance that Cat Mays was already serving as his son's agent, doing his best to get his boy exposure to fulfill what he believed was a major league destiny. The proof is that Sampson said he did lose Mays, not to any white folks' team, but to the ever-present Chattanooga-to-Birmingham pipeline that had existed since Satchel Paige rode it in the 1920s. The Chattanooga Choo Choos paid a small salary, but small was good enough. Mays went off to play for manager Harry Bonds in 1947, one of the countless former fringe players who squeezed livings out of Negro travel baseball. According to Mays, his stay in Chattanooga lasted only three weeks. Sampson, flustered, went back to the Negro Leagues, but never forgot that player who got away from him, always eager to tell anyone who would listen how good that Mays boy had been. Mays said he didn't remember ever playing for Tommy Sampson. But Sampson never forgot Mays playing for him.

Sampson signed with Alex Pompez's New York Cubans for the 1948 season. Part of playing for Pompez was providing information on talented players from other regions. Pompez was well aware of Birmingham's Industrial League talent flow and believed white teams had no concept of the vast player pool, but he needed spies. Sampson spoke of a talented teenage center fielder in Birmingham, who was no secret in his hometown. He realized that making Pompez aware of Mays could enhance his own value. Sampson knew players were pawns, and perhaps he could exact a measure of revenge by stealing Willie Mays from Tom Hayes. A former ACIPCO player who had thought he was going to be a Black Baron for life, he wondered how he would survive after leaving Alabama.

"I had too many guys from Birmingham on the team, the hometown boys, and they were hard to handle," Sampson said. "At first I said, 'I'm taking the job. I'm the same guy you played with, but I can't run around with you guys every day.'" Telling the Black Barons they were night owls, taken care of on Negro Avenue and upstairs at Bob's Savoy, was a mistake. The Black Barons, pitcher Jimmy Newberry in particular, ate Sampson up. "Newberry, he was the main one, he was the hard one to handle," Sampson complained. "He drank a lot. You give him an hour to go out and eat when we're in town, and he may come back two hours later." Hayes watched it unfold and let it happen, for he had the perfect replacement in mind. He contacted Piper, who was playing winter ball for Caguas in the Puerto Rican winter league. Hayes had a proposition for him. Had Piper been upstairs at Bob's the moment Hayes asked him to take the Black Barons, below him he could have seen the masses of coal miners and their sons drinking to escape the misery. He could slowly savor his freedom now, for he had truly escaped his previous life.

At the Negro American League owners' meeting in Chicago in January 1948, several new managers were announced. Among them were Buck O'Neil and Piper Davis. Hayes stepped down from the podium, where he stood as close to Tom Baird as he cared to be. Piper believed the Black Barons needed to develop a different attitude. Winning was never more important. He planned to sharpen the edges of his night owls so he could beat Buck O'Neil and the Kansas City Monarchs. Piper couldn't wait to beat him.

A PIPER KIND
OF TEAM

Before Piper Davis become player-manager of the Black Barons, he had one final exercise in managerial leadership. The lesson came during winter ball in Puerto Rico when he had the opportunity to play for Quincy Trouppe, a switch-hitting catcher who, in the tradition of Negro League baseball, was rightfully considered a proud descendent of the pigtail family tree.

Piper watched and learned as Trouppe masterfully maneuvered a championship team. He observed how Trouppe carefully crafted on-field chemistry, believing winning created camaraderie. Trouppe liked players whose personalities complemented their performances. As a manager, he loved to defy convention and follow his instincts.

Trouppe's confidence was never more daring than in Game 7 of the Puerto Rican winter league championship series at Mayaguez, with Caguas trailing by one run and down to its final out in the ninth inning. He came to bat with a runner on first base, but so far in this game his swings had been futile. Trouppe despised the possibility of going 0-for-5 and losing. He had batted right-handed with no luck, so he tossed logic overboard and turned around to bat left-handed against a left-handed pitcher. Taking a shot at the right-field line 320 feet away, he turned on a down-and-in fastball and sliced the ball over the fence like he was chopping sugarcane.

The genius of black baseball was the willingness to play spontaneously. Piper called it the art of the unexpected. Black players were learning that white folks' ball did not appreciate individual creativity, but the Puerto Ricans loved it. There was no hot box in Puerto Rico, and even though Mayaguez fans were forced to tear up betting slips and toss them into the air as Trouppe rounded the bases, they appreciated his bravery.

Trouppe's team allowed the tying run to score in the bottom of the ninth to force extra innings. Mayaguez scored in the top of the tenth inning, and Trouppe entrusted the lead to pitcher Chet Brewer, who put the tying run on base. Alonzo Perry, a Birmingham boy whose reputation was forged in pool halls, came to bat. Trouppe called on a relief pitcher, Ben Torres.

Piper, playing second base, noted that Perry was a fearsome yet flawed hitter. He was a pitcher for the Black Barons, but Piper believed his future was in the batter's box. The future would have to wait, however, as Torres overmatched Perry with his best fastball to preserve Caguas's victory. Winning was a wonderful feeling, one Piper hoped to bring back to Birmingham. Trouppe said he would never have won the championship without Piper playing second base. Trouppe was made honorary mayor of Caguas and all schools were closed for the day. His home run made him a hero, but his day of legalized classroom hooky made him a legend.

When the series was over, spring in Birmingham meant the Black Barons came home for a family reunion. When the splendid winter ball season ended, six months of segregation and sardines awaited. The spring of 1948 was different from any other. There was home and hesitation, ambition and anxiety. Negro baseball was bleeding and white folks' ball wasn't helping.

Piper Davis stands on the top step of the dugout in 1948, his first season as player-manager of the Birmingham Black Barons.

Players kept a close eye on the progress of blacks in white folks' ball. Jackie Robinson's 1947 season had proved that it could happen, but Piper's experience with the St. Louis Browns was a reminder that black players were still trapped. The Browns had released outfielder Willard Brown during the 1947 season. He played winter ball in Puerto Rico and earned the nickname Ese Hombre, "That Man." The Browns dismissed him as a non-prospect, yet Brown batted .432 and won the Puerto Rican batting title. He hit 27 home runs, establishing a new league record, but nobody in white folks' ball thought he could play, so he resumed playing center field in Kansas City.

As Piper gathered his players, major league spring training had started. In Tucson, the Cleveland Indians brought Larry Doby back, though he struck out 11 times in 32 at-bats in 1947, hitting only .156, faltering as Brown and Thompson had in St. Louis. Piper watched closely, calmly agitated. While Doby was already getting his second chance, Piper wondered if he would get his. The same could be said for Artie Wilson, who had played shortstop for Mayaguez, the team that fell to Piper's Caguas team in the seven-game Puerto Rican winter league championship series. Artie led the league with 102 hits, but Piper was too much of a professional to give Artie a hard time about beating him.

The *Birmingham World* ran a story alongside the Doby update containing news of Branch Rickey's observations of catcher Roy Campanella. Rickey was drawing out the final stages of his long plan, in which he would bring what he considered the premium Negro talent to the majors. A catcher who possessed a superior throwing arm and power bat was going to play in white folks' ball for a very long time. "I want to get Campanella but I can't until I make room for him," said Rickey, who believed in limiting black players on each team, a quota system that was adopted by other clubs. "He was fearful," sportswriter A. S. "Doc" Young speculated, "that trouble might result if three Negroes were placed on one club."

Black players wondered how white folks' ball would make room for the rest of them. It wasn't only race discrimination—it was role discrimination, age discrimination, talent discrimination, and wage discrimination. The only way to control their future was to play well, and though Robinson succeeded, the topic of all black players receiving a fair chance was a sensitive subject. Negro American League president J. B. Martin tried to ease the players with a smooth dose of damage control. He said that Robinson's success was beneficial for Negro League baseball, because white fans would come to black games to watch future stars. He said Negro players should be on their best behavior for white scouts so that "someday a scout may walk up, pat [them] on the shoulder, and say, 'We can use you.'" When players heard that, they rightfully reasoned that Martin, a dentist, had never worn a uniform in his life.

In New York City, Dr. Dan W. Dodson, executive of the city's Racial Unity Committee, spoke in Harlem and wondered aloud if the Yankees and Giants had not only been ignoring black players, but sabotaging Brooklyn's efforts to sign more Negroes. History would prove Dodson to be a .500 hitter on the subject. The Yankees dug their heels in against integration and proved to be highly selective. The Giants, however, had a connection no other club had. Dodson believed the answer was to hire full-time black scouts, which as of 1948 no team had done. A few territory scouts had forged relationships with Negro League bird dogs, but few black voices mattered. Giants owner Horace Stoneham said his team would soon follow Rickey's lead. "We have tried out Negroes for several years," he said, omitting that his most successful player of the 1930s, first baseman Bill Terry, routinely rubbed the head of a Negro boy for luck. "But as yet we haven't found any who would fit in our plans."

Negro League officials wondered if their black teams fit into white folks' ball plans at all. In 1945, two years before Robinson integrated the majors, Yankee president Larry MacPhail urged the Negro Leagues to apply for permission to join the National Association, the governing body of the minor leagues, which would classify Negro teams as members of organized baseball and christen all Negro League players as professionally qualified. It would also mean black teams could sell their best players to major league teams with the promise of adequate compensation. It would also mean a team such as the Yankees could sign a few black players of inferior talent and bury them in the low minors, then point to the inherent deficiencies of black players. It was a practice the Yankees would adhere to into the 1950s. "The Yankee top management had some real sons-of-bitches," New York sportswriter Lester Rodney observed. "George Weiss, the general manager, was an out-and-out racist. Every sportswriter knew it."

In February 1948, Reverend John J. Johnson, president of the Negro National League, went public and claimed that the Negro American and National leagues were denied entry into the National Association. Johnson claimed that the two leagues adhered to MacPhail's suggestions for improvement, but were nonetheless denied classification, organized baseball's gold stamp.

"The Negro Leagues still possess no status, no voice, no rights, no relationship at all to the major or minor leagues," Johnson wrote. He called 1947 a "disastrous season" for Negro League baseball.

When the Negro Leagues were denied entry into organized ball, they were essentially classified as a bastardized league, a place where white teams could plunder players, rob owners, and manipulate formalities with no recourse. Black owners were immediately edgy, and Tom Hayes, in his refusal to sell Piper Davis to the St. Louis Browns in 1947, had established himself as a hard man, though from his perspective he was standing up for himself and his player. That too was a double-edged sword, for not only did a Black Baron ballplayer have to be scouted favorably, but Hayes had to be satisfied. He made it clear that he expected to be adequately compensated for his property. Why then would a white team bother to scout the Black Barons? The Kansas City Monarchs were more than happy to do business and provide scouting reports on players from other teams. The hot box was suffocating.

Hayes's fears were well founded. In February 1948, Monarchs owner Tom Baird was still furious that Branch Rickey never paid him for Jackie Robinson. From his safe perch in Kansas City, Baird was a willing participant in New York City baseball politics. MacPhail of the rival Yankees accused Rickey of the Dodgers of stealing Robinson, a claim Baird called "absolutely true." It cemented Baird's hatred of the Dodgers and loyalty to the Yankees.

"In signing Robinson away from us, Rickey hid behind the alibi that we had no written contract with Jackie," Baird said. "That's true, but our league constitution stipulates that a player agreeing to play by signed letter or telegram is the property of the club concerned. We had Robinson on our payroll in 1945 and we paid Social Security and withholding taxes in his behalf. He was our property all right, and Rickey knew it."

Fitting into a team's plans is the core of a baseball player's career, but it must be achieved within a finite amount of time, while his skills will allow him to compete. Black players tried to block it out and go to work, but it was never easy. In the pages of the *World*, syndicated black columnist Marion E. Jackson wrote a scathing manifesto of the faults of the Negro Leagues, echoing the cries of *Pittsburgh Courier* columnist Wendell Smith as far back as 1938.

"Negro Baseball will not fold up in '48, but here are some 'musts' for the survival of the game," Jackson wrote. "(1) Better publicity. Fans complain when newspapers fail to carry releases of the home team on the road. (2) Too little advertisement with Negro players who must have support through this medium in order to carry comprehensive reports on the games. (3) Too much arguing and bickering among the players. Baseball fans don't go to the ballparks to watch prize fights unless they are advertised as such. (4) Not enough hustle. The players should enliven the game with daring and sparkle. (5) Too much delay in starting games, especially the second game of double-headers. (6) Umpires should be under the jurisdiction of the league and not the owners. As it stands now, the team at home supplies the game officials, and therein lies a long story. Officials should be assigned through the league office and rotated throughout the so-called league. Humans are not infallible and constant umpiring for the home teams tend to develop."

Exposure to white baseball was supposed to create opportunity, but from the southern perspective it had the reverse effect. White baseball exposed the weaknesses of black baseball—organization, cash flow, facilities, behavior, and publicity. No team had its own field, and each was usually subjected to paying exorbitantly high rental fees for the use of major league parks. The great Negro Leagues of the 1930s were reduced to lower than the white minor leagues. White folks' ball succeeded in driving a wedge into the black community, breaking the league as though it were a union, and in pure baseball terms, killing it by attacking its weakness, then sifting through the carnage to sign who it wanted with inexpensive delight. What Negro baseball needed most was a new star, someone who could play at such a high level that the ground below could not contain him, and the glass ceiling above could not limit him.

In the first few months of 1948, Willie Mays was already a high school star. While Piper Davis and Artie Wilson were playing in the Puerto Rican winter league, Mays was flustering flimsy high school athletes who would never see an athlete like him again. While the *Birmingham World* kept an eye on Piper's preparations for spring training, it followed shooting guard Willie Mays.

"MAYS STEALS SHOW . . . Mays started dunking 'em from the outset of the game, never to be seriously threatened for individual scoring honors," the *World* reported. "The first ten points for Fairfield was rung up by this accurate shooting Willie Mays."

Mays was a rising star in Birmingham's buzzing sporting community in 1948. The *World*, which billed itself as a "Standard Race Journal" and a "Newspaper with a Constructive Policy," did its best to spotlight the black sporting environment, which included covering the all-black high schools that the white *Birmingham News* ignored. Mays won the Jefferson County scoring title with 241 points and was the first member listed on the *World*'s all-county team. Mays wasn't the only good basketball player in town, but the *World* thought he was the best. He happily sprinted and dunked, and then, like a million high school jocks before and after him, scoured the pages of the paper to find his name.

Mays had all the physical properties of a splendid natural athlete on the basketball court, a characteristic *World* sportswriter Ellis Jones noted before anyone observed Mays's similar capacity on a baseball field. In comparing Mays to his best high school basketball rival, a forgotten kid named Willie Scoggins of Parker High, Jones awarded Mays the edge, and scouted what Piper Davis would soon observe about him. "The difference in the two players lies in the fact that Scoggins has off nights," Jones wrote. "Mays does not."

It was the ability to be consistent, to rise to the occasion, that was already setting Mays apart. This was an intangible, something few players possess. This quality, paired with pure talent, created the formula for an exceptional ballplayer, no matter whether handling a baseball or a basketball. Jones eloquently captured Mays's gifts. "Mays seldom misses once he breaks through," he wrote.

Mays understood at a young age that breaking through Birmingham society would not be as easy as dribbling past a defender. The city's segregation was legal hatred inspired by fear and enforced by anger.

When Mays was thirteen years old in 1944, Birmingham General Ordinance, Section 859, titled simply "Separation of Races," was authorized by Police Commissioner Bull Connor and made law.

> It shall be unlawful for any person in charge of or in control of any room, hall, theater, picture house, auditorium, yard, court, ballpark, public park or indoor or outdoor place, to which both white persons and negroes are admitted, to cause, permit or allow mixing of races.

Those forty-eight words shaped how young Willie Mays viewed the world around him. Like Piper Davis, he recognized that athletics were his only escape. The external world could not provide him with the means to avoid a laborer's fate, as it had for Piper. For a young black kid growing up in Birmingham, only sports offered that opportunity.

"Everything was segregated," Mays said, "the movies, the restaurants and different things. And you had the bathrooms that had 'colored' and 'white' on it, and all that kind of junk. So you knew exactly what was going on, but you couldn't do anything about it at that particular time. So I think it affected a lot of people at that time coming along. I guess they had to accept what was going on. They couldn't do much about it."

Bobby Veale, four years younger than Mays, remembered how childhood games between black and white children were the first signs of defiance. "We broke the segregation laws way before anyone else because we were playing baseball together," said Veale. "When you were black you had white friends, and when you were white you had black friends. It wasn't the kids carrying the struggle on. It was the adults."

But kids learned that sports were not immune to segregation. Mays remembered mixed games when he was twelve or thirteen, the time when Section 859 made a black boy playing catch with a white boy an illegal act. "They would stop us from playing," he said. "An officer would come down and break us up. We'd go our separate ways."

Those moments built up inside Mays and sports became his refuge. He didn't have much money, he had few rights, he was expected to pick a trade and never make any noise, expected to accept someone else's destiny. His personality was like his body—growing, running forward with slashing moves, and above all, determined to have the right to play what he loved. "I was very fortunate to play sports," he said. "All the anger in me went out."

Years later, when recalling the Negro Leagues, Mays, then seventy-seven, knew very well that Satchel Paige had played not only for the Monarchs but for many other teams as well, "following the money." This was a reality Cat Mays undoubtedly knew. It was a path Willie didn't need anyone to tell him to follow. The system was rigged. The only way out was to cheat.

Piper Davis knew you couldn't cheat or hustle to create a winning team. His first move of the new season was to dispose of the relaxed policy of no spring training and cut short his team's night hours on Negro Avenue. Winning was more important than ever, attendance had to be attained, and players had to be seen, scouted, and sold. Younger players needed to be discovered, polished, and presented. Piper opened tryouts to college players, a first for the Black Barons. This roused the curiosity of the *World*, which decreed, "Who knows? Another Jackie Robinson may be discovered."

All of the fun went out in one loud Saturday bang night upstairs at Bob's Savoy in early March. The bus to Birmingham's first spring training, in a comfortable setup at Montgomery State Teacher's College, would depart early Sunday morning. Piper wasn't at the party, but his line was set and his first rule was to be on time. If the bus was scheduled to depart at dawn, Piper ordered the driver to have the engine running five minutes in front of the sun. When the players boarded, Piper was waiting. He was their friend, but now he was their boss.

Piper had two catchers; the nimble, quick, and thick-boned Herman Bell, an ACIPCO star, and Pepper Bassett, the husky Negro League veteran power hitter. Piper would continue playing second base, as he had over the winter in Puerto Rico, and team with Artie Wilson at shortstop.

Quick of foot, sure-handed, and talented with the bat, Birmingham native Artie Wilson became the home team's starting shortstop, winning fans with his personality as much as his hitting. He was the first of four members of the 1948 Black Barons to play in the majors.

That also meant that he needed a new first baseman. Johnny Britton returned to play third base. Pitching was solid but not plentiful, and so were outfielders. As the bus pushed off from Negro Avenue and headed to Montgomery, Piper knew what he had and what he needed. He hoped some of the answers would come from some of the new players on his bus, some of whom he knew very little about. Tom Hayes had spent the summer dispatching his unofficial scouts to find fresh bodies, but it was Piper's final responsibility to decide who could play and who could not.

Among the first-year Black Barons in the back of the bus was an outfielder from Nashville named Jimmy Zapp, twenty-three, a powerfully built young man with a tan complexion that allowed him to pass in many social circles. He also learned that being light-skinned sometimes meant exclusion from both groups. This hurt and haunted him throughout his early years, but he found complete acceptance in black baseball, and in 1945 he followed his pal Junior Gilliam to the Baltimore Elite Giants.

Zapp's first meaningful moment came against the Homestead Grays at Washington's Griffith Stadium, a ballpark with a cavernous outfield that often turned well-hit balls into frustrating outs. Zapp sauntered to the plate against Roy Welmaker, a hard-throwing left-hander, whose electric stuff forced Zapp to admit that he had never seen pitching like this. Zapp refused to be intimidated, settled in with a smile, and dove for the dirt when Welmaker threw at his head. He dusted himself off and danced back into the box.

Zapp reacted when Welmaker challenged him with a fastball. "There was a screen all the way down from the right-field line to dead center," Zapp said. "I hit it on top of that screen in right-center for a triple. From then on, Buck Leonard would always tell his pitchers, 'Keep that fastball away from Zapp.'"

Zapp believed he could hit a ball as far as anybody, but he wasn't sold on integration. "If I had been a white boy," he said, "ain't nothing would have held me back." He was sold to Nashville in 1946, which he liked because it was home, and wondered if Baltimore had moved him because he was light-skinned and his team questioned his off-the-field decisions.

"When [Brooklyn] signed Jackie, my attitude didn't even change," Zapp said. "I didn't even think about going to the majors. I just kept on doing the same thing I was doing. In Nashville, there was a preacher who would say to me, 'Jackie is in the majors, everyone got a chance now.' I just kept on doing my same thing. I just could not believe that I would have the same chance."

Zapp was traded to the Atlanta Black Crackers in the Negro Southern League, but the experience soured him. The owner, John Harden, "had money, but he was cheap with his players," Zapp said. "He did not like to pay. You had to fight to get your money, so when we went on a road trip east, I quit right there in New York. My mother and sister were there. I thought I was done with baseball. I came back to Nashville and I was standing in front of a nightclub downtown. An old ballplayer came through Nashville for some reason and looked me up. His name was T. Brown. I never did get his first name and I never saw him again. I have no idea who he was or how he found me. He said, 'I understand you have given up baseball.' I said, 'Yes, I'm tired of it.' He said, 'If I recommend you to the Birmingham Black Barons, will you go to spring training with them?' I said yes. So I went to spring training down in Montgomery."

Zapp and Stainless Steele immediately became pals, often engaging in home-run-hitting duels, smiling and swaggering and entertaining teammates. When one of them crushed a ball just right, it created a perfect feeling, and as the ball vanished, so did the pain of discrimination. Piper let his players have those moments, because he was a player too, and he understood how those experiences nurtured the soul. But he was also trying to weed out the weak. "The team is doing a lot of running on the orders of the manager," the *World* wrote. "Piper Davis has sent his cohorts through rigid spring drills in preparation for the coming season."

"I remember that spring training," Zapp said. "Piper had a bunch of guys who worked hard, worked hard and worked hard. If you didn't, you were gone."

Piper prepared his players for an Easter Sunday exhibition game at Rickwood Field against the defending Negro American League champion Cleveland Buckeyes. After that game, the Black Barons were scheduled to play just about every day in April. The Negro American League season would begin on May 1, a Saturday night, also against the Buckeyes at Rickwood Field.

Zapp made the team. He found another running mate in Alonzo Perry, who bounced around black baseball but never settled into success. Perry was a sidearm pitcher who relied more on deception and less on velocity. No one questioned the speed at which he lived his life off the field. Piper didn't care what Perry did away from the field, only what he did on it. A unique dynamic was forming. His players didn't have to love Piper, but they did. Piper's distinct language, his booming voice, and his solid playing skills backed up his presence.

Ed "Stainless" Steele was a mainstay in right field for the Black Barons for nearly a decade, his combination of home run power and arm strength making him a perennial Negro American League All-Star.

Piper continued molding his team around the circumstances of the times. He needed Perry as a pitcher and first baseman. He had seen him flash power in winter ball and believed that he might get the bulk of the innings at first. The Black Barons hired a defensively skilled first baseman from Los Angeles, Joe Scott, who Piper wasn't convinced could hit. Piper hoped Perry would seize the opportunity he seemed certain to receive.

Because most Negro League teams only carried sixteen players, versatility was crucial. Piper was the best example of that. He would play second base in 1948, but could play any infield position, the outfield, and catcher. If Perry was to play more first base, then Piper knew he'd have to keep his eye out for another pitcher. He would be fortunate if he could find one who would provide him versatility—in other words, the ability to swing the bat. It wasn't uncommon for pitchers to be used as extra outfielders and pinch runners. Many black pitchers were exceptional athletes whose skills easily adapted from one position to the next. This kind of player acquisition would be perfect, if he could be found.

After starting the exhibition season with a 12–8 victory over the Buckeyes on Easter Sunday in which Zapp and Steele both hit home runs, the Black Barons embarked on a southern swing through Asheville, Memphis, and back into Alabama. The pitching staff was set with veteran right-handers Bill Powell and Jimmy Newberry to join the tricky, undersized, and relatively inexperienced left-hander Jehosie Heard in the starting rotation. All three were Birmingham boys. Perry, Sammy C. Williams, and Nat Pollard would also pitch, but it wasn't enough. Piper told his catchers to find another pitcher. After all, stealing players from lesser clubs was a way of life.

The Black Barons were eager to report their scores to the *World* while they were on the road trip, with one exception. The team won sixteen games and lost just one, to Asheville, a lower-level team that had no business beating it. In that loss, the Black Barons ran across a young pitcher most of them had never seen before. He had a fast arm to match a fresh, glowing face, and threw a hard, quick curveball that was like a slider. Put a bat in his hands and he could do some damage. Bill Greason had already seen more than he ever thought he would

Right-handed pitcher Jimmy "Schoolboy" Newberry looked like an angel, but he was no saint. The hard-drinking, hard-throwing shine-ball artist was beloved by his Black Barons and derided by others for his mercurial habits.

have growing up in Atlanta. He liked to say that he didn't find baseball. "It found me," he said.

Five years before Piper Davis found Bill Greason, the United States Marines did. Greason soon discovered the worst truth of Iwo Jima. "You see those crosses [in the cemetery]," he said, "and you think that there's only one person under each cross."

By the time Greason experienced baseball segregation, it had nothing on military segregation and the bloodshed he witnessed in the Marines. Drafted in 1943, he learned that white company commanders handpicked black drill instructors to be cruel. A few years later, he had no trouble with Piper's rules because he had met his DI first. "I'll never forget Goins," Greason said. "He was awful. Our boot camp was different. It was very segregated. The whites were hard on the black drill instructors. And they didn't make it no better on us, because we were representing, first of all, this," Greason remembered, touching his hand to his cheek. "We didn't want to disgrace anybody. We had a lot of pride in ourselves and in the Marines. Even now, that's part of me. I'll never lose that. The discipline, the cohesiveness, the camaraderie was something else. They taught us that if one man goofed off, the whole group suffered."

Bill Greason was not an everyday rookie. He was more mature, chose his words carefully, and though he was full of fury, he sought perspective. He had seen racism and death and chose baseball as the means to avoid what befell so many Marines on Iwo Jima. When he came home, he despised racism but didn't want it to lead to a spiritual death. He would do his best to subdue the youthful anger that sometimes appeared during competitive moments, because "once you're dead, you're dead for a long time." Behind the humor was a very subtle defiance to choose love over anger and to overcome all obstacles to become the person he was meant to be.

What he was meant to be was a baseball player. Greason, the middle of five children, who grew up in Atlanta's North Side, said, "We were poor folk." His father, James, was a laborer who made ends meet by working odd jobs. His mother, Lizzie, washed laundry for white families. One day, Greason picked up a tennis ball and began to throw it against the wall. An innocuous act turned into a great moment of invention. He had a slender wrist and instinctively figured out that he could make the ball break. "It was amazing what I could do with it," he said. "With a little thin wrist, I could turn it over pretty good. A little fella named Sammy Haynes—he was a fine brother—he saw me and said, 'Why don't you try throwing a baseball?' He got down to catch me and said, 'You've got something!'"

Greason earned the inevitable nickname "Double Duty" for his pitching and hitting skills and realized he had been given these talents to shape his life. "It was a gift, baseball was," he said. "Once you discover the gift, it's up to you to develop it. That's what I saw. Me, being a poor fellow coming out of Atlanta, at the time after finishing high school, I went into the Marines. I didn't have a chance to pick up a trade or anything. I saw baseball as my future at the time. I developed it. I watched other pitchers. Pitching was my gift that had to be developed."

When Greason beat the Black Barons, Pepper Bassett wanted him. As the story was told to Greason, Bassett said, "Piper, get that boy. We can use him."

"That Friday, the manager came to my hotel and said, 'Bill you've been sold to the Black Barons. They want you to be in Birmingham for the Sunday game.'"

The Black Barons left Birmingham with thirty players and sixteen uniforms. When Greason joined the team, there would be exactly sixteen on this Piper kind of team. He had milked the most flexibility and options out of a small roster built for a six-month season wrought with travel, segregation, and the ever-present hot box. Of course, Piper knew that Buck O'Neil, who finished his first month as Kansas City Monarchs manager, was eagerly building the club he inherited. Piper knew the date the Black Barons would first play the Monarchs, the last weekend in May at Rickwood Field. He wanted to win this season and felt this composition gave him the best chance.

At last, the Black Barons came home, rolling through Negro Avenue, homeward bound to a comfortable world. The Birmingham Barons, the white Southern Association club, had left town for a road trip, and as was customary, the Black Barons came into town to play while the white Barons were gone. Opening day for the Negro American League season was upon the team. Tom Hayes smiled. His new manager had achieved the first order of business. He had shaped a distinctive club, a Piper kind of team, with only one piece missing.

4

THE DEFENDERS OF RICKWOOD FIELD

Rickwood Field was a jewel in its time. A $75,000 spectacle that opened in 1910, it was then only the fifth steel-and-concrete stadium in the United States. The park was financed and conceived entirely by a local Birmingham steel baron, Rick Woodard, who lent a combination of his first and last names to the park's one-of-a-kind title. Woodard consulted with his friend the Philadelphia Athletics owner and field manager Connie Mack to design the specifications to closely resemble Shibe Park, the Philadelphia stadium Mack had helped create to house his team. The result in Birmingham was Philadelphia's twin stadium, a pitching-and-defense-friendly ballpark that discouraged players from swinging for the fences and, not coincidentally, helped keep salaries down.

When the stadium first opened, left field was an unusually deep 470 feet away from home plate. Right field was situated an agreeable

335 feet away, but center field was a graveyard. It was 500 feet to dead center, and nobody ever hit a home run over the fence in that direction. The vast dimensions helped Rickwood Field create its own personality, a hometown feel marked by the nostalgia that already surrounded it. Rickwood represented hope, for the white ballplayers who yearned to make it to the majors, and the black players who longed for baseball to bring them to a better life.

If teenage Willie Mays wanted to run on the outfield grass in the spring of 1948, there's a good chance Eddie Glennon would have let him. Glennon was a rotund, energetic bouncing man of nearly fifty years who never forgot to starch his collar, wear his brown derby, and conceal his true age with the vigor of an ancient ballplayer. He grew up across the street from Shibe Park, wormed his way into Mack's company, and decided he wanted a life in baseball.

After a star career as a high school football player and track athlete, Glennon played in an early professional football league as a quarterback in Mount Airy, Pennsylvania, where he was nicknamed "Shorty." When he was finished playing football, he began selling floor rugs and hated his new occupation. He sought Mack, who introduced him to Bob Carpenter, the owner of the Philadelphia Phillies, who gave Glennon his start as a minor league general manager. By 1940, Glennon was running Mack's minor league team in Wilmington, Delaware. After several seasons in the lower minors, Glennon arrived from New Orleans as general manager of the Birmingham Barons in 1947 and boosted the team's fan base, breaking the franchise's thirty-seven-year-old attendance record despite a sixth-place finish with the inferior players the Philadelphia Athletics provided. Connie Mack still hated paying good money for good players.

Determined to make Birmingham a better team in 1948, Glennon took the initiative. He began by altering the archaic outfield dimensions, transforming it from a dinosaur of the Dead Ball era to a field that better resembled a modern stadium. He ordered the scoreboard repositioned and brought the corners in. The power alleys were less invasive, though they were still an unusually long 370 feet away. Still, the park was cozier for hitters, and it was obvious that no team could win there without a fast center fielder who could catch and throw.

Hitting was difficult, but batters enjoyed playing there. The enormous clock-crowned scoreboard was the landmark in left field. Glennon ordered stars to be painted where memorable home runs were hit. Behind the fence, a row of grass was planted and cheerfully christened "Glennon's Gardens." Rickwood Field, which still stands today and is the nation's oldest major ballpark, two years older than Boston's Fenway Park, was one of those rare fields that felt like home to many players, regardless of race and age.

"I don't know what it is, but when I was playing at Rickwood Field, I was always itching to get to the ballpark," Black Barons right-handed pitcher Bill Powell recalled. "We played all over the United States and when we got here, you loved coming here to play in this park. There was just something about the baseball in that park."

There was a second change that Eddie Glennon arranged in time for the 1948 Double-A Southern Association season. Fed up with Philadelphia's lousy minor league system, he signed a new working agreement with the Boston Red Sox. There was one reason alone for this move: money. The Red Sox spent lavishly on their minor league system, sending the Barons three players they cared about developing: right fielder George Wilson, center fielder Tommy O'Brien, and first baseman Walt Dropo, who on May 21 blasted a memorable 467-foot home run that cleared the forty-foot-high clock tower above the scoreboard. Glennon ordered the first star painted on the outfield wall.

The Red Sox expected all three players to make it from Rickwood Field to Fenway Park by 1950. Red Sox general manager Joe Cronin also promised that the Red Sox would stop and play an exhibition game in Rickwood Field on the way north from spring training. Cronin kept his word, and in the spring of 1948 Ted Williams took batting practice and played left field in Rickwood Field.

The Red Sox visit was part of a banner spring in Birmingham. On April 12, the New York Yankees came to Rickwood Field. That was largely because of Yankee radio broadcaster Mel Allen, who, according to one writer, left town "loaded down with gifts like a bride following a shower." Allen, a Birmingham native who began his sports broadcasting career at the University of Alabama, received the key to the city before the game. A smattering of black fans crowded into the right-field stands as part of the paying crowd of 4,924.

Mel Allen might have been the local hero, but there was no doubt that the real box-office gold was Joe DiMaggio. He was thirty-three in 1948, coming off a 1947 season in which he won his third and final American League Most Valuable Player Award. Willie Mays had been five years old when DiMaggio first came to the Yankees. As he grew up, like millions of other Depression-era boys, he found his big league hero.

DiMaggio could have asked to take the day off in a meaningless game, but to sit out would contradict his elegant image. He collected a single in three at-bats and struck out with the bases loaded in the first inning. It didn't matter. DiMaggio was DiMaggio, and in the spring of 1948, three of the greatest outfielders of all time, DiMaggio, Ted Williams, and Willie Mays, played at Rickwood Field.

In the Barons bullpen, seated on the bench down the left-field line, was right-handed pitcher Al LaMacchia, then twenty-five years old and trying desperately to return to the majors, where he had pitched briefly for the St. Louis Browns and Washington Senators. He trusted his eyes but not his sore arm. He trained his eyes on DiMaggio playing center field. LaMacchia already had thoughts of starting a scouting career when he could no longer pitch and was teaching himself how to accurately judge players. He was convinced that DiMaggio was the best center fielder who had ever played, combining technical perfection with dazzling talent and élan. "DiMaggio had a knack for playing center field," he said.

LaMacchia was fortunate. His bad arm would soon give him an opportunity to become one of the few white Barons to see Mays as an unsophisticated but uncommonly talented teenage Negro League rookie. He would also perhaps become the only scout in baseball history who could accurately address what would become one of the richest riddles baseball has ever produced: Who do you like better in center field, DiMaggio or Mays?

Game day at Rickwood Field in Birmingham, circa 1940s, was the pride of the black community and one of the few times the city's open sores didn't show.

DiMaggio or Mays often became a black-or-white question, but Eddie Glennon didn't care about race. He had no regard for the Red Sox's racist history, which included the infamous workout of Negro Leaguers Jackie Robinson, Marvin Williams, and Sam Jethroe at Fenway Park in 1945 when, according to legend, someone shouted, "Get those niggers off the field!" Soon, Glennon started making a lot of noise about Mays, who he would see play many times in the coming months. Eddie Glennon was the first person to tell the Red Sox about Willie Mays, more than a year before scout George Digby stayed in Birmingham for an extra day to see the Black Barons on Glennon's advice.

Glennon's right-hand man was Bob Scranton, a former college basketball player who described Glennon as a "short, stubby little old man who ran the show." Scranton, then twenty-three, had followed Glennon to Birmingham from New Orleans and became his concessions manager and traveling secretary. Scranton was Glennon's eyes and ears, the man who watched scouts as fervently as he monitored the formula for the ballpark's secret sauce. Scranton insisted Glennon was his own man when it came to racial matters. He remembered sitting in the office at the ballpark in New Orleans with Glennon and former Cardinals scout Roy Dissinger on April 15, 1947, when news came over the radio that Jackie Robinson had made his major league debut. Scranton and Dissinger shared Glennon's disposition and gladly took the bullets that accompanied it.

"Eddie Glennon, being a Yankee, he could care less," Scranton said. "Roy and I and Eddie were in the office at noontime when the news came over about Robinson. A lot of those southern people said, 'Oh, you damn Yankees will be happy he's playing' and all that shit. We Yankees didn't fit in too well in the South in those days."

Glennon's open nature was evident when Scranton observed him interact with Black Barons owner Tom Hayes. Hayes and Glennon got along splendidly, and Hayes knew he had a rarity in Negro League baseball—an amicable, downright normal working relationship with the white team in town. It was a much more constructive relationship than Hayes's other experiences in white folks' ball.

"Tom Hayes was a class act and a fine gentleman," Scranton said. "He was a good businessman, too. We'd run the concession and sell tickets for him. He'd rent the ballpark for something like ten percent of the gate. In those days, it was maybe $5,000 to rent the park and any attendance over 5,000 fans, we'd get another five percent."

Menu prices for black fans were exactly the same as they were for whites. Enjoy the Rickwood Field menu, circa 1948: A hot dog would run you a quarter. A bag of popcorn or peanuts would set a fan back a dime. A Coke was also a dime, but Scranton and Glennon wanted to do better. "Instead of a six-ounce Coke, we sold a twelve-ounce Coke for a quarter," Scranton said. "People would rather have the big double Coke than the small Coke. We were the first to do that."

Scranton's best worker was young Bobby Veale, who, at age thirteen, wanted to play for the Black Barons. He possessed a serious face, yet was developing a coy sense of humor and collecting meaningful observations. He was a pitcher for the 24th Street Red Sox in the Industrial League and was convinced he couldn't be touched. He thought he was "Lefty Grove, a big-time left-handed pitcher," though since he was too young to (legally) talk his way onto the Rickwood Field mound to pitch for the Black Barons yet, he worked the main concession stand. "I could make a Coca-Cola faster that any people Scranton had," Veale said. "I used to run change around to the different concession stands, anything to make a coin." When asked what Scranton paid him, Veale joked six decades later, "A peanut."

Veale's peanuts bought perspective. Young enough to enjoy childhood, he was old enough to recognize segregation. Like Piper Davis, who was his hero, and Willie Mays, whom he emulated, Veale knew baseball was the way out of filling twelve-ounce Cokes for the rest of his life. "If they didn't want you somewhere, they'd put up a sign that said, 'Read, Nigger, Run—if you can't read, nigger, run anyhow.' They had little pictures on the sign if you couldn't read. That was a way of life back there."

Veale was such a good athlete that when the Harlem Globetrotters played at Rickwood Field, Winfield Welch wanted to leave Birmingham with him. But Veale's daddy wasn't hearing any of that. Veale was already focused, and sometimes his serious face was misunderstood. He wasn't mad. He was determined to escape the hot box. He saw white folks' ball scouts come and sit in the press box because they didn't want to sit in the stands with black people. He saw Glennon yell at the Red Sox that summer because they refused to come see Mays. It could happen to any black ballplayer in Birmingham.

When the white Barons were in town, black fans were admitted only into the distant right-field bleachers, which acquired two distasteful nicknames, the "Coal Bin" and the "Crow's Nest." The segregated crowds were the personal touch of former Barons radio announcer Bull Connor. "The white person had the advantage on just about every damn thing," Veale said. "A black person couldn't go sit in the area with the white person. A black person had to go sit in the colored section out in right field. The only time they were allowed to go across that little white fence is when it started raining."

Veale could rarely touch the field when the white Barons were in town, but he could when the Black Barons were home. Though he was four years younger than Mays, Piper Davis welcomed Veale onto the field and made him, for the next few seasons, the team's bat boy. Veale, in turn, became friends with Piper's son, Lorenzo Jr., nicknamed Ruben.

"I used to go out there before games and shag balls," Veale said. "I used to pitch batting practice for the white Barons and come back and do the same for the Black Barons. Then I'd go back out, shag some more, and play around in the ballpark. When the game started, I went to the concession stands and did the things I normally did."

Veale was shagging balls and working the concession stand when Bill Powell was ready to take the ball for Piper Davis on opening night 1948, in the Negro American League opener against the Cleveland Buckeyes. The league opener in Birmingham was scheduled for a Saturday night and was a tremendous civic holiday. A crowd of 8,000 fans flocked to Rickwood Field. Many fans congregated on Negro Avenue in the late afternoon, joining in a parade marching to the gates of the ballpark, led by the Parker High marching band. When the fans streamed through the turnstiles, they found the Black Barons warming up on the field. Batting practice was arranged as one long group, with the starting lineup hitting in order as chosen by Piper, followed by the extra men. After Piper and Artie Wilson had hit, they took infield practice. With rookie pitcher Bill Greason hitting them ground balls with a fungo bat, Artie and Piper turned their flashy double plays into a pregame show. "You want to see something," Greason remembered, "boy, them fellas was something."

After batting practice and infield practice, a pregame ceremony was planned with members of the local Negro chapter of the Veterans of Foreign Wars presenting colors. Powell paused in his warm-ups to join the Black Barons on the third base line for the Parker High marching band to play the national anthem. As the anthem played, the Black Barons stood at attention, caught, like the rest of black America, in a strange paradox of honoring the country that restricted them. That was why these games had such communal meaning. Baseball was freedom. Between the lines, on the field, it was limitless.

· · ·

Though the Black Barons had been playing since April, tonight was the first game that would officially count toward the Negro American League standings. When the national anthem was over, the Black Barons temporarily returned to their bench, the bomb shelter–like dugouts that forced tall players to duck. Piper told his team his seven simple words, a phrase he would only say before games that had significance: "Let's get 'em, men! Let's get 'em!"

The predominately black crowd, with a few curious white spectators seated in the right-field bleachers, rose to its feet to welcome the team that the *World* affectionately called "The Defenders of Rickwood." As quickly as Veale sprinted up and down the grandstand stairs, pitcher Bill Powell leisurely strolled onto the mound. Powell was the hardest working pitcher on the staff. He was a 19-game winner in 1947 and went 7–0 against Negro American League teams. No pitcher did more running in those hot, quiet afternoons at Rickwood Field than Powell, and no Black Baron pitcher took care of his body the way Powell did. Powell was a genial man off the field and called himself a "natural smiler," though he never smiled in team photos, preferring instead to demonstrate his square-jawed seriousness. Powell gave Bobby Veale spare change for his hard work. "Bill Powell was a statesman," Veale said. "He was an excellent pitcher and very congenial."

Powell was slow and nasty on the mound. To the endless annoyance of opposing batters, he took forever between each pitch, as if summoning the energy to throw each one faster than the last. Even soft-spoken Black Barons released their anger on the field. "Powell was s-l-o-w," Greason said. "Oooh, man! Shit, we been in ball games he pitched that lasted three hours. Take him all day. Powell would weigh you down standing out there. It's like it took him a month to throw each pitch."

Stainless Steele made sure Powell didn't have to pitch all day when he knocked a two-run home run to spark Birmingham's five-run fourth inning, much to the delight of the fans. Powell scattered two runs and 10 hits in an 11–2 Black Barons victory against Cleveland's Sam Jones, one of the plentiful power arms in the Negro Leagues.

After the game, Steele was honored for hitting the first Black Barons home run of the 1948 season at Rickwood Field. The *World* eagerly reported the bounty the black community showered upon Stainless: a diamond-studded watch from a local jewelry shop, seven chicken dinners from various local restaurants, and a five-dollar cash reward from a funeral home if he ate himself to death. "One thing about us, we were mostly homeboys," Powell said. "We were brothers. I wish I could go out there and play in that ballpark again. We had the greatest fans I ever seen."

That included the ladies. "You didn't have to look for the date," outfielder Jimmy Zapp said. "The date would come to you." Piper let boys be boys, even though he was married. He kept his eye on the wandering eyes of Zapp, Alonzo Perry, Jehosie Heard, Jimmy Newberry, and Artie Wilson, who picked up the nickname "Squeaky" from teammates who admired his soft voice and debonair demeanor. "Piper told us, 'I don't care what you do off the field, but you better be in shape once you get on it,'" Zapp said. "Pipe knew he had some guys who would run around a little bit, but he set a good example on and off the field for everyone. We never saw Piper running around at night. Never."

The Black Barons were filled with opposite personalities: the aristocratic Artie and passionate Piper; steady Steele and party boy Perry; calm Powell and crazy Newberry; cranky Pepper Bassett and peppery Herman Bell; and the consistent center fielder Bobby Robinson and the devil-may-care left fielder Jimmy Zapp. But Piper quickly proved astute at molding his team's different personalities into one cohesive group, even if he had to tug the reins. And if he didn't humble his players, the fans would. Birmingham fans grew restless and impatient if the Black Barons struggled. Backup infielder Wiley Griggs, a scrappy little hustler who weighed 150 pounds with a roll of pennies in his pocket, remembered a painful batting slump and a fan who wanted his money back. "I wasn't what you called no great hitter," Griggs said. "But when I wasn't hitting, you see a little itty, bitty kid come to the ballpark, tell you what you do wrong."

But the 1948 Black Barons had the feel of a team that could do no wrong, a feeling reinforced on the first Sunday of the season. Sunday was a special day on the Birmingham social calendar, which started with prayers and ended with thanks. When the Black Barons were in town, they always played a double-header against one of the legitimate teams in the Negro American League. The congregations moved from the pews to the box seats. Bob Scranton made sure he had plenty of concessions ready. "On a Sunday, the crowd would come in there and about sixty percent of them would be wearing hats and the women would be dressed to kill coming from church," he said.

The single Black Barons loved it. They would scan the stands during batting practice. The crowds steadily came in before the first game, which would usually begin at 1 or 2 p.m., an hour after Baptist churches let out. Ministers would tell their congregations who the Black Barons were playing. The city ran a streetcar line to Rickwood Field. "In those days, kids ran halfway to the ballpark or they could get a ride on the street car for a nickel," Scranton said. "The city would run special cars, stack them up, and back them into the ballpark."

Veale noted that the black crowds never wavered in their attention to fashion, no matter the heat. "Sunday double-headers," he said, "were always hot as hell, stayed up in the high nineties and low hundreds. You look down in the front row and you'd see the gamblers, the bootleggers, and the ministers sitting side by side."

The crowds were always well behaved. Game days in front of Rickwood Field were one of the few times and places in Birmingham where the segregation ordinance wasn't rigidly enforced, aside from the rule that white fans had to sit in the right-field seats when the black team played. Black customers stood in line next to white customers to buy tickets. Scranton said the Black Barons didn't enforce segregation against white customers the way the white Barons were legally required to. A white scout could walk up to the gate for a black game. Birmingham beat cops worked the area, but Sunday double-headers were fun and happy times that concealed the city's open sores.

"The only thing the police cared about was if people got drunk at the ball games," Scranton said. "We didn't sell beer, but guys would come into the game with the linings of their jackets filled with miniatures. The cops would tell us they worried about people getting drunk and getting in fights, but the crowds were always good. All the police-men were white, naturally, and the crowds enjoyed the game. It was a real social event for the black population." A typical Sunday crowd was between 6,000 and 8,000 fans who came hungry and spent their quarters. "The blacks ate more hot dogs," Scranton reported.

There was no bigger hot dog on the 1948 Birmingham Black Barons than right-handed starting pitcher Jimmy Newberry. Birmingham was his hometown and he had been spinning curveballs for the Black Barons since 1944. Newberry was in his mid-twenties, but he looked so young that the *World* called him "Schoolboy," a nickname so distant from his real personality that it was laughable. Schoolboy Newberry did his own thing. His toothy smile was childish and happy, but he had a quick temper and drank too much. He was friendly when he was in a good mood and was always eager to talk to the ladies. He ran his life on his own schedule, which infuriated everyone outside of Birmingham.

Negro American League batters hated facing Newberry. He gen-erated such velocity that his right arm whipped across his body and allowed him to throw in the low 90s. His fastball danced like rain in the wind and batters complained that his pitches were soaking wet. He often chewed on a piece of slippery elm bark and liberally licked his fingers before throwing the ball. Newberry pitched like a card dealer with a bad attitude, mixed in a curveball he threw from a three-quarter arm angle so he could vary its spin, and could turn a nick on the baseball into a deadly weapon. Opponents were certain his team-mates doctored the ball for him, but most never complained except for Baltimore Elite Giants catcher Roy Campanella, a master at identify-ing a pitch's natural movements. "When y'all don't cut it," he barked at the Black Barons in 1945, "we hit it up against the fences."

The Cleveland Buckeyes were equally irritated on the first Sunday in 1948. "Newberry threw plenty of illegal pitches during his six inning stint," the *World* wrote. "Several times he went to his mouth and got away with it." But Newberry couldn't get away with pitching with a hangover. He made the bus Sunday morning, but had his dark glasses on. Cleveland hung him out to dry, roping 13 hits in a 9–7 victory. Piper loved Newberry's stuff, but he exercised caution because of his drinking habits. Bill Greason was Newberry's new roommate, but Veale observed, "They didn't have no fun together because Newberry had all the fun." Piper tried to arrange the pitching rotation so Newberry never started early Sunday home games again.

Newberry was beaten by Cleveland pitcher Chet Brewer, Piper's former barnstorming teammate and longtime friend. Brewer, like Piper, used experience to compensate for what age stole. He didn't throw as hard anymore, but he still had great fastball command. When he hit a batter with a pitch, it was almost always meant to convey a message. Piper encouraged his pitchers to work with Brewer, who shared many lessons, including how to pitch with a scuffed baseball. One pitcher, Sammy C. Williams, eagerly took Piper up on the offer and said that Chet improved him. Piper would not hesitate to call upon Brewer to help make one of his players better. Brewer, like Piper, gained fulfillment from helping younger players. He was already planting the seeds for a coaching and scouting career when his playing days ended, a path that included a memorable encounter with teenager Willie Mays.

While Mays wasn't a center fielder the Black Barons were concerned with yet, Cleveland Buckeyes center fielder Sam Jethroe showed why he had grand ambitions of playing white folks' ball. He raced deep into the gap to steal a potential inside-the-park home run from Piper. A center fielder like that, Piper knew, could help his team win many games. But Jethroe, a multiple all-star who was already in Brooklyn's sights as a prospect, went 1-for-10 in three games against Black Barons pitching.

Artie Wilson, coming off a 1947 season in which he hit .377 to win the Negro American League batting title, had three hits in three at-bats against Brewer. He was beginning his final push to hit his way out of Birmingham. Zapp banged a long double off the left-field wall, a shot the *World* said "was worth watching." On a team where Ed Steele and Alonzo Perry could both hit the ball for great distances and old reliable Pepper Bassett could still get into one, Zapp, the youngest, might have been the mightiest. He was proving to be a "long ball hitter and probably the most touted newcomer on the squad," the *World* reported. "[Zapp] should prove to be a real crowd pleaser."

As the Black Barons hit the road, touring with the Buckeyes around Alabama the following week before coming home to play the Indianapolis Clowns for the first of seven consecutive games in Birmingham and around Alabama, Piper kept tabs on Buck O'Neil's Kansas City Monarchs. News traveled slowly, and sometimes word of mouth was more efficient than the printed word.

The *World* gave the Negro American League title to the Black Barons, but Piper and his players knew better than to believe that hype before actually playing the Monarchs at the end of the month. Piper wanted his team warmed up and playing well when they met the Monarchs. These were payday games in every way, the highest level of competition each club thought they could face. Buck had been with the Monarchs since 1938 and he knew his 1948 team could win the pennant. According to the *Kansas City Call*, Kansas City's black newspaper, Buck was calling the race before it started. "So well has the team performed," the *Call* wrote on April 30, "that skipper O'Neil has gone out on the limb to say that the team that wins the Negro American League pennant this year will have to beat the Monarchs first."

The Kansas City Monarchs always had a regal look about them. Buck liked outfielders with power and speed, and he had one of the best in center fielder Willard Brown. He liked fast middle infielders with sure gloves and surprising pop. He had rookie shortstop Gene Baker, who possessed a promising package of speed and quickness. O'Neil loved Baker and thought he couldn't miss in white folks' ball. The *Call* noted Buck's admiration, writing that Baker had become "Manager Johnny O'Neil's golden boy." Baker teamed with another rookie, second baseman Curtis Roberts, to give the 1948 Monarchs a rarity, an all-rookie double-play combination. Buck considered the younger Roberts and Baker combination superior to Birmingham's older combination of Piper Davis and Artie Wilson. Roberts and Baker, the *Call* reported, was "said to be just what the doctor ordered."

The addition of Baker and Roberts pushed the talented Hank Thompson to the outfield. Thompson, who like Brown and Piper was property of the St. Louis Browns for a few weeks in 1947, was a younger version of Piper, but with more power. Veteran third baseman Herb Souell returned after two years away from the Monarchs.

Buck, a flare hitter with limited power and a sure glove, knew that he was on the downside of his playing career. He began sharing playing time at first base with Tommy Cooper, priming himself for a major league managing career. Like Piper, Buck realized that Negro League baseball was shrinking, and he knew that his best chance for success in white folks' ball rested squarely on assembling the best team he possibly could. He knew he had to win games and send players to white folks' ball. The result was his 1948 club, an intriguing mix of veterans and rookies, the kind of team that could tease one day and frustrate the next. Among the young players was a rookie from St. Louis, Elston Howard, who had started working out with the team and would join the Monarchs during the summer. Buck wasn't sure which position the kid would settle in at, but he was convinced Howard would hit.

Then there was the pitching. The greatest pitching name, Satchel Paige, was off barnstorming across the country, a freelance ballplayer following the money, with Tom Baird serving as his booking agent. Baird kept Satchel's address and home phone number on the front page of his personal address book, and as Satchel "folded his crane-like legs into his 1948 Lincoln Continental and headed South," according to the *Call*, he had more freedom than any other Negro League player.

Hilton Smith was still on the team but his age and sore shoulder combined to create swiftly declining effectiveness. Buck pitched him sparingly and trusted him as a pinch hitter. Smith was not the same dominating pitcher of whom Philadelphia Stars infielder Mahlon Duckett said, "I would rather face Satchel eight days a week than Hilton six days," nor was he what he had been when Buck described him in a scouting report as a "front line first division type pitcher—Two fastballs—Overhand riser—3/4 sinker—Excellent curveball—Great competitor."

The modest left-hander Jim LaMarque was Buck's pitching ace. LaMarque never threw hard, but his beautiful sweeping curveball got him many looks from white folks' ball, though he realized that Baird zealously blocked his future by putting too high a price tag on him. Thin and wiry, light-skinned, LaMarque was a well-paid and highly respected veteran who was the leader of an impressive collection of pitchers that included Connie Johnson, Gene Collins, Ford Smith, and Gene Richardson. The death call for the Negro Leagues had been summoned, but the battle between the Birmingham Black Barons and the Kansas City Monarchs was building. The last great summer of Negro League baseball was about to begin.

"The Monarchs have a good hurler in LaMarque, but the rest of the staff does not appear to be first rate," the *World* reported. "Defense is rated fair. The team is likely to battle Cleveland for the second spot."

The Black Barons did nothing in May to discourage that thought. Piper set up his pitching rotation so Bill Powell always had a Sunday game, and two weeks later the Black Barons were back at Rickwood Field against the Clowns. Powell pitched a seven-hit shutout and struck out eight. The game ended when he induced a double-play ground ball, with Artie and Piper turning the second of what the *World* called their "lightning-fast twin killings." Piper had learned his lesson about Jimmy Newberry. Sometimes he skipped pitching him altogether on Sundays at Rickwood Field. In the second game of the double-header against the Clowns, Piper called on the little left-hander Jehosie Heard.

Compared to the other pitchers on the Black Barons' staff, Heard was a newcomer. He discovered his talent for pitching during World War II and pitched in the Industrial League when he returned to Birmingham. His talent guided him from slabs in the South Pacific to the mound at Rickwood Field, and he signed with the Black Barons in 1946. On his 1937 report card from Parker High in Birmingham, his teacher noted that Heard's underachieving performance in school wasn't indicative of his intellect, writing one word in the comments that well described Jehosie on and off the mound: sly. Said Veale, "Jehosie Heard was a hell of a left-hander. He was raw-boned, had a good curveball, and he had some heat, too. By the time you were through watching his curveball he'd blind you with his fastball."

This time, Heard gave up four consecutive hits and two runs without retiring a batter in the first inning. Piper had seen enough. Heard was nursing a leg injury that would hinder him throughout the season, which made signing Bill Greason even more important. Piper had not started Jimmy Newberry at home that day, but he called upon him to shake off his hangover and pitch in relief. Newberry responded to Piper, pitching six and two-thirds innings of a game that was shortened to seven innings.

The Black Barons left town with a record of fifteen wins and eight losses. They met up with the Clowns in Centralia, Illinois, and Piper gave the ball to Newberry for what became a pitching duel against rookie Laru Velasquez. For sixteen innings, Newberry knocked down zeroes like whiskey shots. Finally, in the seventeenth inning, the Black Barons scored six runs. Newberry took the mound in the bottom of the inning and completed a seventeen-inning shutout. He may have been crazy, but when Jimmy Newberry put his mind to it, he could pitch.

Newberry's bold performance showed the durability and determination prevalent among black pitchers. They worked fast. They wanted to throw the ball the moment the catcher got it back to them, and under no circumstances did they care to leave the game. "We got mad thinking someone would have to go into the bullpen to relieve us," Greason said. Few pitchers worked faster than Newberry. Greason emulated his style. "Newberry and myself, we were quick and aggressive," he said.

The Black Barons aspired to play quick and aggressive baseball when they faced the Monarchs at Rickwood Field in the last weekend of May for the first time in the 1948 season. It was an opportunity to play well at home and send a message to their rivals that Piper Davis's Black Barons were ballplayers first and night owls second. Between the players, it was never personal. There was mutual respect for the talent on the opposite side of the field, yet the Black Barons reasoned that Monarchs owner Tom Baird was advocating his own players and disparaging Birmingham players to white folks' ball. That added conflict to these games, which were suddenly about not just winning, but escaping a dying league. "We respected their ballplayers and I think they respected us," Greason said. "They had a lot of talent and so did we. A lot of us played together in winter ball over the years. Black ballplayers, we typically stuck together. We didn't dislike the Monarchs, but we disliked how their owner seemed to think of us. We were about beating the man in the suit."

That man was Tom Baird, who could also see the end of the Negro Leagues coming and wanted to establish his reputation inside white folks' ball as a valuable source of accurate player information, not only about his Monarchs but about what he perceived were the shortcomings of Birmingham players. Baird, in short, was in business for Baird, yet he was regarded as trustworthy while Alex Pompez, the owner of the New York Cubans, was frowned upon by most in white folks' ball because of his race and past. Baird also showed signs that he did not care for Pompez and his business associates, who included Latinos, blacks, and Jews. These games between the Monarchs and Black Barons were not just a rivalry on the field, but one that encompassed the world around them, the battle to escape the hot box, and the route a tremendously talented young center fielder needed to take to escape Birmingham. If there truly was an Underground Railroad from Negro League baseball to white folks' ball, Tom Baird was going to be certain that any player who was not a member of his own Kansas City Monarchs was not going to get a ride. That feeling of rivalry between the Monarchs and the Black Barons was growing in 1948 and not lost on the team's young bat boy, Bobby Veale. "They weren't just another team coming into Birmingham that needed to get the shit kicked out of them."

Bill Powell lumbered to the mound, and the right-hander waded through the dangerous lineup on a soggy Saturday night. He entered the game with five victories and no defeats, but the Monarchs made him work, none more than center fielder Willard Brown. As Brown dug his cleats into the soft clay of Rickwood Field, he reveled in the opportunity to face a hard thrower. It was power against power when the two faced each other. Powell reached back and threw each pitch faster. Brown tried to hit each pitch farther. Their duels usually resulted in either a strikeout or a fly ball. Brown had three hits that night, including two home runs and an RBI double, and watched Black Barons center fielder Bobby Robinson bring back another drive with a galloping catch. When Brown put his mind to it, he was also a top-notch defensive center fielder. Years later, when Buck wrote a scouting report on Brown penned in terse yet elegant language, he described a rare breed: "Soft hands and quick feet—Got the good jump on the fly balls—Could close the gaps right and left. Outstanding offensively—Home run power to all fields—The ability to steal 50 bases per season—Very desirable."

Powell held his own against the Monarchs and pitched the Black Barons to an 8–6 complete-game victory. Brown handled Powell, but he couldn't do it by himself. The Monarchs knew they needed at least a split in the Sunday double-header to avoid what would be an embarrassing sweep in Birmingham. Brown and Thompson, outfield partners and drinking buddies, didn't help the cause when they ventured from Fourth Avenue's Rush Hotel to Bob's Savoy and came away with a fuzzy memory of a Saturday night.

A strong, well-dressed, and happy crowd of 8,000 fans awaited the Black Barons and Monarchs at Rickwood for their Sunday double-header. Bob Williams—"Savoy Bob"—sat behind the Black Barons dugout in his customary seat, wearing his favorite white fedora that matched his loosely kept white linen shirt. Sunday was the only day of the week Bob didn't wear his tie. He peered through his wire-rimmed glasses and smoked a good cigar that at the end of the day was burned to a nub.

The Black Barons delivered the message Piper Davis wanted them to send. Bill Greason took the ball in the first big-game assignment of his career. Piper gave him a 1–0 lead in the first inning when he drove home center fielder Bobby Robinson with a clean base hit against Monarchs right-hander Ford Smith. Greason was "awful" against Brown, who did not touch him, but he was not invincible against the rest of the lineup. His snappy right wrist left a pitch hanging for catcher Earl Taborn, who doubled over Robinson to tie the score in the fifth inning, but Greason stranded Taborn at second base to end the inning. Ford Smith, proving that many Negro League pitchers could hit, doubled in the seventh and scored on second baseman Curtis Roberts's single, giving the Monarchs a 2–1 lead. But Greason pitched with uncanny moxie for a rookie and kept the game close with sliders and savvy.

In the bottom of the seventh inning, the Black Barons provided the first memorable moment from 1948. With Ford Smith still on the mound with a one-run lead, the twenty-nine-year-old right-hander couldn't protect it. Bobby Robinson slapped a single to reach first base and represented the tying run. With the right-handed-hitting Jimmy Zapp coming to the plate, Piper called for switch-hitting Alonzo Perry to bat left-handed against the right-handed Smith. In center field Brown drifted back a few steps and told left fielder Hank Thompson to do the same.

Ford went to his strength and threw a fastball. Perry uncoiled with a long, loose, effortless swing and tore into the pitch. Thompson watched the ball fly over his head and plant in Glennon's Gardens. Bobby Veale hurried out to see the ball rocket out of Rickwood.

The pinch-hit home run sent the crowd into a frenzy, sent the Black Barons streaming out of the dugout to welcome Perry when he crossed home plate, and gave the Black Barons and Greason a 3–2 lead. The hometown gamblers in the front row were pleased. "Perry wasn't nothing but muscle," Veale said. "If he didn't get around on a fastball, he could hit it out to left field. I've seen him hit it over that brick wall in Rickwood, not the one inside, but the one about a hundred feet behind the fence."

The jubilation caught up to the Black Barons in the eighth inning, when Greason promptly gave up a double to Baker and watched him score when the normally reliable shortstop Artie Wilson made a bad throw first baseman Joe Scott couldn't dig out of the dirt, allowing Baker to tie the score, 3–3.

But the Black Barons were at Rickwood and had the final at-bat. Pepper Bassett led off the inning with a base hit. Clearly tiring, Smith refused to leave the game. He got one out, and then walked the next two hitters to load the bases. Sometimes, pride mattered more than strategy. Smith lost his touch and walked Bassett home from third base and the Black Barons had a 4–3 victory. Greason had pitched a nine-hitter and given up only two runs to earn the first important victory of his Black Barons career.

There would be only enough time for seven innings in the second game of the double-header. Seven innings for the Black Barons to wrap up a three-game sweep and send Buck back to Baird with a safe message that the Kansas City Monarchs weren't the only team to beat in the Negro American League. Perry, the hero of the first game, started the second game on the mound. He made it through five innings and left with the score tied, 3–3. Piper proved he knew how to run a pitching staff in a game situation. Jimmy Newberry pitched the sixth inning and gave up one run. Piper pulled him, telling Jehosie Heard, "You got the seventh." Heard responded with a shutout inning. That gave the Black Barons a chance to win in their final at-bat. Though Rickwood Field had lights, they were an expensive luxury, and owner Tom Hayes rarely paid for them to be used. If the Black Barons were going to win, they had to do it before sunset or settle for a tie, which would provide the Monarchs with a moral victory.

The thought disgusted the Black Barons. Joe Scott, the little first baseman who had to be worried about keeping his job after watching Perry's home run, began the seventh inning by walking against Monarchs starting pitcher Gene Collins. Baird considered Collins better than any pitcher who had ever come out of Birmingham, including Dan Bankhead, who pitched for the Brooklyn Dodgers in 1947. With Pepper Bassett at the plate, Piper put Scott in motion. Bassett struck out, but Scott beat Taborn's throw and stole second base, avoiding the double play, giving Ed Steele a chance to hit with the winning run on second base. Stainless found a pitch he liked from Collins and roped it into left field. Piper, standing in the third base coaching box, eagerly waved Scott home. As he dashed home and scored the winning run of a 5–4 victory, the Black Barons' second one-run victory over the Monarchs in the day, the Monarchs turned and walked off the field in disgust, for they were rarely embarrassed. The Birmingham faithful's prayers were answered. The Kansas City Monarchs weren't supposed to lose games like this, and they certainly weren't supposed to lose them to the Black Barons. "Failure to hit in the clutches proved the undoing of the Kansas City Monarchs here Sunday," the *Call* reported.

When the game was over, the crowd didn't want to leave. Faye Davis, Piper's daughter, remembered how the crowds would jam the driveway on Twelfth Street alongside the ballpark, and when the bus turned right on Third Avenue West, the fans would still be lined up, cheering and proudly waving good-bye to the Birmingham Black Barons as they hit the road. The crowds would mob the players as they made their way to the bus, shoving pieces of paper under their noses for an autograph, trying to shake their hands, rub their shoulders, or

Sundays in Birmingham meant two places to be: church and Rickwood Field. The well-dressed crowd of 1948 includes injured Black Barons pitcher Nat Pollard looking forlorn in street clothes (bottom right).

just graze their shirtsleeves. Bobby Veale remembered that feeling of watching his heroes drive away to parts unknown to lead a lifestyle he dreamed of living. "Everyone wanted to be a BBB," Veale said. "If not a BBB, a BDF—a Brooklyn Dodger Fan."

It was the best weekend the Black Barons had ever enjoyed against the Monarchs, prompting the *World* to report, "This was the first time that any Black Baron team has been so successful in a series with the Monarchs."

Piper's team ended the month in first place in the Negro American League with a 24–10 overall record and a 17–7 mark in the American League, and the weekend series sweep carried enormous significance. All the Black Barons had to do was play solid baseball for the next month and they would capture the first half of the NAL season, which would ensure them an automatic playoff spot. If they won the NAL second half, they would advance directly to the Negro League World Series, but if they lost the second half, they would face a playoff series against the second-half winner. The Black Barons knew their sweep virtually ensured the first-half title. The night owls roamed and a sense of complacency set in during June.

Piper hated when his players slacked off. The June slump wasn't a disaster, but it showed Piper that to be better, the Black Barons needed a push. Piper knew the Monarchs were thirsting for revenge when the Black Barons played in Kansas City in August. This was Piper's club, but something was missing. The solution, he learned, was riding the bus from Birmingham to Chattanooga.

Willie Mays was playing high school baseball for Fairfield when he wasn't playing low-level Negro ball on the side. After leading Jefferson County in basketball scoring, he was first noticed not playing center field, but pitching. This might be expected, because everyone in Birmingham knew that Willie's granddaddy had been a pitcher. Ellis Jones, the *World* writer who was frustrated that he still had to cover high school sports, reported on Fairfield's first game. He didn't miss the best player because he knew about the boy's pedigree. Jones couldn't have missed Mays throwing a fastball. If his eyes were closed, his ears would have told him.

"Fairfield, with Willie Howard Mays doing the tossing, was too much of a team for the Muscoda lads," Jones wrote. "A keen judge of baseball talent could possibly spot a future ballplayer here and there on the two teams." But these accomplishments meant nothing to the Black Barons. Mays was a high school kid playing for cash under the table with traveling teams, something they had all done. He hadn't established himself in the Industrial League. They were the big, bad Black Barons who swept the Monarchs. Mays was a kid who hadn't proven anything, even if Birmingham baseball fans knew what he was capable of doing. "Everyone here knew who Mays was," ACIPCO outfielder Jessie Mitchell said. "He wasn't no surprise. Everybody figured it was a matter of time before he started playing with the Black Barons."

But the 1948 Black Barons never thought he would become a rookie on their veteran-laden team. Willie already knew he was a good ballplayer and yearned for another challenge. His desire was about to collide with their careers. Willie had enormous confidence in his abilities. Some wondered if his adolescent awkwardness masked a kid who believed he belonged with the men.

When the Black Barons barnstormed into Chattanooga in June, Willie was waiting for Piper. When he saw him in the hotel, he made a beeline right for him. Willie had a knack for going right to what he wanted. When Piper met him, his first thought was of how much he reminded him of Cat.

"THE BEST LITTLE BOY ANYBODY EVER SEEN"

Willie Mays laughed when he saw Piper Davis, but it wasn't because he was embarrassed. He wore the Chattanooga uniform he had played in during the day, his wool flannels wrinkled with dust and retaining the odors of sweat, grass, and pine tar. Mays had turned seventeen in May, but he looked so young that many Black Barons assumed he was twelve or thirteen. It was a joke in their hard-edged world to think a child could simply walk up to the highly respected manager of a Negro American League team, flash a smile, tell him, "I got my own bat and my own glove," and ask him to play.

But the boy had something going for him: His last name was Mays. The Black Barons had played against Cat for years in the Industrial League.

The Mays family was a baseball brand name in Birmingham, like the Hairstons and Veales, a legacy that did not begin with Willie, but culminated with him. He was so eager to chat up Piper that he giggled through his grin and the words came out of his mouth almost as quickly as he could swing a baseball bat. He walked with the contradictory waddle of someone whose legs were impatient with the speed of the rest of the world but were forced to keep pace with it anyway. When he appeased his legs and ran, he could only be compared to a buck, so they called him Buck Duck. "He ran like a buck. He walked like a duck. Buck Duck," Bobby Veale said.

Piper saw how Willie shared Cat's personality, but he also knew Willie possessed something Cat did not. Cat was a great baseball player, but he never took it seriously. He knew he would never play white folks' ball, so instead of living a life of regret he played baseball like he hustled pool, purely for fun and profit. Discrimination in baseball was as sure as a dull pool cue in a strange hall, but Cat played anyway. Willie played baseball like there was no beginning and no end, where the only thing that mattered was the happiness he felt when he could show everyone that he was right about how good he was. Willie reminded Piper of himself. Willie's glee hid his fear. Cat Mays never had Jackie Robinson to inspire him to be more than a tin mill ballplayer, but then Cat never had to escape the hot box.

Willie didn't want to work in the mill any more than Piper wanted to work in the mountain. People often misunderstood that. Willie loved to play because he wanted to escape. Piper knew that feeling. Bobby Veale saw Cat play as an old man and watched Willie play as a young man. "Buck had a tenacity to succeed that his daddy didn't have," Veale said.

Willie loved ballplayer hours, the late, late nights and the noon wake-up calls. When he found Piper in the lobby past midnight that night in Chattanooga, Piper knew who he was. Willie's distinctive high-pitched voice was all his own. It became one of Piper's favorite stories.

"Hey, Piper!" he said.

"Boy," Piper replied, "don't you know if you get caught out here playin' ball for money, you can't play no high school next year?"

"I don't care," Mays said, his words as impatient as his legs.

A week later, Willie found Piper again. His persistence won Piper over.

"I see you're still out here," Piper said.

"Yeah, Piper, I'm still playing," Mays said.

"Okay," Piper said. "If you want to play with us and your daddy lets you play, have him call me Sunday morning at 10 a.m."

On Sunday morning, the phone rang. It was a very short conversation.

"If he wants to play, let him," Cat said.

"Have him at the ballpark at noon," Piper said.

Mays lingering around the Black Barons presented an intriguing problem. The moment anyone saw him working out with the team, he would undoubtedly lose his amateur status. But there was an easy way around that. Piper began working out Mays outside of Birmingham. Piper needed a fourth outfielder, and if Willie could catch the ball like Cat, he would be perfect. "I worked him out because I needed an outfielder," Piper said. "I'd heard he had a good arm. Then I saw him throw."

Mays threw harder than any man. Everything was on a line, and fast. Nothing was on the short hop. As soon as Willie threw, Piper knew it wasn't a question of if Mays would play. It was a question of who wasn't going to play. He was willing to tolerate the growing pains that would surely accompany inserting a teenager into a lineup of grown-up, carousing, embittered, scowling veterans who were terrified that white folks' ball would never give them the honor of treating them like trash. But the Black Barons immediately recognized that Willie had the talent to break the rules. The unique dynamic of the 1948 Black Barons was born.

"I ain't never seen a ballplayer like that in my life," Bill Powell marveled. "When he was coming up as a little boy, his pants were too big for him and his bat was too heavy. We played in this cornfield in a small town. I never forgot, one night we're playing out there and the ball was hit to him left-center. He was out there like a cat. What he did, he just turned and ran straight across and picked the ball up. When the guy got to third, [third baseman] 'Brit' [Johnny Britton] put the decoy on like that ball wasn't coming. When the guy got to third, Brit had the ball waiting on him."

"The best little boy anybody ever seen": Willie Mays, age seventeen, officially signed a standard Negro American League contract with the Birmingham Black Barons on July 4, 1948, beginning his career as an American legend.

It seemed too strange to be true. Here was this little boy next to these men, holding a bat that looked like it swung him, wearing a baggy gray flannel uniform he couldn't fill out and a hat that somehow never seemed to stay on his head. Yet Mays had something else, something the Black Barons knew they had never seen before. He was baseball's Mozart, a child prodigy gifted well beyond ordinary youngsters, whose talents exceeded those of most adults. He was a raw natural resource of a ballplayer who lacked polish but was too gifted to spend his entire career playing in the dying Negro American League.

"His abilities were incomparable," Greason said. As rookies, Greason, Mays, and Jimmy Zapp took turns showering last and carrying the ball bucket and water pail. But Greason and Zapp also knew that contained in the gangly personality of an awkward adolescent was talent that the Baptist preachers said could only come from God. "Mays was an unusual young fellow," Greason said. "For his age, he was what we call a phenom."

Zapp was astounded when he saw Mays throw. "Mays had one of the greatest arms I ever seen, period," Zapp said. "Some people used to say Carl Furillo used to throw as well or better, but I never thought so. Nobody threw as well as Mays. Not a chance."

When the first workout was over, Piper took Willie back to Birmingham with him. He began to travel locally to play with the Black Barons on weekends, but not at Rickwood Field. In all likelihood, Piper probably made sure that Tom Hayes gave Mays some money under the table to replace the income he had been making at Chattanooga. *World* reporter Ellis Jones, who knew Mays because he had seen him play high school football, basketball, and baseball, noticed him working out with the team at Rickwood Field on a Tuesday night in late April, perhaps during spring break, against the Indianapolis Clowns. But Jones did not say if Mays played, and if Mays did, Jones might have been intentionally doing Piper a favor by not reporting it. "The young fellow fans saw working out Tuesday night with the Barons was Willie Howard Mays, [seventeen-year-old] Fairfield Industrial Student, who plays a lot of football and basketball. When school days are over, the young one might catch on with the Barons."

Piper was way ahead of Ellis. He was the only manager in Negro baseball to ever steal Willie Mays, and he wasn't even trying to. That's because he was trying to help Mays even though he hardly knew him. When it was finally decided that playing for the Black Barons would be worth sacrificing his high school sports career and making it official, Willie Mays was no longer a college basketball or a college football prospect. He was a baseball prodigy. He played with the Black Barons for most of June but not in any recorded Negro American League games. He may have suited up in early May when the Cleveland Buckeyes were at Rickwood, but because classes were still in session and he was still playing for the Fairfield High School baseball team, his activities were limited and unannounced.

Mays spent those first few weeks performing under an assumed name in the wilderness. Here, the memories of playing with him began to build up long before he made his official Negro League debut. "He had the arms, the legs and the talent," Greason said. "He just didn't connect a whole lot when he began."

When he came to bat, Mays already had a wide-open stride. He spread his legs wide apart and triggered his swing by lifting up his front foot and putting it down so quickly that it barely looked like it moved at all. His swing was all in his wrists. The Black Barons used store-bought ash bats produced by Louisville Slugger, but some players fashioned their own bats from a railroad tie. They would cut an eight-foot log and narrow it off, treat it with cooking oil, and lay it in the sun. Most of those bats were made of oak. They were heavier and almost never cracked. Players used to say they didn't break those sturdy bats, they just wore them out. Mays didn't care what bat he used. He was always in attack mode at the plate, but he was learning that Negro League pitchers were going to attack him first.

While Mays was already a man as a defensive player, the fast arms of Negro pitchers were something he had never seen before. As a rookie working out with his new teammates, he surely faced the most "awful" pitching he had ever seen, superior to what he faced in the Industrial League. When he faced Jimmy Newberry in batting practice, Jimmy most certainly was not smiling, and his hair-trigger temper might be sparked by the wide grin on Mays's face. Then Newberry might snap his curveball and that would be the end of the discussion. Mays could have stood in against Bill Powell and seen what the fastball of a Negro American League All-Star pitcher looked like. He could have faced Greason's sharp slider. Jehosie Heard could have thrown him a sly curveball that started at his eyes and ended at his knees. Piper understood that Mays would need the breathing room to accumulate the at-bats he needed to speed up his swing in order to face the top-notch Negro pitchers awaiting him, especially those belonging to the Monarchs. "When he first got here," Jimmy Zapp said, "he wasn't the hitter he became."

Piper carefully chose Willie's first games, letting him cut his teeth away from Rickwood Field against small-town teams far away from the Negro American League games. Piper didn't take Willie on any long road trips until school was out. It was already established that Mays was going to graduate from high school.

The Black Barons played better in the middle of June than they had at the start of the month. Though Mays wasn't starting, he was sparking the veterans. There was a 5–4 victory in which Johnny Britton hit a three-run home run and Ed Steele hit a two-run home run. There was also a wild and crazy 13–12 victory on a Saturday night at Rickwood Field in which Jimmy Newberry got hammered on the mound. Center fielder Bobby Robinson got the game-winning hit in the tenth inning of a game in which Piper and Artie each had four hits. The victory shared space in the *World* with the dying Babe Ruth's last curtain call at Yankee Stadium.

The Black Barons brought down the curtain in the first half, playing well enough to clinch the first half of the Negro American League pennant. Buck O'Neil's Kansas City Monarchs had slipped to third place with a 20–17 record, an inconsistent mark reflecting rookie mistakes. But Buck also expected his team to be better in the second half. The learning curve was over as far as he was concerned.

The learning curve for Willie Mays was just beginning. Piper, though, had a problem. Where was he going to play Mays? Bobby Robinson hadn't played his way out of his starting center-field job. According to the official league statistics of June 30, Robinson was hitting .291. But Piper had made up his mind and spoken to Tom Hayes. The Memphis Red Sox were scheduled to come to Rickwood Field for a July 4 double-header. It was the official end of the Negro League first half. Because the Black Barons had formally clinched a playoff spot, the games were essentially meaningless. Piper had picked the perfect time for Mays to make his official debut in Birmingham.

Hayes rarely ventured from his Memphis office to Birmingham, but he did send a standard Negro American League contract dated July 4 through September 6, calling for a salary of $250 a month, a robust sum for a player who had just completed his sophomore year at Fairfield High. Hayes filled out the top three lines of the contract as he did for all of his players. It read, "The Birmingham Black Barons, herein called the Club, and Willie Howard Mays Jr. of Birmingham, Ala., herein called the Player," agreed for Willie's services with paydays on the first and the fifteenth of the month. The contract folded into three halves so it would fit into a player's pocket like a bus ticket. On the final page, Hayes wrote biographical information in longhand, citing

Mays's birthday in Westfield, a neighbor of Fairfield, as May 8, 1931, not May 6, as historically recorded. He noted William Mays and his aunt, Sarah Morris, as legal guardians and said Mays had four years of baseball experience, probably pulled from some combination of his time with the Fairfield Stars, Chattanooga, and other lesser-known teams. Mays said that he never signed a contract, but a signature marked "W.H. Mays" appears on the dotted line, perhaps signed by Cat.

Negro League players didn't always trust the validity of their contracts, but owners did. Birmingham players believed Tom Hayes was fair with his players and Mays was included in this, especially with Piper watching Mays closely to be absolutely certain that everything was completed legally. Piper knew that Buck would have to have all of his ducks in a row when white folks' ball called. Piper saw to that because of his wounds. He didn't have to look very far into his own past to realize that a white team could shoot down a black player for just about any reason it wanted. From that moment, for the next two seasons, but especially in 1948 and in June 1950, Piper Davis was Willie Mays's baseball godfather. Every fan who ever loved Willie Mays should thank Piper Davis, who brought him out of the trees and the tin mills, to the Negro Leagues, and to the larger world awaiting him.

When the Black Barons first discovered Willie Mays's name in the starting lineup of the second game of the Negro American League doubleheader against the Memphis Red Sox on July 4 at Rickwood Field, they were not eager to welcome him into the lineup, despite the fact that they had become familiar with him over the past few months. The veterans weren't convinced Mays could hit. They had seen him struggle against good drop balls and chase rise balls at his eyes. His running and throwing were exceptional, but he had to hit. Piper wrote out the lineup card with Mays hitting seventh. He handed it to Roosevelt Atkins, a former Industrial League player who served as the team's trainer, and told him to pin it on the dugout wall. When the Black Barons read Piper's lineup card, they were stunned. The odd man out was not center fielder Bobby Robinson. It was left fielder Jimmy Zapp.

Zapp was furious. Piper had a strict rule forbidding swearing, but Zapp broke it the moment he read the lineup card. His anger boiled at being benched. "Great temperament is not something I always had," Zapp said. Piper got a dirty look from right fielder Ed Steele, who wondered what had happened to coming up the hard way. Alonzo Perry defiantly glared at his manager. Bobby Robinson, the center fielder, was upset. The outfielders viewed this decision as an insult to their livelihoods. The rest of the players wondered if their jobs were safe. Potential didn't matter, only performance, and enthusiastic or not, Willie Mays hadn't shown them anything.

But Willie had shown Piper enough. Piper knew his decision to play Mays wouldn't be popular, but he refused to tolerate any dissension. Mays looked sheepishly at Piper, who reassured him when he spoke to his team. "That's the lineup!" Piper bellowed. "If anybody doesn't like it, there's the clubhouse door. You can pull that uniform off if you want to."

The Black Barons won the second game, 8–5, in seven innings. The box score wasn't recorded, but Artie Wilson hit an inside-the-park home run and Piper belted a shot over the 407-feet sign in left field. When

The other first-year Black Baron in the outfield for the 1948 team, Jimmy Zapp had tremendous home run power and a fiery temper to match.

Mays came to bat for the first time as a Black Baron at Rickwood Field, he heard the first applause of his career. Fittingly, an American legend's baseball career officially began on the Fourth of July. "Were those Fairfield admirers hand-clapping when Willie Mays of their community came to bat?" the *World* reported.

Even when he didn't do enough to make the newspaper, Mays did enough for the Black Barons to recognize that he was not an ordinary teenager. His arms flailed back and forth when he ran, like he was endlessly treading water, but he could get from the right-hand side of the batter's box to first base in less than four seconds. His feet moved so fast that it looked like they barely touched the turf. Sometimes he would make base-running mistakes born of aggressive inexperience and find himself trapped in a rundown. Then his teammates sat back and watched Mays escape the hot box. His body would jerk to a sudden halt and he would swim back to first base. If the first baseman got the ball, Mays would change direction on his tiptoes, turn on the gas, and blur past the second baseman chasing him. He would dive headfirst into second base, his wiry fingers fully extended until they latched on to the base. The shortstop would catch the return throw by the time dirt caked the word BIRMINGHAM on Mays's uniform, and his teammates would sit back and laugh. There was no use fighting or resenting him. Mays was Mays.

"More than once, that would happen to him," Zapp said. "Perry turned to me once and said, 'How'd he get out of that?'"

Eventually, Perry couldn't resist Mays's energy. He warmed up to him and started treating him like a little brother. "Perry used to wrestle Mays all the time," Zapp said. "He was kidding around with him. At least I think he was." In turn, the other Black Barons kidded with Mays. Sometimes they called him Willie. Sometimes they called him Buck. "We called him Mays most of the time, really," Zapp said. "Sometimes I call him Willie if he deserves it."

The Black Barons realized that this kid who had been showing up on the weekends was not just an ordinary fill-in player, but one who was going to help them win the Negro League World Series. They realized that his extraordinary skills made him an extraordinary weapon. Bobby Robinson was still the starting center fielder, but Mays occasionally played a few innings there. First baseman Joe Scott, who was having one of his worst hitting seasons, remembered playing right when Mays was in center field. At Rickwood Field, a ball was hit into the right-center gap. Scott gave pursuit and closed in on the ball at about the same time as Mays. "I sure couldn't throw as well as him," Scott said. "I beat him to the ball, but I was going away from the infield, so I just flipped it to him so he could throw it to second." Piper took the incoming throw and the runner stayed put at first base.

It was an easy first week and must have felt like heaven to Mays. He was out of school for the summer and was getting paid to play baseball. The Black Barons played locally that week, with Mays getting used to playing every day. Piper knew that the real challenges were ahead of Mays, but Mays was having too much fun to think about what was next. That was Piper's place and he took it very seriously. And while Mays started to grow up, sometimes Bobby Veale would sneak into a game in the summer, finding his way onto the mound while he was a minor and pitching innings that, like Mays's at-bats with the Black Barons during the school year, would never be logged and would never officially exist. Like Mays, Bobby Veale's first taste of faster competition vanished into the Alabama woods amid the mosquitoes. "You go someplace, they gonna give you a dollar to play and a dollar for meal money," Veale said. "But a growing kid need more than that."

Soon, Mays would need more than the local Alabama sandlots to develop his talent. He also learned that there was more to becoming a baseball player than simply being a baseball player. There were life lessons and a socialization process awaiting him outside of Birmingham, new perspectives that would be introduced to him at a young age. Inside that bus so boldly decorated with the words BIRMINGHAM BLACK BARONS BASEBALL CLUB, Mays was about to learn about more than baseball. Piper told his men to make sure everyone paid attention on the next road trip, so they didn't have a repeat of the incident late in May when thieves broke into their bus during a Sunday doubleheader at Rickwood Field and stole two catcher's mitts, a fielder's glove, somebody's spikes, and several hats. Tom Hayes did not replace that equipment for his players and they had to buy their own. This was Negro League baseball—every man for himself. Yet somehow, Piper Davis had turned his team into a group that would play for one another, and above all, play for Willie Mays, because he was the boy who could escape the hot box. If somehow he could escape, then perhaps a little bit of each of the Black Barons would go right along with him, not only to white folks' ball, but to the big leagues itself.

"Mays, his was a gift," Bill Greason said. "Nobody taught him. He could play. It was a gift that he took and developed. Being around all these good ballplayers at an early age helped him to develop his gift." And as the players boarded driver Charlie Rudd's bus for a road trip that would begin in Memphis and take the Black Barons to Chicago and Cleveland and many points in between before returning to Birmingham at the end of the month, Mays was certain to be on time when the bus pulled up in front of Bob's Savoy on Negro Avenue. As a rookie, Mays got the worst, most uncomfortable seat, but the players were astounded at how he laughed and didn't care. He may not have been as good as he could be, but he was slowly becoming one of them. "I tell you what," Zapp said. "Mays was the best little boy anybody ever seen."

6

READIN' THE HOPS

The first man Willie Mays saw when he boarded the bus was driver Charlie Rudd. His tan slacks were always impeccably pressed and his tie neatly displayed inside his Ike jacket. He wore his driver's cap crusher style, like the bomber pilots. Rudd never carried maps because he knew where Negroes could travel and where they could not. The itinerary was folded in his pocket, the detailed game schedule owner Tom Hayes would devise with promoter Abe Saperstein, who called himself the proprietor of "America's Ace Attractions." Saperstein's connections allowed him to book games in small towns between the Black Barons' bigger games slated for the three-week road trip. Most days, the Black Barons would play twice, but if they played three times, it wouldn't have been unusual. Abe made sure Tom broke even, with a tad of profit on top and a chance for the Black Barons to pass the hat.

The bus was a twenty-two-seat model with no air conditioning, so the good seats away from the wheel wells and near the windows went to the team veterans. The smart players never left their vital gear in the cargo hold. They carried a roll and placed their spikes, jock, jersey, pants, and glove into it, then fastened it with their uniform belt. The roll became a pillow. Some players brought their bats on board.

The Black Barons took their road gray uniforms and wore the hats marked BBB, new for the 1948 season, which were blue with a red bill. Somebody had to score the games, so a college student named C. Eric Lincoln was hired to be the road secretary. He carried a score-book and a pencil, but nobody thought statistics meant anything and the majority of games were forgotten as soon as they were finished. They played in small towns against semipro, factory, and town teams, against white teams and black teams, on gravel and in carved-out corn-fields, where if a town's ball field had portable lights it was considered a desirable place to play a game. Many times, Studebakers, Packards, and Model Ts would form a ring around the field and turn on their headlights, and in many small midwestern towns the lights shining on black players exposed what to the townspeople was an anomaly, dark-skinned southern blacks from an exotic destination. The posters, placards, and sound cars would announce the arrival of the "Negro American League First-Half Champion Birmingham Black Barons." This was Willie's first taste of a new world. The closest he ever came to these fields again was when he flew above them in the big leagues.

But that first summer, Mays was greener than cow pastures in Kansas. He wasn't going to develop his skills against the inferior small-town talent, but he was going to develop stamina and strength. He was also going to learn firsthand about how the men who played before him lived. He was going to learn the language, some of which he had undoubtedly picked up in the Industrial League. Inside the bus, Mays learned words like "kick-ya-poo" and "crumb snatcher," learned new card games, old songs and some new ones, and some southern folklore. He learned about his teammates, where they had been and where they hoped to go, what motivated them and what made them who they were. He learned to speak the black baseball language that had its beginnings in Birmingham. No one spoke it better than Piper.

Piper kept Willie close to his seat at the front right side of the bus. He never worried about the youngster developing the physical aspects of baseball. He wasn't even worried about him figuring out how to hit.

He was more concerned that Willie develop the discipline that he felt his rookie left fielder needed to survive. So Piper purposely made himself a presence Mays could not ignore. When Mays set foot on the bus, there was Piper waiting with the first lesson. "White ballplayers have one expression and black players have another, but they be talking about the same thing," Piper said. "Take a white ballplayer, he be keeping his eyes on the ball, but we be 'readin' the hops.'"

"My daddy was a character," Faye Davis said. "Funny, funny man, but whatever he would do, if you look back at it, you would find that it all taught you a lesson."

This bus was Piper's classroom. On the road to Memphis, he began his discourse. Charlie Rudd could read the rough roads from rural Alabama into rural Tennessee. The man could do two things exceptionally well. One was drive and the other was talk. To pass time between

The only girl on the team: Charlie Rudd's bus was the safe haven for the Birmingham Black Barons, and her driver, Charlie Rudd (pictured), could fix her with a hairpin and drive his way out of any dangerous situation.

destinations, the conversation rolled like the hills. Perhaps the bus might pass the place where the engine had once failed when a lift pin and a valve lifter had broken. Piper had bellowed at Rudd and told his team, "It was the bus driver's fault, now everybody got to get out and push." Rudd parked the bus and went for a walk. He knocked a board loose from a farmer's fence, shook the nail lose, shaved off the head, stuck it in the engine, and got the Black Barons to the next game. He was well worth the $500 a month Tom Hayes paid him. For the record, the bus driver was making more than Willie Mays. "God bless him, he saved our lives many a day," Piper said. "He could drive. He could drive."

Piper might turn his attention to the studious young Lincoln, who passed his time reading and writing in his journals about experiences that formed the foundation of an academic writing career. He too was trapped in the hot box, though his future was not in baseball. "What did it matter if you could hit the ball and run the bases?" Lincoln wrote of his youth. He recalled the first time he learned that society considered black children different from white children when he stepped forward in the vaccination line, unaware that whites were to go first, and was chastised by a nurse who bellowed, "All niggers have to wait! Wait! Nigger, wait!"

Southern blacks seemed to have to wait for their chance in white folks' ball, yet sometimes it seemed tantalizingly close. But Willie made the Black Barons feel like they were closer to the front of the line than they really were. His enthusiasm dulled some of the pain they had felt over the years. "We knew what it was all about," pitcher Bill Greason said. "Baseball was not movin' up. It was comin' down."

So Piper told Mays never to let his level of play come down no matter what he heard from the fans, no matter how much more talented he was than many of the people who called him names. That way, when he played at Memphis, Chicago, or Cleveland, his own level of play would be movin' up and not comin' down. As the bus motored into Memphis's Martin Park on East Crump Boulevard, Piper told him something very important. "Somebody is watching you," he said. "Somebody is always watching."

• • •

If Tom Hayes had been watching Willie Mays before he stepped on the field when the Black Barons arrived in Memphis, Hayes's hometown, he might have been surprised to be reminded that he was paying someone so young. Mays had moments of acting so childishly impish that Hayes might have wondered whether his $250 a month was spent at the candy shop. But there was a difference. When Mays was off the field, he was a boy. When he was on it, he was something else. The Black Barons' visit to Memphis was the first time Hayes watched him play. "Mays was a happy-go-lucky kid," Zapp said. "But I wouldn't say he was green. He didn't act like a kid on the field. That was the difference. He acted like a veteran on that ball field. Other than that, Mays was a baby."

When Mays was a baby, Memphis's Willie Wells had already been one of the best shortstops ever to play in the Negro Leagues. Piper told Mays to watch closely. Buck O'Neil's scouting report on the hard-nosed, outspoken Wells reflected many of the qualities young Willie Mays was developing: "Most intelligent player I've ever played against—Great eye sight—Picked up ball off bat and rotation of ball from pitcher's hand—Excellent bat control—Line drive hitter to all fields—Soft, quick hands—Made all the plays—Very desirable."

Memphis first baseman Bob Boyd was such a good hitter that he was nicknamed "the Rope" for the way he sprayed line drives all over the field. Piper told Mays to watch Boyd's hitting approach. Piper was only focused on teaching Willie how to be a ballplayer. He omitted the fact that in black lingo, a "rope" was a marijuana cigarette. Black ballplayer code called for nobody to question off-the-field habits, which once caused Baltimore manager Felton Snow to say, "We've got so many guys who just wouldn't act right."

Piper taught Mays to think before he acted. He wanted Mays to make good decisions and to stay away from an off-the-field reputation that might doom him. Black players, he said, were given the smallest margin for error. So, Piper told Mays, keep it simple: Play hard. Play with passion. Play the game right, because you never know who is watching. "We always felt that if we were going to be scouted," Greason said, "that our best chance to be seen was on the road instead of in Birmingham because of the segregation."

Piper encouraged Mays to play well in front of Tom Hayes, who controlled his baseball destiny. Mays took Piper's advice, took his bat to the plate, and looked for fastballs. When he got them, he didn't miss them.

Most black pitchers didn't take long to learn that trying to throw a fastball past Mays was a bad idea. Instead, they threw him every form of breaking pitch they could concoct, from slippery elm balls to thumb tack cutters. While Mays learned to identify curveballs, he was making defensive plays that ordinary outfielders couldn't. His athleticism overwhelmed his inexperience. He had no concept of how to pursue balls by taking the shortest route to them. As a result, he misjudged some fly balls, but had the athletic skill to make up for his mistakes. He outran balls he got a bad jump on, but he could also chase down balls others could not. Many times Mays made catches not with his glove but by reaching out his throwing hand and snagging the ball out of thin air. "A lot of times he'd catch the ball with his throwing hand," Zapp said. "He also might catch a hit bare-handed on the first bounce and throw it in. It would seem like the ball would take off by the time it got to the mound. The catchers had to be quick to stay with him."

Mays moved faster than Satchel's Paige's fastball. On the road from Memphis to Chicago for the weekend series at Comiskey Park, word reached the Black Barons bus that a momentous occasion was to occur in Cleveland that weekend. The Brooklyn Dodgers were going to play the Indians in an exhibition game. Everyone expected Satchel Paige to pitch for the Indians. When he did, it would mark the first time four black players would be on the same major league field at once: Paige and Larry Doby from the Indians and Jackie Robinson and Roy Campanella with the Dodgers. For the players on Charlie Rudd's bus, white folks' ball again felt attainable. Paige had made his major league debut on July 9, just five days after Mays's official Negro American League debut. Paige's long-awaited debut led him to comment, "Twenty-two years sure is a long time to be a rookie," but the Black Barons were proud. Though most of the country knew him as a Monarch, Willie's Boys considered him a Black Baron.

It was a long time to wait for something that might never happen for most of the Black Barons. The plight of Negro players in white folks' ball had the same feel as an old southern story that was one of Rudd's favorites to tell on long drives. Two slaves stole a sack of potatoes and decided that the safest place to divide them up would be in the graveyard at night. The two slaves started dividing the potatoes, singing aloud, "You take dis one, I'll take dat one." Another slave passed beyond the fence and decided that it must be God and the Devil dividing up the souls. He fetched his master, who threatened a whippin' if the slave was lyin'. When they reached the graveyard, they hid behind the fence, saw two potatoes roll near them, and heard the voices again, singing, "You take dis one, I'll take dat one." When there were only two potatoes left in the sack, one slave said, "I'll take dese two, you take dem two over by the fence." Clearly traumatized, the master and the slave ran away, lest they be handed over to the Devil.

The story always got a big laugh the way Rudd told it, but there was worry beneath the humor. The ballplayers felt like the potatoes on the plantation, with the big league scouts dividing up them up. "You take dis one, I'll take dat one." But it wasn't just white scouts who were trying to take the best black players to enhance their reputations. It was also black players trying to steal black players from other black teams. Chances are that Piper already knew that his manager in Puerto Rico the previous winter, Quincy Trouppe, had tried to steal his crumb snatcher.

Trouppe, the experienced and highly regarded catcher who was managing the Chicago American Giants in 1948, passed through Birmingham with his team in late June, before Mays started playing with the Black Barons regularly. After the twelve-inning, 13–12 Black Barons victory on June 26, Trouppe was hanging out, most likely at Bob's Savoy. A ballplayer Trouppe knew gave him a tip on a young outfielder with an "awful" arm. Intrigued, Trouppe tracked Mays down. He found him in a hotel room and asked him if he wanted to come to Chicago for a tryout. Mays didn't sign anything. He spoke to Cat, and when Trouppe returned to Chicago, there was a letter from Mays's home in Westfield asking for a $300 salary to join the American Giants, $50 more than he was making with the Black Barons. Mays may have been Birmingham's little brother, but he wasn't above jumping the team for more money.

But the American Giants refused to spend that kind of money for a teenager. When the Black Barons reached Comiskey Park following the games in Memphis, Trouppe was eager to see Mays play for the first time on a major league field. Comiskey Park's occupants, the Chicago White Sox, were off because of the major league all-star game. On a Sunday double-header, the Black Barons split the twin bill, with Greason improving to 7–0 to earn the only victory. Trouppe had a nice long look at Mays. He saw a fastball he liked from Greason and drove it deep into center field. Mays, playing left field, raced all the way over to center, called off Bobby Robinson, and made the play.

Trouppe was convinced he had an easy double, but when he pulled into second base, Artie Wilson was waiting for him. "Mays got it," he said.

"Man, oh man, what a prospect," Trouppe said. "And the Chicago American Giants had just let him go by."

There was no way Piper Davis was going to let his little crumb snatcher get away from him, especially in Chicago, the first big city Mays had traveled to. Piper took special care to make sure Mays couldn't shake him. That was the special kind of bond that led Bobby Veale to observe, "Mays was tight under Piper's wing. Pipe was on him like a hawk on a sparrow." That was a good thing, because on Saturday night in Chicago, the night owls flew the coop. Piper knew his players were sick of being caged up on the bus for the past few weeks. He knew they would hit the town, but all he asked was that they be responsible and be on time. Don't bring a hangover onto the field. Don't let a light or a shade interfere with work on the field. So while Alonzo Perry, Jimmy Newberry, Jehosie Heard, Squeaky Wilson, Jimmy Zapp, and others hit downtown, Piper made sure Mays was occupied in his hotel room.

Third baseman Johnny Britton, nicknamed "Brit," liked to read out-of-town newspapers because he liked to follow the major leagues. Some players, especially Heard, who Piper said spent "every dime he made," mercilessly poked fun at Brit for wondering what Joe DiMaggio's batting average was. "Always reading about them damn white boys," Heard would say. "Why don't you do something yourself?" Mays, for his part, wanted to know. He took Brit's newspapers in the hotel room with him. Brit, however, was hanging out with the boys in downtown Chicago, where Newberry was drowning in the kick-ya-poo juice.

Piper explained to Mays that a road roommate was a way of life in Negro baseball, where players often had to "sleep in the same bed, like husband and wife," he said. "I slept in the same bed as Ed Steele. When I started, Tommy Sampson was my roommate and then Steele. We got along very well, yes-sir-ee." One player Mays often spent time with on the road was pitcher Nat Pollard, Piper's longtime friend. Pollard so frequently quoted scripture that teammates nicknamed him "the Prophet," but the Prophet couldn't pitch very much in 1948 because of a sore arm that forced him to watch Sunday afternoon double-headers behind the dugout at Rickwood Field, dressed for God.

The Black Barons dressed for the ladies on Saturday night in Chicago. Brit and Squeaky were roommates who, Zapp said, "dressed sharp all the time." Brit thought Wilson was the greatest hitter who ever lived and considered it an honor to keep Artie's company. Zapp would run with Perry and Scott. Newberry and Heard were joined at the hip, with Greason the quiet third wheel, but that didn't mean he didn't keep his eyes open too. Even when the players sought nightlife, Greason said they took Piper's advice to look out for one another. "If we saw one of our teammates drinking, we'd tell him, 'Man, you aren't gonna make it like that,'" Greason said.

Kick-ya-poo juice was the hardest whiskey a man could get, moonshine even, and Newberry drank the hard stuff until it lived up to its nickname and kicked him square in the ass. He would never turn down a free drink, either. Greason lost track of how many times he got his roommate out of trouble, or caught him with a rope, including that Saturday night in Chicago when Newberry managed to get several players in trouble when they went to a club with some members of the American Giants. Greason spent most of his meal money on cab fares that night.

Even away from the field, Piper had influence. His players respected his wishes because they understood that he didn't want to deprive them, but he didn't want to see a bad decision cheat them out of

Pensive and fiery, Black Barons right-hander Bill Greason was a top rookie in 1948 and later became the first black pitcher for the St. Louis Cardinals.

white folks' ball. "Piper expected us to be gentlemen when we went out," Greason said. "We didn't get to go out much on the road, and when we did, you didn't know we were there. We never did tell people that we were there or ask the band to play one for the Black Barons. If you go out drinking late at night and somebody at the club saw you, the next day, everybody would know because you'd hear the fans yell, 'Hey, you were drunk!' So we used to tell guys, if you go to a club, just get in the corner. If you got a girl, get on out of there."

The girls were easy to come by. While Mays slept near Piper and the Prophet, Perry and Zapp sought the lights and shades. "Most of us loved the women," Greason said. "Oh, we loved the women! We didn't even have to hunt for them. If they knew you played baseball, wherever you were playing, they would come. And you knew to take care of yourself. You didn't want to come down with no clap, as they called it then."

Mays never had the chance to be tempted. "I don't think Piper would have let him go out," Zapp said. "We never did see him out anyplace. If we had, Piper would have taken him back to the hotel. Those guys were so much older than Mays, and even me and Greason, as rookies, were four and five years older than Mays. He never did go out with the boys and I don't think he ever wanted to. Most of the time in the big cities, Mays would be around the hotel with Pollard."

Somebody was always watching Mays. Sunday morning at Comiskey Park, Piper saw Abe Saperstein. There, he learned that Saperstein's longtime traveling manager of the Harlem Globetrotters, Winfield Welch, had been hired by Alex Pompez to manage the New York Cubans. Saperstein wasn't the type of person who could accurately judge ballplayers, even if he was scouting black players for Cleveland Indians owner Bill Veeck and had his eye on Birmingham shortstop Artie Wilson. Piper knew Welch would do his best to grab Birmingham players and bring them to New York. The first long road trip of Willie's Negro League career also contained one of his first important moments as a ballplayer, when Piper, with one trusted word, made sure that Saperstein and Welch knew about Mays. Eventually, Piper's tip was handed through the scouting grapevine to two teams: the Cleveland Indians and the New York Giants.

Piper purposely helped plot Willie's future, but he always stayed in the background. "Piper never talked to Mays about any of that stuff," Greason said. "All he wanted him to concentrate on was becoming the best player he could be." Mays's ability to quickly adjust stunned his older teammates. The curveballs that consistently baffled him were still a challenge, but were no longer foreign enemies. "The thing that surprised the older guys the most was how fast Mays came as a hitter," Zapp said. The scorebooks C. Eric Lincoln kept were thrown away as quickly as they were filled, but the lessons from Willie Mays's rookie summer stayed with him when he pressed his image into the American psyche.

Piper pressed himself into Willie's mind. When he had a few extra minutes during batting practice, he would seek Willie. "When I was in the outfield with him, we'd talk," Piper said. "I showed him how to come in on balls. Pick a hop so you don't let it get by. Don't make a practice of throwing the ball no way but one way from the outfield.

If you can, this is what you do: get the ball like that and pull down on it." Piper spoke with sound effects to prove his point—*whish!* and *snap!* to describe what he could make the ball do. If Willie did that, Piper assured him, people would notice. Piper reminded Mays to play hard and hustle. "You never know who is watching," he said again.

Mays showed signs that he was a better hitter than some veteran pitchers were giving him credit for. To his credit, Piper was wise enough not to tamper with Mays's unusual swing. What he stressed instead was one minor alteration in hitting approach. "Willie, you have a thing you do," Piper explained, holding a bat in his hands. "You step away from the ball with your left foot. If the pitcher is throwing here, you can't reach that ball. Close your shoulder and point it at the pitcher. If the ball is in here"—Piper gestured to the inner half of the plate—"stay inside and go to left field. If the ball is out here"—he gestured to the outer half of the plate—"shoot it to right field, just off changing that part of your stance."

So Willie absorbed Piper's advice and began to work on it. Piper made it simple. "Aim," he said. "Don't peek!" Mays already did everything else naturally. Piper respected his natural ability to keep his hands back despite his long stride. He hit against a firm front side that allowed him to get great torque with his hips and create a direct path of the bat to the ball. His hands were so fast that they blurred when he swung. Mays got great extension through the ball at contact. In time, Piper felt he would hit home runs. He noted that despite all the moving parts in Mays's swing, his head *never* moved. He always stayed down on the pitch. White folks' ball called it "having a quiet head." Piper called Mays's talent a gift to be left alone. He admired how Willie attacked the ball. Each time he came to the plate, he seemed to have a vendetta against the pitcher. Perhaps it was the years of segregation boiling up in him or the observations he had made. He was there to hit, not to be cheated.

When the Black Barons boarded Charlie Rudd's bus for several weekday games before the road trip concluded the following weekend in Cleveland, Piper was pleased. Willie was learning to read the hops, but Piper was not finished preparing his team. He knew the schedule like Rudd knew the roads. At the start of August, the Black Barons would travel to Kansas City to play the Monarchs again. Piper wanted his players ready.

So while Piper taught Mays, he didn't stop teaching the other players. Sometimes his players hated how intense Piper would get, but they realized what Faye Davis knew about her daddy. Everything Piper did had purpose. The lesson was always there. Zapp remembered how Piper tore up Ed Steele, his longtime friend and road roommate, when Steele failed to score from third base on a line drive hit to the left fielder. The left fielder threw the trail runner out at second base to complete the inning-ending double play, while Steele stood there like a tourist. "Piper ate his butt out in front of all of us," Zapp said. "He said, 'You weren't hustling. You turn your uniform in.' I never forgot that. Piper demanded the highest effort all the time. And most of the time, he got it."

"He'd get up in your face, too," Bill Greason said. "But he never cursed you. I remember, I was pitching in a close game. Johnny Britton played it cool and a ball went through his legs at third base. Brit got me behind in the game. The way I saw Brit nonchalantly play that ball angered me. On the next pitch, I began to wind up, and Piper had run in from second base and was standing in front of me. He shouted, 'What's wrong with you? Do you think Brit tried to miss that ball? Now take that ball and pitch!' Boy, I was hot, but Piper said, 'I don't want to see that no more.' So I said, 'Okay, Skip.' That taught me something there."

While Mays learned, the Black Barons bonded. Mays learned that pitcher Sammy C. Williams, whom his teammates affectionately called "Sammy C.," had driven DUKWs (pronounced "Ducks"), amphibious trucks, in the South Pacific. At night, players took turns standing next to Rudd and talking to him so he could stay awake. When Rudd finally needed a nap, Sammy C. would take the wheel of the bus. "That was the best team I ever played on," Sammy C. said. "We all got along just like brothers. We were a close group and it meant something."

Mays learned never to ask Pepper Bassett if Pepper was his real name. "My name is Pepper Bassett," Pepper liked to say, "and my mama's name is Lillie." That was Pepper's way of saying don't ask again. He picked up the nickname "Rocking Chair Bassett" because once on a dare he caught a game while sitting in a rocking chair. The one-night gag became his career calling card. Sometimes, fans would bring a rocking chair and ask Pepper to catch in it. He would play along. "Pepper could catch, now," Bobby Veale said. "He'd get back there in that little rocking chair and pick you clean behind the plate."

Pepper could hit a ball a mile and punch out a grizzly bear if he had to, as Mays learned one night on the bus when he woke him up to ask him to move his legs. Before Pepper's eyes opened, he took a swing at Mays, who saved himself with his reflexes. Buck ducked and Pepper's throwing hand hit the luggage rack. His scream woke up half the team and his sore hand was the reason Herman Bell caught most of the games on that road trip. Mays learned his lesson: never, ever aggravate Lloyd Pepper Bassett.

On the base paths, Mays had a natural tendency to aggravate opposing teams. When he reached first base, he took such huge leads that Piper said he needed a lasso to keep Mays still. He slashed more than

Pepper Bassett was one of the toughest, most durable, and most unheralded catchers from the Negro Leagues. His trademark act of catching in a rocking chair was as notable as his home run power.

he ran and when he dove into second base he made a noise like a saw. In the outfield, there wasn't a ball hit into the air that Mays didn't think he could chase down. If he was playing deep left field and there was a pop-up to shortstop, Artie Wilson had to watch his back, and scream at the top of his lungs to call off Mays. And at the plate, Mays was feeling his way. If the pitch came where he could reach it, he would remorselessly cut at it. He was as unforgiving as a rookie could be.

From game to game, Mays learned to hustle with the Black Barons and worked up a sweat. If the players were lucky, they might get a bath before the game. Many times, they traveled from game to game without washing. The summer heat made the stench on the bus worse. The side of the road was their best friend. If players could do laundry, they often held shirts and underwear out the bus window. "In twenty minutes," Veale said, "your shirt be bone dry."

Yet despite the hardships, Mays made this team special. Though white folks' ball scouts and Negro League players from outside of Birmingham were only now becoming aware of Mays, the Black Barons knew what they had on their bus. They watched Piper nurture him and followed his lead. "We all believed he would play in the big leagues," Greason said. "You see a rare gem? That's what he was."

Mays was indeed a rare gem, but the polishing was not limited to playing baseball. The older players knew he was putting pressure on himself. "Piper had to encourage him so he knew he was worth something," Greason said. "He was trying so hard for a young fella." Greason sensed that Mays, just below the surface, was an insecure child who was trying to reconcile how his life was going to be so much different than those of the men around him. To be a baseball star in the big leagues, his future was going to have to be in the prim and proper white man's society, which in the rural worldview of Westfield felt terrifying.

Piper knew this distinction would eventually separate Willie from the Black Barons, so Piper raised Mays like he was his own son, with lessons Cat could not share. Piper had seen so much more of the world outside of Birmingham, his experiences wide-ranging. There had always been stories about Willie's childhood, rumors that stayed in the community, willfully hidden in the trees and lost to time where nobody could find them, even if they knew where to look. Piper put that aside and, like he had always been, became a role model for his team. They followed him step by step, and Willie became their little brother and favorite son. They didn't want to see Mays fall. They wanted to see him fly. "So we took care of him," Greason said. "And learned how to take care of each other."

The teaching extended from the trees and into the night. When Rudd was awake, Piper had a very direct rule to avoid the white cops who might be happy to pull over a bus full of black ballplayers. "If the speed limit was thirty-five, he did thirty-four and a half," Faye Davis said. "He wasn't going to break any laws, so you better not break any." Every lesson had something in common: watch your back and have one another's backs. "We learned, being black and from the South, how not to get angry just because somebody called you a name," Greason said. "If you know who you are, you don't have to worry. That n-word, anybody can call you a nigger, so we didn't let it bother us. We stayed focused."

Greason was as focused on playing in the big leagues as Mays was. The rookies spent time talking on the bus. Mays loved to talk about hitting. Greason loved to tell Mays how he could get him out if he ever got the chance. He also described the honor code among black pitchers. "You got two strikes on a guy and he got to be pushed off the plate," Greason said. "If you hit one of ours, we hit one of yours. We never threw behind a guy, always in front. You knew if he was throwing behind you, he was throwing to hurt you. We never tried to do that. We'd come in, brush him back and knock him down, but we'd never try to hit him."

As the Black Barons came to Cleveland to face Piper's old friend, right-handed pitcher Chet Brewer, Mays was about to learn exactly what Greason meant. Faye Davis remembered how Chet was an odd sight on the mound, so thin that he practically wore his pants up to his armpits. Mays didn't know one pitcher from the next when he was a rookie, but he had surely heard of Chet, who was Satchel's shadow in Kansas City during the 1930s. He didn't know that Brewer was so precise with his pitches that Frazier Robinson, his former catcher with the Monarchs, believed that "if he hit you, it was no accident."

The first time Mays faced Brewer, Piper shouted, "Aim! Don't peek!" That was code. Brewer wound up with a high leg kick in which the tip of his big toe went above his head, and found a touch of his old fastball. He drilled Willie in the ribs like he was shooting darts. The pitch knocked the breath out of Willie and he fell to the dirt. The Buckeyes laughed at him on the bench and Brewer stood on the mound with his hands on his hips. The Black Barons were quiet. Mays looked at his bench, but none of his teammates charged onto the field. He looked at the third base line, where Piper was coaching, and Piper pointed to first base. Greason had been right: Brewer had thrown in front of Willie, not behind him.

But Willie sat on his behind for a few moments. A funny man with a serious side, Piper walked down the line until he lorded over Mays, as Bobby Veale described, like a redwood. "You got plenty of trees, but that's the tallest." Veale said, "Piper let his actions speak for him," but this time he let Brewer's fastball do the talking. Mays still sat in the dirt when Piper arrived. His manager seared him with his dark eyes and deep voice.

"You know where first base is?" Piper asked.

Mays nodded yes.

"Get on up and get down there," Piper said. "When you get to first, steal second. When you get to second, steal third. When you get to third, steal home."

Of course, Lincoln's scorebook was in the trash, so nobody remembered what Willie did after Brewer hit him. But as Piper walked back to coach third base, Greason swore he saw a glimmer in his eye as he looked directly at Brewer, hid a smirk, and shouted, "Don't let that guy make a fool about you!" Greason remembered how Brewer covered his face with his glove so nobody could see him laugh. Piper Davis was a funny, funny man. Willie Mays was a better ballplayer because of it. Mays, Piper, and Brewer never forgot that moment. Piper and Brewer liked to tell the story as though it was a complete coincidence, and the joke never got old.

"My daddy saved that newspaper clipping until it was orange and falling apart in his hands," Faye Davis said. Piper had chosen his moment. He had asked Brewer to throw at Mays on the road, not in Birmingham, where fans would have relentlessly attacked the pitcher with a verbal barrage or worse. Piper's lesson was as precise as Brewer's pitch. The lesson stayed with Mays long after the Negro Leagues died. "They were teaching me to survive," Mays said. "That's all it was."

After splitting a Sunday double-header with Cleveland, the Black Barons and the Buckeyes toured out to the countryside, playing each other for a few more days as the Black Barons played their way back to Birmingham. Along the way, Mays began to settle in. Soon he might find himself singing on the bus, a favorite hobby in the Negro Leagues. Jimmy Newberry might imitate Cab Calloway's scat songs, but his heart was in the South. He'd get together with his polar opposite, pitcher Bill Powell, and his soul brothers, Alonzo Perry and Jehosie Heard. Other players took turns filling in, singing traditional southern songs they all knew. "They could have a glee club if they wanted to," Bobby Veale explained, before singing:

You get a line and I get a pole, honey, honey
You get a line and I get a pole, babe, babe
You get a line and I get a hole, we'll go down to the crawdad hole
Hoooney, baaaaaby, miiiine.

Sometimes Piper and Rudd might share stories of road trips that hadn't been as dangerous as this one. "He could tell you stories like they was happening now," Veale said. "He could tell you about the hardships, the trials, and the tribulations—walk a mile to try to get somewhere to sleep, sleeping on the side of the road or on the bus. Eating sardines out of the can. Going without a bath sometimes all night, you have to wait to get to the ballpark and shower. You smell good before the game, and after the game, forget it."

Mays wasn't always sitting next to Piper now, instead milling his way around the bus to talk to the other players. He began to get the hang of the unexpected. When the players got hungry, they would stop at a country grocery store even if they had to enter through the back door. "One of us would buy bread, one would buy cold cuts, one would buy a jar of mustard, and one would buy drinks," Greason said. "We'd hop back in the bus before they ever knew we were gone. We'd have a 'Dutch Lunch,' knockin' down the highway, eating sandwiches, and not worrying about a thing."

There was another unwritten rule among the players, something distinctly southern. Nobody liked to be mistreated, but the Black Barons knew they had better lives than many other black people. It didn't mean they had to accept it forever, but they shunned segregation and collectively inhaled the moment. "We had a lot of fun on the bus," Greason said, even though, as Zapp pointed out, "We played in so many games, you couldn't keep track of them all." That was another reason why the 1948 Black Barons could read the hops. "It was not so tiresome," Greason said. "We were always laughing and talking."

And now that Mays had a better grip on the language, Piper let him in on why he called him a crumb snatcher. It was an old black-folk term for a child. Piper applied it at his own dinner table, where he told Faye and Ruben that he "played ball to take care of his crumb snatchers." Years later, Faye said she told Piper, "I was proud to be your crumb snatcher." That Piper would equate Willie with one of his own children made him more than a baseball manager. And just as Piper's own children learned more geography at the dinner table playing a game called "How Come?" with their papa, Willie learned more geography in Charlie Rudd's bus than he would ever do anywhere else.

Rickwood Field was awaiting the Barons the next weekend, where a Sunday double-header against the Newark Eagles was scheduled. But one last lesson of this road trip awaited Mays on the bus. Piper, of course, already knew the answer to his question, but that didn't stop him from asking.

"Mays," Piper said, "how much you makin'?"

"Two hundred and fifty a month," Mays said. He was sure of that.

"My first contract," Piper said, "I was makin' ninety-one dollars a month playin' for Omaha. That was in '36. You got it better already."

Mays had been playing baseball for what seemed like twelve days. Piper told him the secret to making more money. Willie listened.

"I played against white boys when I was growing up," Piper said. "All the white boys played with ACIPCO's white team because they wasn't good enough for white folks' ball. I knew one of them boys real well. I said, 'You'd never beat us if we played each other.' I said, 'We'd run you to death.' And he said, 'Oh nooooooo!' I said, 'Oh yeeeeeeeeees.'

"So when the time comes for you to go to white folks' ball," Piper said, "you run 'em to death."

Mays listened and intently nodded. "What they did for me," he said, "I'll never forget." On those bumpy bus rides over dirt roads, from one backdoor kitchen to another, amid countless card games, songs, and drowning in kick-ya-poo juice, the torch from the black leagues to the big leagues was silently passed.

7

WHAMMY ALABAMA

Bitter Battle Expected" was the headline that greeted the Black Barons in the *Kansas City Call* when the team arrived on August 1 for a Sunday double-header against the Monarchs at Blues Stadium, the minor league ballpark that housed the second of two Triple-A teams the wealthy New York Yankees operated. The Monarchs secretly wished they could take on the Blues, a club that featured Hank Bauer and Al Rosen, two future major league regulars in 1948. The Monarchs' desire to play their white counterparts mirrored the Black Barons' wish to take on the Birmingham Barons. Once, Piper and Ed Steele held an impromptu home-run-hitting contest in the company of Barons first baseman Walt Dropo. Piper assured Dropo that the Black Barons would win if they played each other, because the Black Barons would run the white Barons into the ground.

The Monarchs longed to grind the Black Barons into the ground, but Birmingham had other ideas. The Black Barons needed to win the series at Kansas City to secure the second-half championship. If they lost, the Black Barons and the Monarchs would meet in a playoff series at the end of the regular season to determine the Negro American League champion and the league's representative in the Negro League World Series. If the Black Barons could beat the Monarchs this weekend, they would all but clinch the second-half title.

It was a tantalizing possibility, but winning in Kansas City wasn't easy. The crowd was always hostile (returning the favors bestowed on the Monarchs by the Birmingham fans at Rickwood Field) and the umpires were former Monarch players. Gambling was plentiful as sunshine and nobody bet against the home team. The Monarchs, fresh off beating the Indianapolis Clowns in six out of seven games, desperately wanted to force a playoff series against the Black Barons. While young Willie Mays was breaking into the Black Barons lineup and learning how to play with men, the Monarchs had made an immediate statement, rushing into first place in the second-half standings with a 16–4 record before the Black Barons arrived at Blues Stadium.

John I. Johnson, the sports editor of the *Call*, did his part to help the Monarchs invigorate their fans. Johnson believed it was his responsibility to drum up publicity to help the Monarchs boost sagging ticket sales. Any gimmick was a good one. The bathing beauty contests proved to be especially popular and the swimsuit-clad girls were eagerly anticipated. Kansas City fans, like the Birmingham faithful, found special social meaning in their baseball games. "Probably no club in either league has a more enthusiastic backing of fans than the Monarchs," Johnson wrote. "They have a loyal booster club that works constantly and efficiently to pull fans into the park and to give whatever it needs to win."

Tom Baird wasn't pleased when he surveyed the crowd of 5,044 who had made their way from church pews to box seats in anticipation of the 2 p.m. first pitch. Twelve thousand empty seats proved to be a much smaller crowd than Baird hoped for, though his decreased cash flow had been enhanced recently. On July 13, he had received a check for $5,000 from the Cleveland Indians for pitcher Satchel Paige. Baird had split the money evenly between himself and previous Monarchs owner J. L. Wilkinson. While Baird studied the crowd, he kept his eyes open for white baseball scouts, men he eagerly courted to purchase his best players. They were impossible to miss and Baird hated it when they escaped his detection. He meticulously monitored every scout, making mental notes of the players they liked and his asking prices. Baird had his own idea of how to escape the hot box. He would run a pawnshop disguised as a baseball team, attempting to auction off his best players to some combination of the highest bidder and the buyer Baird felt was best for his post–Negro League baseball career. At the bottom of Baird's priority list were his players as people. He was a white owner who fancied himself a champion of the black race, but money was his motivation. Once he sold a player to white folks' ball, he wrote the player a letter of release, tacked the player's name on his résumé, and tried to convince every major league baseball team that the only Negro ballplayers worth hiring played for the Kansas City Monarchs.

The first time Baird looked at the Black Barons Sunday starting lineup, "guided by wily manager, Piper Davis," according to the *Call*, he noticed a player who would have looked great on his résumé. Baird may have been surprised to see rookie left fielder Willie Mays batting eighth. He already knew the name.

Cool Papa Bell, the former outstanding center fielder who was now the player-manager of the Kansas City Stars, the Monarchs second-team squad where Baird housed younger players until they were ready to play for the big Monarchs, had tried to steal Mays from the Black Barons. Bell had spotted Mays when the Stars played the Black Barons in July. Bell was no longer the player he had been in the 1930s or as recently as 1944, when as a member of the Homestead Grays he rolled a bases-loaded single in the eleventh inning to beat the Black Barons in Game 2 of the Negro World Series. His sad decline had continued in 1945 when writer Sam Lacy declared, "He could no longer worry the life out of pitchers once he got on base."

But Bell saw how Mays could worry everyone he played against. Cool Papa, whom players universally called Cool, was "getting old, but he could still motor," said Piper, who played with Cool and several Black Barons in the winter of 1945. Piper never doubted Bell's ability to spot a ballplayer, and when the Stars played the Black Barons in July, Cool saw many familiar faces including Piper, Artie Wilson, Pepper Bassett, and Ed Steele. The Black Barons raved about their new outfielder. Cool had never heard of Mays, but when he saw him play, he never forgot him. He knew that Mays was going to learn how to hit, and when he did, he offered talents that Cool knew he never possessed. Bell could run and he was a slap hitter who almost never hit out-of-the-park home runs. He possessed an ordinary arm, but used his speed as the equalizer. Mays was raw and strong, but what separated him was his power—his strength at a young age, his quick muscles, and his aggressive nature. Bell wanted to retire because his legs ached and he was tired of wrapping his ankles. He was at the end of the line and he knew it, but he needed to find a replacement for himself to play center field for the Stars. When he saw Mays, he wanted to sign him away from the Black Barons, spend the rest of the 1948 season tutoring him on the Stars, and then hand him over the 1949 Monarchs. The Monarchs would provide the Stars with a replacement outfielder, and at long last, Cool Papa could rest his weary feet.

It was a perfect plan, but Bell didn't anticipate Baird's distaste for southern black ballplayers. He was a white supremacist from Missouri who left his closet open just wide enough for his Ku Klux Klan robes to be seen. Baird didn't care for Birmingham players, and Bell's reputation and favorable scouting reports weren't enough to sway him. Bell's enthusiasm for a rare player was ignored. It wouldn't have taken much more than $250 a month.

"Willie Mays played in Birmingham," Bell said. "Our owner was told that there was a great ballplayer down there. He couldn't hit the ball, but he could run and throw. He swings level. All you would have to do was just bring him up. But [Baird] wouldn't take the chance on Willie Mays."

Bell pleaded with the owner, even asking William "Dizzy" Dismukes to change Baird's mind. Dismukes, an Alabama native who had been a submarine pitcher for the Black Barons in the 1920s, had divorced himself from Birmingham and won Baird's loyalty. Baird trusted Dismukes almost as much as he trusted his field manager, Buck O'Neil, calling the tandem his "Board of Strategy." Dismukes was always dressed in a suit, so Baird described his longtime traveling secretary as someone who looked "like he came out of a band box." Cool Papa Bell shrugged his shoulders and surrendered. "Look what a ballplayer Mays made," he lamented.

Baird, however, was particularly interested in watching his August 1 starting pitcher, Jim LaMarque. The crafty, red-tinted left-hander took the mound against the Black Barons with a 10–4 record, his best Negro American League season. Baird believed he could sell LaMarque, whom he described as "an intelligent looking Negro, in fact, he might pass for Indian." Although Baird assured his ballplayers that he would try to help them break into white folks' ball, LaMarque mistrusted him, a sentiment that he concealed. Baird was quick to point to the sale of Satchel Paige as proof that he held the black players' best interests at heart, but his rejection of Mays showed otherwise.

LaMarque dreamed of joining Paige, but Paige was dealing with his own cultural acclimations in his first month as a major leaguer. While Bell was denied the chance to steal a player he had correctly scouted, Paige was deprived of the opportunity to throw his famous "hesitation pitch," his trademark delivery in which he paused in mid-windup to vary the pressure points on his fingertips to change speeds on the pitch to fool the batter. American League president Will Harridge declared Paige's delivery illegal after numerous hitters complained. Many players were convinced that Paige was doctoring the baseball, but none of them could prove it. The hesitation pitch was Satchel's mind weapon, which had more to do with deception than velocity, like speaking in his rich Alabama dialect about pigtails and "awful" arms. He reveled in the confused looks he created in white folks' ball. *Call* sports editor Johnson scoffed at white folks' ball, writing in a column in letter form to Paige in which he urged him to carefully choose his trick pitches. "I advise you not to use your Whammy Alabama," Johnson wrote. "Maybe you'd better not display your other pitching tricks you've picked up on a thousand diamonds."

Bill Powell yearned to put the Whammy Alabama on the Monarchs when he pitched Game 1 against LaMarque, hoping that white scouts would see him, too. When LaMarque and the Monarchs took the field against the Black Barons, all Baird had to do was look at 12,000 empty seats to realize that he had to find another way to make money, but the best chance he ever had to achieve that goal vanished the moment he decided to ignore Willie Mays.

LaMarque threw his curveball like he was spinning a yo-yo, up and down with ease, putting it at the knees or in the dirt if he pleased. He pitched two scoreless innings before Mays came to bat to lead off the third inning and chopped a base hit past rookie shortstop Gene Baker to get the Black Barons rolling. Powell sacrifice-bunted Mays to second and Artie Wilson slapped a single to left to score Mays and give the Black Barons a 1–0 lead.

But Powell lacked his typical fastball command. Though he entered the game with a record of 9–1, he was incredibly hittable. Hank Thompson hit a two-run inside-the-park home run. Willard Brown then doubled to left and came around to score when rookie Elston Howard, a northern black from St. Louis whom Cool Papa Bell had been allowed to sign, singled to give the Monarchs a 3–1 lead. Piper and Artie shared a worried look. The fans grew noisier.

Kansas City put Game 1 out of reach in the seventh inning when LaMarque's run-scoring double and Baker's run-scoring single against reliever Alonzo Perry sparked a three-run inning. Piper misplayed a hot ground ball off Thompson's bat. The ball went through his legs and the game got away from the Black Barons. The Monarchs had a 6–2 victory and LaMarque's value increased another notch with his eleventh victory, a six-hitter with six strikeouts, enhanced when he pitched around a triple by center fielder Bobby Robinson and a double by Mays.

Baird was closely watching Elston Howard, whom O'Neil started in left field to get his bat into the lineup. Baird had dollar signs in his eyes when he watched Howard hit, and envisioned him in pinstripes, playing the vast center field in Yankee Stadium, despite the fact that Howard was clearly not fast enough to replace Joe DiMaggio. While he ignored Mays's two hits, he dreamed that Elston Howard was his ticket to a job with the Yankees.

While Baird was daydreaming, Bill Greason longed to deal his best stuff and beat the Monarchs in Game 2. There would almost certainly be a Negro American League playoff between the Monarchs and the Black Barons at the end of the regular season if the Black Barons lost this game. Greason had beaten the Monarchs and his mound opponent, Ford Smith, at Rickwood Field in June. Jimmy Zapp, Alonzo Perry, and Pepper Bassett decided to help Greason. They snuck over to the other side of the field and stole Willard Brown's bats. "He never did figure out who took 'em," Zapp said.

For six scoreless innings in the afternoon shadows of Blues Stadium, the Monarchs could not figure out Greason. He reached back, threw hard, and snapped his curveball. He struck out five, scattered three hits, and approvingly slapped his glove when Artie and Piper turned an "awful" double play behind him. But Smith, another player Baird hoped to pawn, answered. He stopped the Black Barons cold, including Mays, who went hitless in two at-bats. Through six innings, Smith allowed only a pair of harmless singles to right fielder Ed Steele.

In the bottom of the seventh inning, with night falling and what was left of the tiny crowd hurling insults at the Black Barons, Greason allowed a single to Willard Brown. From Greason's point of view he was angry that he had allowed the leadoff hitter to reach base in a scoreless game, but pleased that he had managed to keep the powerful Brown inside the park. Working with his favorite catcher, Herman Bell, he knew it was a matter of time before Brown tried to steal second. Even the Monarchs fans were sometimes annoyed by his cavalier play, leading the *Call* to write, "Brown walks as if he has sore feet, but he plays his position as if he has wings."

Bell was a strong-armed catcher who honed his strength working at the Mobile docks in the winter. His father had played for the Black Barons. He too sensed it was only a matter of time before Brown tried to steal second base. Greason stopped pitching out of the windup and moved to the stretch, where his slidestep allowed him to get rid of the ball quickly. Brown edged off first base, taking an extravagantly

The "guys who threw nothing but hard": the talented, tumultuous 1948 Birmingham Black Barons pitching staff. Top row from left: Sammy C. Williams, Alonzo Perry, Bill Powell. Heard later became the first black player for the Baltimore Orioles. Bottom row from left: Nat "Prophet" Pollard, Jehosie "Little Jay" Heard, Jimmy "Schoolboy" Newberry, Bill "Grease" Greason.

aggressive lead. Greason raised his front leg and threw the pitch as soon as he whipped his arm past his ear, but Brown was dashing for second the moment Greason made his first move to home plate. The hitter, Elston Howard, took the pitch for a strike, and Bell threw a hard shot from his knees to Piper Davis covering second base. Brown went in spikes first, showering dirt and pebbles into Piper's face. Piper retaliated by slamming his glove on Brown's shin and was convinced Bell's throw had beaten Brown. But when Brown was called safe, Piper's temper burned like hot coals. The six-foot-four former basketball player loomed over five-foot-nine umpire Wilbur Rogan, better known as "Bullet Joe" in his two decades as a star pitcher for the Monarchs.

Piper's protest went "without avail," according to the *Call*. Rogan, of whom Buck O'Neil later described in a scouting report as "not a big man" but possessing "broad shoulders and muscular forearms," simply folded his arms and told Piper to play ball.

Greason thought Brown was out, but he battled his temper and bit his tongue. Piper had urged him never to let his emotions coax him into throwing a bad pitch in a big situation. Though Greason felt pinched by the umpires, he bore down to retire Howard and first baseman Tom Cooper. One more out and he was out of the inning. But emotion slipped into Greason's game. He put too much on a slider that ran into the dirt and eluded Bell. Brown, the potential winning run, advanced to third base.

The batter was Curtis Roberts, the feisty rookie second baseman. Roberts didn't have a lot of pop but he knew how to play. Greason was confident that he could overmatch him with his fastball, but he didn't anticipate that Roberts could make contact if you tied his hands together. Greason jammed Roberts with a hard fastball in under his hands, but Roberts fisted the ball on a few hops to third base. Johnny Britton charged and scooped up the ball with his bare hand as Brown made a mad dash to home plate.

Britton made a split-second decision to throw to first base, where his throw would nullify the run if he could nick Roberts. But Britton's arm strength was only average and Roberts was an exceptionally fast runner. Piper knew Britton's throw wouldn't beat Roberts, so he shouted at first baseman Joe Scott to come off the bag, intercept the ball, and make a return throw to Bell.

Scott nimbly set his feet, caught the ball, and fired a bullet to Bell. He was positive that his swipe tag caught Brown before he streaked across the plate. The home plate umpire was former Monarchs catcher, manager, and fan favorite Frank Duncan, who ruled Brown safe. The Monarchs had a 1–0 victory and a double-header sweep.

This time, Piper threw his patience out the window. He never swore, but he ran from second base to join Bell at home plate. They bellowed at Duncan, a local tavern owner working for Tom Baird's cash under the table. The fans loved it, and as Baird smiled, Greason fumed and walked off the mound. Trailing behind him, quietly dejected, was rookie left fielder Willie Mays.

"There are many fans who think the Monarchs will win the 1948 pennant and probably the World Series," the *Call* declared. There would now be a Negro American League playoff series in September between the Birmingham Black Barons and the Kansas City Monarchs. As the Black Barons boarded Charlie Rudd's bus, not one player was late. "I don't remember where we were off to next," Greason said. "But it took forever to get there."

"A PLAYER WHO SHOULDN'T HAVE BEEN THERE"

Piper pondered the direction of his team as he flopped into his seat on the bus, wearing the residue of Kansas City's sweep on his uniform. The Black Barons traveled back home on a journey that would have them on the road for the next two weeks before the New York Cubans arrived at Rickwood Field on Friday, August 13. Losing a Sunday double-header to the Monarchs stung their pride, but there was no time to dwell. The Homestead Grays, the eastern power that was based in Homestead, Pennsylvania, but played league games at Griffith Stadium in Washington, D.C., awaited five days later in Dayton.

The Black Barons and the Grays knew each other well. The Grays had beaten them twice in the Negro League World Series, including the painful 1943 series in which they defeated the Black Barons in the deciding seventh game. The 1944 series had been even worse, with the Grays winning handily in five games, and the Negro National League's publicity officer, Frank Forbes, Alex Pompez's Harlem confidant, on hand to cover Birmingham's demise for the *Chicago Defender*. Willie Mays was just thirteen years old in 1944, but he knew who played for the Grays, a team convinced that they were better singers, better dressers, and better hitters. Black Barons center fielder Bobby Robinson, who broke in with the team in 1944, liked to tell a story about the time Josh Gibson hit a ball at him so hard that if he hadn't caught it at eye level, he feared the ball would have killed him.

When the Black Barons arrived in Dayton, it was Mays's first look at one of black baseball's finest talent collections. Gibson had died in 1947, but his replacement, Luke Easter, possessed a swing that was as big as his mouth. The astute Sammy Bankhead, shortstop and manager, firmly of Birmingham descent, governed his players with respect and talent. Center fielder Luis Marquez, Cool Papa Bell's heir to the position, was so fast that white folks' ball coveted his speed. The lanky third baseman and pitcher Wilmer Fields learned from Bankhead how to study his opponents. He thought Mays couldn't hit a curveball. Bob Thurman, a left-handed power hitter, could also be called on to pitch. Venerable Buck Leonard was the first baseman. His joints were creaky but he remained the hinge of his lineup.

Piper gave the ball to Jehosie Heard, the little left-hander with a big curveball, and told him not to throw anything straight. But Heard gave up runs like he spent money, forking over four in the first, and Piper had seen enough. He pointed to Bill Greason, who responded with five shutout innings. The Black Barons lost 6–2 and had failed to deliver another message. They boarded Charlie Rudd's bus, drove most of the day and all of the night, and two days later were back in Montgomery to play the Cleveland Buckeyes, who by now were without center fielder Sam Jethroe, sold to the Brooklyn Dodgers for $5,000 in July in an effort to keep the Buckeyes in business.

Alonzo Perry was barely staying in business as a pitcher. Throwing any pitch from any angle, he pitched like he lived his life, "always dibbling and dabbling," according to Bobby Veale. Perry had help from his infielders, who cut the ball behind him, and he wasn't afraid to throw whatever it took. "Perry was gutty," Jimmy Zapp said. "Some guys in our league knew what Perry was going to throw and they still couldn't hit him." The Buckeyes roped him for nine hits that day, but he finished the job, beating Cleveland 4–3 for a much-needed victory. He was 9–2, placing him among the league leaders.

Four days later in Memphis, Mays found himself on the bench, undoubtedly one of Piper's lessons. Sammy Williams pitched into the tenth inning tied against Ernest Long of the Buckeyes, 5–5, but "Willie Mays, rookie outfielder, pinch doubled in the tenth to send Alonzo Perry across the plate," according to the *World*'s wire story. Two days later in Tuscaloosa, again against the Buckeyes, Mays hit his first officially recorded home run as a professional baseball player when his solo shot tied the score, 2–2. "Rookie Willie Mays homered in the second inning," the *World* reported. The paper wasn't aware of what every Black Baron knew was significant about Mays's home run. He had hit it against Chet Brewer, who most assuredly had already done his part to teach Willie to read the hops. Or had he? Perhaps Piper needed someone to help Willie snap out of his slump with a nice fat confidence-building fastball before the New York Cubans arrived, a series of games that Mays had no idea how important would be to his future.

By the time the Black Barons arrived home to play the New York Cubans, Mays had given Harlem's strong Birmingham connection plenty to talk about. Though he was a streaky young hitter, he was gradually developing consistency because he never ceased to attack the ball. His throwing arm was already the best in the Negro American League and his quickness allowed him to compensate for just about any error his inexperience created. The arrival of the Cubans in Birmingham was a tremendous civic event, both for the Black Barons and the Cubans, who had a strong Birmingham flavor in 1948. Amid celebrations and festivities, the Cubans' stay in Birmingham began to shape Mays's future. The New York Cubans, Harlem's black baseball team, would receive help from Piper Davis to begin the process that delivered Willie Mays directly from the Birmingham Black Barons to Harlem's white baseball team, the New York Giants, who called the Polo Grounds home.

W. S. Welch, Lyman Bostock, and Tommy Sampson were thrilled to return home, where they were welcomed as heroes when they returned to Rickwood Field as members of the Cubans. "The Cubans bring with them three former idols of the Black Barons," the *World* reported. Welch, the former field manager who had guided the Black Barons to the World Series in 1943 and 1944, was to be honored. Bostock and Sampson were both favorite sons, former ACIPCO players, each with intimate knowledge of young Willie Mays and his father, Cat. On Friday the thirteenth Mays hit his home run against Brewer in a day game at Tuscaloosa and the Black Barons played that night against the Cubans at Rickwood Field. For Mays, it was the chance to play against the men he had grown up admiring.

Sampson had loved Mays the moment he first saw him, though he lamented for years that he was unable to lure him away from Birmingham before Mays played in Chattanooga. Piper had played with Bostock and Sampson. Piper and Welch were close from their days with the Globetrotters. They were the last three Black Barons managers. And in the crowd, bringing with him a full-time scout from the Cleveland Indians, was the white folks' ball bird dog and Black Barons and Globetrotters promoter Abe Saperstein, who was always trying to sell a player and make a deal.

Bostock remembered how he had given young Mays hitting lessons long before Mays wore a Black Barons uniform, often sharing the story with his son, Lyman Jr. After Lyman Jr.'s parents separated, his mother raised him in Los Angeles, where father and son shared little in common except sporadic telephone conversations and baseball anecdotes. Lyman Jr. didn't know many of the players his father was talking about, but he recognized the names of scouts Chet Brewer and Quincy Trouppe when they came to see him play college baseball at California State University Northridge. Brewer and Trouppe told

Lyman Jr. about his daddy, demonstrating characteristics remarkably consistent with one of Piper Davis's elders. "They said they had never heard [my father] swear," Lyman Jr. said. "Chet said he saw something in me like my father. They said he could run and throw. And he was a gentleman."

Though Lyman Jr. had no concept of what playing for a place called ACIPCO meant in Birmingham, he tried to grasp his father's time. "I've tried to learn what I could about what life was like in the Negro Leagues in those years," he explained. "He accepted the conditions just like every black player then. They knew it shouldn't be like that, but he couldn't change it himself."

What Lyman Bostock Sr. could do was help change Willie Mays's future. He had all the information he needed from Piper and his eyes would tell him the rest. Alex Pompez needed to know the name Willie Mays so he could tell the New York Giants, just as Piper had made Saperstein aware of Mays in Chicago.

Lyman Jr. also shared Piper's qualities of humility and sharing. Thirty years later, in April 1978, having signed a five-year, $2.25 million contract with the California Angels, Lyman Jr. felt so guilty for his salary received at the expense of the men before him that he plummeted into a depression and a 2-for-38 batting slump that left his average at .147. He went to the general manager's office and said he couldn't accept his monthly salary. When the Angels wouldn't take his money back, he donated it to charity. Lyman Jr. never lived Lyman Sr.'s life, but he tried to live like his father. He understood how much it meant to him to help Willie Mays. He noticed how proud his father was to have left a tiny fingerprint on the direction of Westfield's favorite son. "My father helped teach Willie," Lyman Jr. said in March 1978. In September of that same year, he was shot and killed at age twenty-seven after only four major league seasons. Lyman Sr. wept for the son he hardly knew and never forgot the son who wasn't his own.

Bostock and Sampson recognized the value of recommending young players to their owners for the benefits of their own careers. In the period after Tom Hayes fired him as Black Barons manager in 1946 and before Alex Pompez signed him in 1948, Sampson, eager to avoid returning to ACIPCO, said he let Mays play on his team for meal money and a pair of shoes. "I asked him, 'Would you like to play for my team?' He said, 'Yeah, I'd love to.' I said, 'Can I talk to your mother?' He said, 'I stay with my aunt.' See, his aunt raised him. Harry [Bonds, or possibly Henry Barnes] went over and talked with her. We had to beg her and finally she gave her consent that he could go with us. So I said, 'I'll take care of him.' I bought him spikes and everything. He was just a kid."

Mays was still a kid by the time Sampson saw him on Friday the thirteenth, but it wouldn't take him long to see what he needed to, even though Mays sometimes sat on the bench to keep Jimmy Zapp sharp. The Black Barons beat the Cubans 5–4 on Friday night. Sampson and Bostock were surely eager to hit Negro Avenue and visit Bob Williams upstairs at the Savoy, where information flowed like kick-ya-poo juice and Willie Mays was no longer a secret.

Connections from Birmingham to New York were everywhere. Wiley Griggs's brother Acie was playing for the New York Cubans. Another brother, Bennie, played for the Cincinnati Crescents, the team Welch quit to manage the Cubans and probably a player he signed himself. Welch, Saperstein, and Pompez had all known each other through baseball and basketball bookings for years, and at some point interacted with Frank Forbes, the Harlem sporting legend associated with the Cubans who had coached college basketball against Piper. Pompez, who expected his baseball players and his promoters to be as reliable as his numbers runners, would have to wait no time at all to be told which player he needed to tell the New York Giants about. And when anybody had any questions, the person they would come to was not Cat Mays, but Piper Davis, the tallest tree in the forest and a soothing sound of reason in a troubled time. He would tell everyone about Willie Mays, not because he was thinking about advancing his own career, but because Piper knew it was the right thing to advance Mays's career. Piper never took credit for his contributions. Instead, with his rich and booming voice and a wondrous glimmer in his eye, he would simply smile and assure anyone who asked that Willie was going to be just fine and bellow, "The Lord is in the plan!"

Patricio Scantlebury and Jose Santiago were in the plan for the New York Cubans to face the Black Barons on Saturday and Sunday, respectively. They were to pitch for Cleveland Indians scout Bill Killifer, who was meeting Abe Saperstein and Winfield Welch. Killifer's first priority was to evaluate New York Cubans outfielder Orestes Minoso, a dark-skinned Cuban whom Indians owner Bill Veeck wanted to purchase, but Mays also caught his eye. Killifer had been on the scouting trail since Welch brought the Cubans to his hometown of New Orleans. There, Welch defied Pompez's orders. Pompez wanted to limit Santiago's innings so he could pitch more in Birmingham, but Welch granted Killifer's request to see Santiago pitch before that. Pompez was so angry at Welch that he assigned his veteran backup catcher and former manager Jose Fernandez Sr. to look over Welch's shoulder as the team played into Birmingham. But if Welch had lost any influence with Pompez, he still had an army of ballplayers to back up Welch's appraisal of Mays. "Welch probably thought he knew more than Pompez anyhow," Jimmy Zapp said.

While Killifer was in Birmingham scouting the Cubans, Pompez requested $25,000 from the Indians for Scantlebury and Santiago. But Pompez made the mistake of asking for major league money for what white folks' ball considered minor league talent. The typical Class C player in 1948, four levels below the sixteen-team major league level, sold for $5,000. No Negro team owner believed his best players were worth minor league money, but the black owners were swiftly learning that integration, while magnanimous to the black population, was thievery of their best property. The black club owners were trapped in the hot box, pressured by their own black newspapers. "Negro Club Owners Fail to Deal Fairly with Major Leaguers," a *Chicago Defender* headline pronounced, before admonishing owners for overpricing the merchandise. "The majors want to do business in a legitimate manner," the *Defender* wrote. "And if not, no business at all."

Killifer, best known in his Dead Ball era playing career as Grover Cleveland Alexander's personal catcher, didn't want to deal for the touch-and-feel lefty Scantlebury, who defeated the Black Barons and Alonzo Perry, 7–3, on Saturday night. The victory was fueled by two home runs from catcher Ray Noble. But Killifer loved the live-armed Santiago, who claimed to be a teenager, even though Bill Powell beat him 8–2 on Sunday afternoon. Killifer also had his eyes on shortstop Artie Wilson for the Indians, another Birmingham player the Cuban contingent was eager to funnel to the New York Giants via Pompez. "The Cleveland Indians have expressed an interest in Mr. Shortstop and may bid on him at any time," the *World* reported.

Though Mays didn't make the write-ups in the *World*, it is highly unlikely that Piper benched him for the entire weekend audition for the Birmingham contingent of the New York Cubans. Saperstein, ever eager to gain footing and respect within Bill Veeck's organization, was not the kind of man to keep quiet when he believed he had valuable information. "Saperstein did a lot of plugging for [Larry] Doby," Fay Young wrote in the *Chicago Defender*. "He was doing something to get a Negro player in the majors. He did much for [Piper] Davis although it turned out futile."

Piper was not the kind of manager to steer Saperstein wrong. Killifer either never told the Indians about Mays, didn't think he could hit, or didn't think they would sign another black outfielder. Killifer signed Minoso that weekend in Birmingham. He was the second black outfielder, after Larry Doby, whom the Indians now owned. Mays was still a minor and it was unlikely that the Indians would sign a third black outfielder.

Veeck, who had hired Saperstein in May, may have also rejected Mays because he was leaning toward more experienced black players he felt could help his major league team win immediately. He also needed to at least look like he was complying with the quota system. Veeck announced the purchases of Minoso and Santiago from the Cubans for $7,500 on September 3, but the Cleveland Indians had missed Willie Mays.

Officially, the Cubans–Black Barons games didn't mean much in the standings. The Black Barons knew they were going to play the Monarchs in the playoffs and were playing out the season, though Piper demanded hustling at all times. On Thursday, August 19, Birmingham held Black Barons appreciation night for its playoff-bound team.

The Black Barons, distracted by "gifts of money, jewelry and merchandise," donated to an "Appreciation chest," according to the *World*, promptly rewarded their faithful fans with a 7–3 loss. Scantlebury pitched eight shutout innings and Minoso banged a two-run double off the left-field scoreboard. Though the Birmingham fans loved the local boys, Nashville native Jimmy Zapp delightfully recalled that it was he and Joe Scott, the light-hitting first baseman from Los Angeles, who "got more presents than anybody."

Tommy Sampson and Lyman Bostock Sr. left a parting gift in that game, a perfectly executed ninth-inning double steal, resulting in Bostock taking third and Sampson safely sliding under pigtail Pepper Bassett's pud to steal home plate. Among the young fans in the crowd of 4,126 was Benjamin Givens, an ACIPCO ballplayer who dreamed of playing for Piper Davis and the Black Barons. He watched what the *World* called "a near perfect night," but he sensed fear. Artie Wilson was batting .406 and wasn't sure if he had a future. Piper was batting .363 and had no idea if he would get out. Even Mays had come alive, raising his average from .146 to .226 in a matter of weeks. It was easy to identify a scout like Killifer, a former big leaguer sitting in the press box or away from the black fans on the third base side. "We had ballplayers should have got signed," Givens said. "They didn't get signed because they didn't have the right people behind them, pushing them. Willie Mays, for instance, he was an offensive ballplayer, a powerful young man. He was a player who shouldn't have been there. Anybody can tell you that."

Piper hated it when the old guys beat him, but he had done what he set out to do. The black baseball underground that would pull Willie Mays from Birmingham to New York City was steaming forward, safely pushed along by the right people behind him.

9

"A HORSESHIT SCOUT"

While the New York Giants were soon to have Willie Mays placed in their hands, the Boston Red Sox began the process of ignoring him so many times in the next several months that Barons general manager Eddie Glennon shook his head in dismay and wondered why racism mattered more than baseball talent. There were only two members of the Boston Red Sox organization in 1948 who saw Mays, but they had no authority. One was white Barons pitcher Al LaMacchia and the other was Barons catcher Joe Stephenson, who had broken his leg in a home plate collision earlier in the season. Both men were on the backside of broken-down minor league careers in which they didn't stay long enough in the big leagues to check their bags. Both men wanted to become scouts.

When the white Barons were on the road in August, LaMacchia couldn't stand being away from the ballpark. He had once pitched exhibition games against the Chicago American Giants and Memphis Red Sox, Negro American League teams, but he had never been to a Negro game as a spectator. Sore-armed and in dire need of a ballpark fix, LaMacchia headed to Rickwood Field. "I just told the guy at the gate, 'My name is LaMacchia, I'm a pitcher for the Barons.'" He didn't have to pay admission to watch the greatest player he had ever seen.

He moved freely among the black crowd before choosing a seat on the first base side. His observations were typical of a white person who had never been to a Negro League game. LaMacchia sensed the energy of the black fans, but he saw differences between the white and the black game. "I was curious to see how they played," he said. "It was a little different. I don't know that they were so strict about who got hits. They seemed to give certain guys hits. It was like they wanted everybody to do well."

LaMacchia was not judgmental, nor was he educated on the black experience. He didn't know about the Industrial League or the role of the Black Barons in Birmingham's community. The two teams shared the same park but lived in different worlds. The white *Birmingham News* was distributed in his team's locker room. The black *Birmingham World* was not. The *News* sometimes mentioned Black Barons games, but the *World* never mentioned white Barons games. LaMacchia knew he was a visitor and didn't mind exploring this parallel world, but he was a ballplayer who wanted to be a scout and not a sociologist. So he thought like the pitcher he was, put race out of his mind, and started sizing up players.

"They were pretty good players, but they weren't outstanding," he said. "There were those who were standouts, but there was only a few. I could see where the black fans were coming from. That's what the fans saw as good players. As far as they were concerned, some of the ordinary players to me were really good players in the Negro League. But I thought some of those ordinary players weren't as good as they were told they were."

In a few innings, Al LaMacchia had given more thought to race and baseball than the Red Sox would in years. He had pitched at Rickwood Field with the Coal Bin at his back. He noticed that there were rarely black fans at white Barons games. "I don't know that they had the money to get in," he said. "Even now, how many black fans do you see when you go to a ball game?"

He thought Piper Davis was "just an ordinary player, but in the Negro Leagues, he was considered a great player." He noticed Alonzo Perry hitting. "Alonzo was a big guy," LaMacchia said. "Perry had a lot of power. Yeah, he could have played in the big leagues." Then he saw the rookie left fielder and wondered why some guy named Bobby Robinson was playing center field. "There was only one guy that really stood out," LaMacchia said. "Mays.

"People said he lunged. Well, shit, look where his hands were! His body was out in front. He was the best overstrider you ever saw. He was a little bit of a wild swinger, but he wasn't afraid to swing at bad pitches. That's what made him a good hitter when he grew up. You cannot survive if you cannot hit bad pitches. If I ever saw a guy take a ball up around the eyes, I'd shoot him."

LaMacchia couldn't understand why Mays was still playing in Birmingham. He knew it was a matter of race and not talent. "I knew there were certain clubs that weren't going to sign black players," he said. "They didn't get interested in them until they realized they could play. When you broke down Jackie Robinson, he wasn't that great. He was an aggressive hitter and an aggressive base runner. He was an athlete, but he was just an ordinary second baseman."

The Black Barons, especially Piper, had learned that the moment white folks' ball defined a Negro player as ordinary, the hot box closed forever and their chances of playing in the major leagues were gone. But Piper's dream burned on, a willingness to take abuse and take chances to feed his crumb snatchers. Eventually, he knew Willie would find his way without him, but he felt obligated to steer him toward open-minded people to look after him until his personal maturity caught up to his physical maturity.

"The first thing you would write up was how aggressive Mays was," LaMacchia said. "Everything he did was aggressive. Willie had such a quick bat. His swing was a little longer, but he could get to a pitch that was 92 miles per hour. You could see then that he already had an idea of how to make adjustments. He had a live body, a very supple body. He was a tremendous athlete. The ball was hit and he was react-ing to the ball. That is natural. You try to teach that and some guys can't retain it. Everything Mays did was natural."

The Red Sox had no idea how close they were to discovering Mays in 1948, months before they finally made an effort. On August 19, while the Black Barons were playing their night game at Rickwood Field against the New York Cubans, Red Sox scout Roy Dissinger was only a few blocks away at a Birmingham high school field conducting the second day of a three-day amateur tryout camp that concluded on August 20. But Boston's blood order to avoid black players dated back to at least 1945, when then general manager Eddie Collins subtly pointed out that "very few players can step into the majors from college or sandlot baseball." In the same *New York Times* story, New York Giants owner Horace Stoneham called the signing of Jackie Robinson, a player the Red Sox ignored along with Sam Jethroe and Marvin Williams, "really a fine way to start the program. We will scout the Negro Leagues next year, looking for younger prospects." Three years later, the Giants scouting staff didn't know the Negro Leagues any better than when they started, but Alex Pompez was forging a relation-ship with Carl Hubbell and the Giants. While Boston was posturing in its rigid stance, Pompez was maneuvering with cunning grace.

Yet deceit abounded on both sides. Black players felt they were bet-ter than ordinary players. They thought they weren't getting a fair look. Every full-time major league scout in 1948 was white and the majority of them were former major league ballplayers, which meant they were white southerners. The old battle lines of the South were drawn again. The right to determine the value of property and who it belonged to, the right of one man to choose the fate of another, and the belief inherent in generations of white southerners that black southerners were there to serve them, and if not, to be ignored, permeated the play-ers and the scouts. Jackie Robinson didn't know what was going on in baseball below him in 1948, that for every one player who received an opportunity he had created, dozens more would not. Willie Mays was experiencing one of the several occasions when he was nearly a casualty of Robinson's war.

Owners sparred over dollars and destiny. There were white scouts for black players and black players currying favor with white officials by degrading the talents of other black players. Kansas City Monarchs owner Tom Baird wrote to New York Yankees farm director Lee MacPhail in February 1948, observing, "It seems as though ethics are about the same with club owners where there are a few dollars involved, whether they are black or white."

In 1947, Boston-born Lenny Merullo, a veteran infielder for the Chicago Cubs, played against Robinson and remembered how the Cubs swore at him and tried to spike him. When Robinson came in hard on Merullo at second base, they almost fought. "Robinson got up with fire in his eyes," Merullo said, "then gave me that good look and went right back to the dugout."

Merullo suspected the Red Sox weren't giving the good look to black players. "I heard so many things about the Red Sox always being against signing black ballplayers," he said. "Many ballplayers originally played for the mills in the South. They were not for black ballplayers. It was inborn nature for them. You could get the feeling on the bench, if the players were from the Deep South, that they didn't like this. There was a lot of open mouthing and it wasn't pleasant to hear. We fellows from the other part of the country, we didn't understand exactly the feelings they had. We couldn't imagine the language that was being used on our bench by our own ballplayers who were from the South. The clubs had to be very careful of who they signed, black or white—more so if black."

LaMacchia shook his head. "I know guys who didn't sign black ballplayers and guys who weren't allowed to sign black ballplayers," he said. "All I know is this: You'd have to be a horseshit scout to pass up Willie Mays."

The scouts dressed up for the East-West All-Star Game at Comiskey Park in Chicago and dressed down if they happened to be watching

Mays and the remaining Black Barons at home against the Cleveland Buckeyes. While Ed Steele, Norman Robinson, and Willie Mays patrolled the outfield for the Black Barons at Rickwood Field, Piper Davis, Artie Wilson, and Bill Powell were selected as Negro American League starters for August 22.

Eddie Glennon tried to make another move. Red Sox farm director George Toporczer, who got the nickname "Specs" because of his thick eyeglasses, was due to scout the white Barons at home on August 23. Rickwood Field manager Bob Scranton remembered Glennon pleading with Toporczer to come a day earlier to see what he could of Mays. Instead, Toporczer arrived as scheduled.

Black players couldn't miss the white scouts, who attired themselves in some dour combination of dressy and dumpy, wearing straw hats, bowlers, or fedoras, and in every case lying to one another as surely as they were lying to the players. They spoke with the same southern accents, never removed their sport coats when they perspired, and wore monotone neckties. In many cases ancient rivalries from their playing days seeped into scouting and they fought to settle old scores.

Black players felt uneasy. They looked into the stands and wondered if the reason they were permitted to play in the majors had nothing to do with talent and everything to do with the 42,099 mostly black fans at Comiskey Park whom white folks' ball seemed eager to pilfer. One scouting proverb held that two scouts watched a pretty girl walk down the street. One scout said she was drop-dead gorgeous. The other scout said he was drop-dead blind. Black ballplayers couldn't tell if they were pretty or the scouts were blind.

"I can tell you this," Pirates manager Frankie Frisch said in 1942. "Any move I make will be calculated to help our team and the game. I am not going to hire a player only because he's colored. If we hired a colored player who doesn't quite make the grade, I suppose we'll automatically be accused of discrimination."

Yet nobody wanted to be wrong on a black player. When discussing his starting catcher, Earl Taborn, with Yankees farm director Lee MacPhail in 1949, Baird discounted the advice of Buck O'Neil and Dizzy Dismukes, and concluded, "Perhaps you big leaguers can see things they can't."

Just as LaMacchia was culture shocked when he went to a Black Barons game, white scouts were befuddled when they experienced black baseball and black social gatherings for the first time. It was a phenomenon that persisted inside the game for decades and created tension on both sides. "A white person comes into the ghetto, does a job and then he can go home," pitcher Bob Gibson said. "The Negro in the ghetto does the same job and then he is home."

Lou Johnson was a fourteen-year-old athlete in Lexington, Kentucky, who worshipped Jackie Robinson but saw the hot box long before he became one of the last Kansas City Monarchs and before he spent seven years in the minor leagues. "In the first place, the only reason they signed Jackie was the money the black teams was making on Sunday," Johnson said. "But most white scouts didn't know what to look for in black ballplayers. When they did, we was so natural, everything that they was teaching us, we can do. Our longevity as black folks, we can be forty years old still playing like we're twenty-five. They couldn't understand that."

Piper attempted to bridge the cultural gap by playing younger than his age at the East-West game. He stole a base in the third inning. Then, batting in front of Monarchs cleanup hitter Willard Brown, he doubled into the left-field corner in the ninth inning and scored on Bob Boyd's sacrifice fly. In the bottom of the inning, Piper and Artie turned a game-ending double play to preserve a 3–1 win and give Bill Powell the victory for pitching three scoreless innings as the American League's starting pitcher. Owner Tom Hayes had come to Chicago for the game to protect his property. White scouts were in such unfamiliar territory that they often had no idea who to contact if they liked a player. The *Chicago Defender* received a phone call from an unidentified scout requesting information on Powell. The *Defender* reported that Hayes asked for $5,000 for Powell, one of his top pitchers. The deal never happened, and once again, Tom Hayes was gaining the reputation as a stubborn man among black media and white scouts. Hayes felt it was a matter of professional courtesy and adequate compensation he felt he had yet to receive from white folks' ball. He would continue to proceed cautiously when teams wanted to buy his players.

Artie Wilson knew that plenty of white folks' ball scouts were on him in Chicago, so he fumed when he went hitless in three at-bats and vowed to play as well as the .400 season he was producing when the Negro American and National leagues played another East-West game at Yankee Stadium two days later for the league to drum up support. But when the players stepped onto the Yankee Stadium grass and realized that there were 49,000 empty seats, the drums were playing a funeral dirge. The game drew only 17,928 fans, a drastic display of the economic troubles facing the Negro National League teams in the Northeast.

The small crowd was further dulled when a moment of silence was called to honor Babe Ruth, who had died eight days earlier, with grief matching a "personal loss one feels when advised of the passing of one's kin or dear personal friend," according to Fred Lieb's obituary in the *Sporting News*. Ruth belonged to white folks' ball, though black folks always wondered if he had a trace of them somewhere in his past. The *Chicago Defender* wondered why if Ruth was honored, there wasn't a moment of silence for Josh Gibson, the so-called Black Babe Ruth, who was said to have once hit a ball completely out of Yankee Stadium and who had died in January 1947. "Maybe [Gibson] didn't amount to much in the eyes of the owners and promoters of the game," the *Defender* wrote, "but the baseball fans wondered why."

Wilson made noise with his bat at Yankee Stadium when he collected three hits in four at-bats against three pitchers white folks' ball coveted, Max Manning, Dave Barnhill, and Joe Black. Though his team lost 6–1, it meant nothing. Artie was flying high as Piper, Powell, and catcher Pepper Bassett, who had joined them in New York, headed back to join the Black Barons and prepare for the playoffs against the Monarchs. Before the series, the Black Barons decided to look in on a player they knew had already escaped the hot box.

After the final game of the regular season in Chicago on Friday, September 3, the Black Barons checked Johnny Britton's newspaper and learned that Satchel Paige was pitching Saturday night for the

Cleveland Indians in St. Louis. That was too good of an opportunity to pass up. With no game scheduled, the Black Barons made a slight detour to Sportsman's Park in St. Louis on the way home to Birmingham to play the Kansas City Monarchs in the playoffs. They took Willie Mays to see his first big league game.

Piper, who knew black hotel managers in the big cities, got his players last-minute rooms. "I didn't know Satchel personally," Jimmy Zapp said. "But Satchel and Larry Doby were staying in the same hotel as us in St. Louis when we went to that game." It was the first Saturday the team had had off since March. In Paige's last start at Washington, outfielder Ed Stewart had reportedly called him a "black son of a bitch." In his prior start, he had pitched in Boston's Fenway Park, a hostile environment that led Paige to remind reporters who wanted to know if there was additional pressure pitching in a city that was resisting black players, that even in Fenway home plate was still sixty feet six inches away. His finest moment came in Cleveland on August 13, before 78,382 fans, when he outdueled Chicago White Sox pitcher Bill Wight, 1–0, leaving Wight in admiration.

"Paige was smooth as glass," Wight said. "You would hardly ever see a spike mark. He would warm up and then they would throw the ball out. I got a chance to warm up with those balls, but I never got to throw them in a game. I don't know what the hell he did, but he did something. I could grip it real good. You had to have an unusual arm and an easy way to throw to survive for that long. God, almighty, I don't know how old he was when I faced him."

Since the Browns and the Washington Senators were the last two major league teams that enforced segregated seating, the Black Barons sat in Sportsman Park's version of the Coal Bin. They watched as Paige's self-proclaimed pitches the "blinkless breeze," "whamless wonder," and "whiff woofer" weren't as effective as their alliteration. Paige had as many nicknames for his pitches as he had inaccurate birth dates, but the Black Barons didn't mind. Amid a crowd of 17,092 watching the woeful Browns, Piper had a painful reminder of the team that had rejected him in 1947 and released Willard Brown and Hank Thompson after only one month.

Brown had hesitated to sign in the first place, but he went because he knew the Negro Leagues would not last. He was so certain that he would never play in the Negro Leagues that he didn't take his bat and Baird had told him the Browns would give him bats. But Brown was wrong on both counts. When he went to the Browns, he couldn't find any position players who would let him use a bat, nor would the club furnish him one. He used light pitchers' bats, but hated swinging with them. After a few weeks, he scavenged a discarded bat used by Browns outfielder Jeff Heath, major league trash because the knob was snapped off the end. But to Brown it was pure gold. He grabbed the bat and wrapped athletic tape around the bottom, fashioning a crude knob. Thrilled to be hitting with a bat that he could get into a pitch with, Brown hit a game-winning inside-the-park home run, becoming the first black player in the American League to hit a home run. When he returned to the dugout, he received handshakes from everyone but Heath, who grabbed his garbage bat and in front of the entire team shattered it on the top step of the dugout. Then he gave the handle back to Brown, who never forgot that moment, and never played in the major leagues again.

The Black Barons boarded Charlie Rudd's bus and left St. Louis headed south, away from a baseball community that still believed in the Confederacy. "Missouri is a border state," the *Sporting News* wrote. "Many of its inhabitants are descendents of Confederate sympathizers during the Civil War." Willie Mays was safely aboard the Underground Railroad as the Kansas City Monarchs rolled toward Birmingham with anticipation to match their enormous talent. The Monarchs had grown up under Buck O'Neil, learning from their humiliation at Rickwood Field in June to sweep the Black Barons in August. The Monarchs had finished as second-half champions with a 26–10 record to Birmingham's 20-8 mark, partly thanks to several rainouts.

The 1948 Monarchs were "said to be the best in the history of the club," according to the *Kansas City Call*, bringing a "caliber of ball-hawking artists and long-ball clouters" that made them a team of "seasoned players and brilliant rookies." Tom Baird surely sent his team to Rickwood Field with marching orders to decimate the Black Barons and uphold what he called "the million dollar name, Kansas City Monarchs."

What Baird and Buck and the rest of the Monarchs didn't know was that the Black Barons had a million-dollar ballplayer. Mays had improved as a hitter since the Monarchs faced him in August, raising his batting average again, this time from .222 to .246. He was still playing left field as late as August 29, when before only three thousand fans at Chicago's Comiskey Park, the *Chicago Defender* noted, "McCurnie flied to Mays in left" while the Black Barons played the American Giants.

But by the time the Black Barons played at Comiskey Park on September 3, the lineup had changed. Jimmy Zapp was back in left field, Ed Steele was still in right field . . . and Willie Mays was the starting center fielder. Bobby Robinson had broken his foot when he stepped in an outfield pothole. He had played 69 games and batted .298 in the last statistics published August 27, but his ankle injury ended his season. Losing the starting center fielder before a playoff series would be a devastating blow to any baseball team with aspirations to win the World Series. But the Black Barons had somebody no one else had. His teammates were ordinary players next to Mays, but they could not resent him for his ability, and they were glad he was from Birmingham. He was one of them, and that was better than playing for Tom Baird.

When Piper wrote out his lineup card for Game 1 of what was scheduled to be a best-of-seven Negro American League playoff series, no Black Baron was shocked to see what had stunned them on the Fourth of July. Not only was Mays the starting center fielder, but Piper challenged him to elevate his game yet again. Piper's lineup card said it all:

Wilson, SS
Britton, 3B
Davis, 2B

Mays, CF
Steele, RF
Zapp, LF
Bassett, C
Scott, 1B
Powell, P

Willie Mays had arrived as a man, batting cleanup against the mighty Kansas City Monarchs. Piper gathered his players in the dugout moments before the first pitch of Game 1. "Men," he said, "let's get 'em!" Mays and Piper led the charge out of the dugout as the Black Barons took the field to the rousing applause of 7,000 hometown fans. Willie was one of their own, and when they envisioned his future, they wondered if theirs too might be better. The world was changing, baseball was evolving, and white scouts were ready to say Willie Mays couldn't hit a breaking ball. None of that mattered when Piper stood at second base, saw Artie to his right, saw Willie behind him, and gestured at Powell on the mound. "Man!" Piper said years later. "We started rollin'!"

10

"COME ON, WILLIE!"

Willie wanted to run down every ball the Kansas City Monarchs' lineup could lift into the air. It didn't take long for Piper to realize that right fielder Ed Steele and left fielder Jimmy Zapp were waiting for the checkered cab in center field to pick them up. Piper hated it when his players didn't hustle and he voiced his displeasure. Steele, his longtime road roommate whom Bobby Veale described as a "thickly built guy who wasn't too fast and was on the quiet side," was his first target.

"The ball goes out to right-center," Piper said to Steele. "I hear, 'Come on, Willie!'"

Piper faced Zapp with his impatience burning.

"Ball goes out to left-center, I hear, 'Come on, Willie!' He's breaking his neck going after those balls. You boys better start earning your money and stop running that boy's legs off."

"Piper was firm," Zapp remembered. "I was very temperamental. Joe Scott, my roommate, a sweet guy, he could always cool me down.

He'd say, 'Let's get a beer and everything will be okay tomorrow.'"
Mays wasn't old enough to drink, but he was old enough to fly. "He
could cover the outfield grass like the morning dew," Veale said.

The Monarchs wanted to leave the Black Barons all wet. The Monarchs had won the Negro American League championship five times
since 1939, the first of four consecutive years the Satchel Paige–led
club won the crown. They also swept the Homestead Grays in the 1942
Negro World Series. The teams were about to begin the third series of
the season, the one that would determine the Negro American League
championship. Of the five earlier recorded contests between the two
teams, three had been one-run affairs. Each team swept the other on
its home field. Each team brought a powerful lineup, speed, and strong
pitching. "There wasn't no pretty good ballplayers," Birmingham
utility infielder Wiley Griggs said. "There was only good ballplayers."
It was anticipated to be a highly competitive best-of-seven-game series,
of which the *Chicago Defender* wrote, "Hustling, bang-up games can be
predicted. It should be a series worth traveling miles to see."

Center fielder Willard Brown and right fielder Hank Thompson
were Kansas City's feared home run hitters, but the Monarchs had
yet to fully comprehend Mays's talents. They had only seen him play
a few games in August in Kansas City, when he was playing left field
instead of center, and when he was figuring out how to speed up his
bat against faster pitching. Mays was already better than he had been
a month earlier, his abilities allowing him to improve much faster
than he should have been able to. He had helped the Black Barons
sweep a seven-game series against the Chicago American Giants a week
before the playoffs. "A few of Tom Hayes's protégés may not be batting
as well as those Monarchs demons," the *Defender* reported. Brown was
the one hitter in Buck O'Neil's "pepper-pot, spark-plug" lineup that
worried Piper. The two center fielders were the best players on the field
when the Black Barons and Monarchs played. Brown announced his
team's intention when they arrived in Birmingham.

"Brown made a comment, 'When the Monarchs leave town, you
guys won't be laughing too loud,'" Zapp said. Piper and Artie had led
the Barons to new respectability, but the Monarchs were still favored.

The Black Barons were the most dangerous kind of opponent, the team that didn't know it was expected to lose. "We didn't know what an underdog was," Zapp said.

Bill Powell started Game 1, having completed the regular season with an 11–3 record and a 1–1 mark against the Monarchs. He was matched against left-hander Jim LaMarque, who led the Negro American League with a 15–4 record in the best year of his career. The *Call* described LaMarque as "cool-headed" and "nerveless." LaMarque didn't throw hard, but his fastball always moved. Over the years he had learned to survive, though the modest velocity of his pitching around the plate meant he would be hit. With a fastball that couldn't puncture skin, LaMarque learned to thread the needle. "I guess my top speed was maybe 80 or 85 miles per hour," he said. "So I learned to have real good control."

The Black Barons tried to take control of Game 1, but found that LaMarque made it difficult. The Monarchs defense was extremely fast, with rookie shortstop Gene Baker, who according to the *Call* "covers short with professional skill," and second baseman Curtis Roberts, described as "fast, accurate and consistent," combing the infield with center fielder Willard Brown closing the gaps when he felt like it. Birmingham took the lead in the fifth inning. LaMarque's command temporarily deserted him when he hit Zapp with a pitch and walked Pepper Bassett. He then allowed a single to Powell to load the bases, bringing Artie Wilson to the plate. Wilson slapped a single to left field, scoring Zapp to give the Black Barons a 1–0 lead.

Wilson's hit emphasized what he had accomplished, but barely a soul knew about it. Wilson had completed the quest to bat .400, winning the Negro American League batting championship. In the final recorded statistics, he was credited with 134 hits in 332 at-bats, good for a batting average of .402. Considering the pressure inside the hot box, Wilson had arguably produced one of the best individual hitting seasons in Negro League history, if not one of the best hitting seasons in baseball history. Ted Williams batted .406 in 1941, the last white man to hit .400, but he never had to play a single day with the prospect of never playing again because of his race. "A chill goes up and down my spine when I realize that it all might have been denied to me if I'd been black," Williams said in 1969. Artie Wilson became the last professional hitter to bat .400 in a season, and even if organized baseball never dared consider the Negro American League on a par with the lowest Class D team, the players, black and white, knew better than that. "Ted Williams was the best hitter I've seen," Piper said. "And Artie Wilson was the best singles hitter I ever saw." Ballplayers knew that Artie Wilson was a born hitter. "I don't care who was pitching," Artie said. "I always wanted to play ball."

So did the Black Barons. After LaMarque retired Britton, who went 0-for-6 in Game 1 and was the only Black Baron who couldn't solve the lefty, Piper promptly banged one of his four singles to load the bases again for rookie center fielder Willie Mays. The mosquitoes buzzing inside Rickwood Field scared Mays more than LaMarque's pedestrian fastball. LaMarque hadn't been able to get Mays out in Kansas City and he couldn't figure him out this time either. Mays drilled LaMarque's first pitch for a base hit, scoring Bassett to give the Black Barons a 2–0 lead. Ed Steele followed with a sacrifice fly to score Wilson and give Birmingham a 3–0 lead.

Bill Powell waded through the middle of the Kansas City batting order in the top of the sixth. Right fielder Hank Thompson, batting third, hit .375 during the season, finishing behind Artie Wilson and Memphis's Bob Boyd (.376). Thompson always gave Powell trouble and drew a walk, bringing Willard Brown to the plate. Brown was the most productive outfielder in the league, finishing fourth with a .375 batting average and first with 19 home runs. In the last week of the season, he was edged out by Piper Davis for the RBI lead, with Piper winning the title with 69 RBI to Brown's 68. Piper also finished fifth in the league in hitting with a .354 average.

Brown was dangerous. Like Mays, he had grown up around his hometown team and had become the center fielder. Like Mays, he was aggressive and didn't care where the pitch was thrown. White folks' ball called it a lack of discipline, but black ballplayers thought being too picky gave the pitcher the advantage. "I didn't care if it was up there, I could hit that ball that was over my head over the fence,"

Brown said. "Ball hit the ground, I don't know, I just followed it." The veteran Black Barons remembered the time in Birmingham a few years earlier when one of their pitchers bounced a drop ball in the dirt and Brown chased it "just like a golf ball or something" and hit it over the left-field scoreboard. "Never will forget it," Brown said. "The pitcher folded up his glove and put it in his belt, walked off and he ain't pitched another game."

Powell dodged a Brown bullet, most likely with one of his eight strikeouts or on a fly ball to Mays. Zapp might as well have sat in a beach chair in left field. He caught only one fly ball in Game 1 while Mays ran down five. But Powell had more work to do against Elston Howard. Like Mays, Howard had grown increasingly comfortable at the plate, evidenced by a deep drive in Kansas City a week earlier when the *Call* said he "blasted a triple against the center field fence 425 feet from home plate and saved from being one of the longest home runs by a few inches of top boards." Powell managed to get Howard to keep the ball in the park, but he allowed a single to Roberts and catcher Earl Taborn, slap hitters at the bottom of the batting order, to tie the score, 3–3.

Laboring into the eighth inning, Powell found more trouble. Brown singled and stole second against Bassett. Powell retired Howard and first baseman Tom Cooper for two outs, bringing contact-hitting Curtis Roberts to the plate, but Powell couldn't get a fastball past him. Roberts lined a single to right field and Brown didn't loiter. He beat the throw home by Ed Steele and the Monarchs pulled ahead, 4–3. The Rickwood Field crowd was silent.

But in the bottom of the ninth, the crowd rose as LaMarque tried to finish off the home team. He had turned back a steady stream of threats and the Black Barons had left several runners on base. Bassett, frustrated that he had not been able to throw Brown out, sought revenge and drilled a double to begin the bottom of the ninth. With one out and Powell due to bat, Piper made the first of two clever managerial moves. He pulled Powell from the game and told Bill Greason to grab a bat. "Double Duty" Greason couldn't wait. He knew he could hit and he loved beating the Monarchs. Still seething at his 1–0 loss in Kansas City and aware that LaMarque had struck him out as a pinch hitter the last time they battled, he internally boiled. "If you can't stand the heat in the kitchen," he said, "get out." LaMarque didn't throw heat, but he threw everything else. Greason found a good pitch and drove a single. The Black Barons thought they had never seen Pepper Bassett run as fast as he did when he scored the tying run. LaMarque slapped at his leg with his glove while Greason remembered mouthing to LaMarque, "I gotcha!" Artie Wilson, who knew a thing or two about hitting, loved what he saw. "William Greason," Artie said, "was a super hitter."

Greason pitched a scoreless tenth inning against LaMarque, who finally left the game after pitching ten innings, striking out eight, and scattering fifteen hits. The Black Barons had stranded twenty runners on base. LaMarque's replacement was Gene Richardson, whom Tom Baird described as "a left-hander with perfect control. He has a good curveball but his fastball is not too hot." The Black Barons eagerly greeted Richardson, but couldn't touch him in the tenth.

Still tied 5–5 in the top of the eleventh inning, Piper made his second clever move. He had saved Jimmy Newberry to pitch in relief. Piper intentionally wouldn't start Newberry at home in the playoffs because he couldn't tell if "Schoolboy" would be sober, but Newberry laid off the kick-ya-poo when it mattered and kicked the Monarchs with a scoreless eleventh.

The Black Barons sensed something might happen in the bottom of the inning. Joe Scott, who according to the *World* "hasn't hit well enough to make his job at first base secure," singled against Richardson, whom Baird was trying to sell partly because he was "light in color and looks like a white man from up in the stands." Richardson ignited Newberry's white-hot temper when he got him to pop up to shortstop Gene Baker for the first out. Richardson, who Baird wrote "never gets excited," intentionally walked the always aggressive Artie Wilson. Then, perhaps fatigued after a long season, Richardson walked Johnny Britton to load the bases. "I advised him last fall that he should chop wood or do some shoveling or any type of work," Baird wrote. "He wrote to me that he had cut down two trees and cut them into firewood and said that he was going to have a good year."

Now the ravenous Rickwood Field crowd let Richardson have it as Piper Davis came to the plate. Perhaps Richardson's performance-enhancing chopping benefited him, as Piper popped up to second baseman Curtis Roberts for the second out of the inning. That left the inning squarely on the shoulders of Willie Mays. It didn't matter how you pitched to Mays because he didn't care. He hit like he was trying to hurt someone. This time, Mays hit a full-count pitch hard behind second base. Roberts was extraordinarily fast, so he was able to scramble to his right to knock down the drive as he slid on the seat of his pants. He stopped the ball but could not control it. When he saw Mays dashing down the first base line with the hat flying off his head, he knew he no chance to stop Scott, who charged home with the winning run in Birmingham's dramatic 5–4 victory.

The Black Barons streamed from their dugout and surrounded Mays on the infield grass, celebrating the child, who basked in the moment. "He was the most exciting player," Bobby Veale said, "just like you saw in the majors." Willie sensed that he had the gift to make people happy by doing what he loved most. He loved the feeling of making his teammates feel good about winning. His passion bubbled to the surface. The Black Barons drank from his well.

The Monarchs were only beginning to learn how Mays could change everything, but they tried to alter the course of the series in Game 2 against Alonzo Perry. With a 10–2 record, Perry was among the league leaders, but his sidearm throwing had taken a toll. Though Perry's elbow was killing him, Piper hoped he could nurse seven innings out of him, especially because Jehosie Heard and Nat Pollard were both injured and not available to pitch. But Perry gave up solo home runs to Gene Baker and Willard Brown and, despite Piper's home run, trailed 3–1 after three innings. Piper brought back Bill Greason in relief for the second consecutive game, on Sunday afternoon. Greason kept the game close, dueling against his nemesis Ford Smith, and the Black Barons closed the gap to 5–4 entering the bottom of the ninth inning.

Greason began the ninth inning by grounding out to shortstop Baker, but Artie Wilson slapped a double to left field. Johnny Britton grounded out to second baseman Curtis Roberts and the Black Barons were down to their final out. But Piper had been creative when he wrote his lineup card. He moved Mays from the cleanup spot to third in the batting order and dropped himself to fifth to offer protection for Ed Steele. That foresight brought Mays to the plate when it mattered most. Smith wasn't the kind of pitcher to mess around. He went right at Mays, who went right back at him, slashing a double. Wilson scored standing up and the Black Barons tied the score, 5–5. Smith retired Steele on a ground ball and the game went to extra innings.

Greason needed help to escape the tenth inning. Gene Baker bunted to third baseman Johnny Britton, who in his haste fielded and threw the ball away, allowing Baker to advance to second base. Curtis Roberts followed with a single to right field. Baker never doubted for a second that he wouldn't score, but right fielder Ed Steele charged the ball and picked it up on a good hop. Steele's shot to pigtail Pepper Bassett never touched the turf. As Baker raced home, his eyes widened when he saw Pepper waiting on him. "Edward Steele cut Baker down at the plate with a line peg for the most beautiful play of the game," the *World* reported. Said Greason, "Ed Steele had a great arm. I was glad he did."

Steele kept the score tied so the old guys could make it happen in the eleventh. Piper, leading off the bottom of the inning, reached first base when Monarch third baseman Herb Souell committed an error. Piper took second base on Joe Scott's sacrifice bunt. Then Piper jumped off the bag with a daring and aggressive lead, ignoring Baker and Roberts swooping in behind him and slapping their fists into their gloves in an attempt to distract him and minimize his lead. Piper was too experienced to bite, and as Buck's rookies buzzed him, he edged off the bag some more, as if communicating to Buck and the Monarchs that the Black Barons would not be contained.

Bassett was serene with a bat in his hands, calm as an old man sitting on the porch with a beer. Smith had a great fastball when he was fresh, but in the ninth inning some of its sting had abandoned him. He refused to dabble with breaking balls and tried to bury Bassett with inside fastballs, but instead threw a pitch where Bassett could unravel his arms. His forearm muscles, visible in his elbows and biceps, were strewn together like a wicker basket and tightened as his bat found the ball. Piper ran before the echo resonated through Rickwood Field, cutting past third and anticipating the charging Hank Thompson's throw from right field. He arrived in front of Thompson's throw, his spikes leaving the ground as he slid safely, and Rickwood Field exploded again. The Black Barons had a 6–5 victory and a 2–0 lead in the best-of-seven series.

Game 3 was moved to Memphis because the white Barons were scheduled to play the Southern Association playoffs at Rickwood Field. Officially, it would be Birmingham's home game, but to the teams, staying in the same hotel tantalizingly close to Beale Street's nightlife, it seemed more like a holiday. The game afforded an opportunity for Memphis-based owner Tom Hayes to watch his team in person and witness a game the players would remember as a special moment. In the end, it led to a jubilant celebration photograph that captured young Willie Mays in his happiest moment, surrounded by his boys, the team that made him a man, and told the story of the outcome of the game more conclusively than newspaper accounts.

Beneath the team's joy rested a tangible tension. Contradictions surfaced about how the game ended, who was the hero and who was the goat, how it was reported, why and by whom. The only thing that added up was the final score, a 4–3 Black Barons victory in the bottom of the ninth inning that gave Birmingham a commanding 3–0 series lead. The win foreshadowed the friction between the rivals as they played their way back to Kansas City with the Monarchs one game from elimination.

Connie Johnson, a lean and loose right-hander, started Game 3 for the Monarchs and pitched well. Jim LaMarque entered the game in middle-inning relief. In the bottom of the ninth inning, he was attempting to preserve Kansas City's 3–2 lead. The Black Barons and Monarchs would argue for decades about what happened next. What was clear was that Willie Mays was again in the middle of it.

According to a non-bylined story in the *Kansas City Call*, "an error by Curtis Roberts, Monarch second baseman, let the winning run

Celebration in Memphis: Joyous Black Barons celebrate Jimmy Zapp's game-winning home run against the Kansas City Monarchs in Game 3 of the 1948 Negro American League playoffs.

cross the plate." The *Chicago Defender*, in another non-bylined story, reported that "Jimmy Zapp opened the home ninth with a homer to tie the knot. Then, with two out, second sacker Roberts errored, allowing the winning run to score." Finally, in a *Birmingham World* wire story, "Left fielder Howard Zapp's ninth inning home run enabled the Black Barons to defeat the Kansas City Monarchs 4 to 3 here Wednesday night."

Dizzy Dismukes of the Monarchs likely reported the non-bylined stories in the *Call* and the *Defender*. Dismukes was a college-educated, meticulous man who kept Kansas City's scorebooks and had scored thousand of games. He knew the difference between a double and an error. Dismukes would also cover the 1948 Negro League World Series for the *Defender*, which he expected to be in Kansas City. No reporter from either city had traveled with the teams and the Black Barons were notoriously bad about reporting their results. Through the years, the story of Roberts's error costing the Monarchs the game seemed to become accepted as truth. The Black Barons wondered if Dismukes had thrown Roberts, one of his own players, under the bus rather than give Mays and Zapp credit for yet another Birmingham victory in a series they weren't supposed to win.

The closest account was in the *Birmingham World*, though the *World* again consolidated Willie Howard and Jimmy Zapp into the erroneous "Howard Zapp." According to the Black Barons, the *World* had Zapp's game-winning home run on the final pitch of the game correct even if they had his name wrong. Mays and Zapp tried to solve exactly what happened for years. When the Kansas City account, which appeared in the *Defender*, a national black paper, surfaced, Mays said it was wrong. "Don't believe everything you see in the papers," he said.

Roberts apparently did make the error, but not as the last play of the game. It could have been a ball Mays hit that Dismukes credited as an error rather than a double. "The way I remember it, I came up with two out," Zapp said. "Mays said that he was on base."

"I doubled before he did," Mays said. "I hit the double and Zapp hit the home run."

"Buck O'Neil always said Gene Collins was his ace, but we thought it was LaMarque," Zapp said. "I was guessing curveball and he threw me a fastball and I half swung. So he threw me another fastball. I half swung again and fouled it off. He had two strikes on me. Now I got to look for anything. So he threw me a fastball and I hit him over the left-center-field fence for a two-run home run and beat him, 4–3. That was my biggest thrill in Birmingham. We had them down three games to nothing."

Zapp said, "Buck O'Neil always said I should have never come to bat. Me and Hank Thompson were good friends. We went down to Beale Street that night. When we left, the Monarchs were still sitting around the lobby arguing about what pitch they should have thrown me. I just laughed and went out and had me a beer."

Before the team left the ballpark after the game, they piled into Martin Stadium's cramped dressing room. Two celebration snapshots, most likely taken by Memphis-based photographer Ernest Withers, who chronicled the Negro Leagues before his celebrated work documented the civil rights movement, captured the moment. Tom Hayes hurried into the locker room to crowd into the photograph, ducking underneath the wire clothes hangers racked on a water pipe across the wooden ceiling. In the first shot, Ed Steele, Artie Wilson, and Alonzo Perry surrounded Mays, who looked at the camera and didn't smile. Steele, Perry, and Wilson stretched their arms out to pat the head of a player whose face is distorted. Beaming next to the distorted player is Bill Greason, who pitched in relief of Jimmy Newberry to earn his second consecutive victory. Herman Bell, the catcher who never smiled, did this time. He stood next to Greason, who was beside Piper Davis, showing the proud and happy glare Faye Davis called "my daddy's good look."

Withers set his flash and moments later snapped another shot. This time, Willie's smile showed happiness that he never wanted to end. Steele, Perry, and Wilson looked at the camera and the player on whose head their hands rested was clearly shown. It is young Jimmy Zapp, the hero of the moment. It wasn't simply another picture of a happy team. It was a family portrait. "That was a very close-knit team," Zapp said. "And I'll tell you what. I miss 'em."

The Black Barons arrived in Kansas City hoping for their greatest achievement yet, a sweep of the mighty Monarchs. "The Black Barons are set to bring the Negro American League pennant, the Negro League World Series and the Negro World's Championship to the Vulcan City," the *World* reported. "This is the year and Piper Davis and his teammates are the team."

But the Black Barons had to win at Blues Stadium, which was a fortress laced with pitfalls. The chief umpire for the series would again be Frank Duncan, the former Monarchs field manager who was the home plate umpire when Bill Greason lost 1–0 on a close play at the plate in August. To make matters worse, the weather in Kansas City was cold and miserable and the teams played under the constant threat of rain. Tom Baird harbored a secret disdain for the Black Barons and couldn't stand the thought of losing to Birmingham. Piper put the baseball in

Greason's hand and asked him to close the door. When he walked onto the mound and bounced the rosin between his fingers and rubbed up the ball, Greason grew increasingly determined to throw the best game anyone had ever seen.

The Black Barons had won three consecutive one-run games in their last at-bat, bruised the pride of manager Buck O'Neil and his Monarchs "with flying colors," and watched Willie Mays change all three games. To complicate matters, second baseman Curtis Roberts was out of the lineup for unspecified reasons, forcing Hank Thompson to move from right field to second base. Catcher Earl Taborn, who hadn't caught since he took a foul ball to the throat by Gene Richardson's wild pitch in the eleventh inning of Game 1, returned to catch Game 4. Rookie Elston Howard moved back to left field, where he was playing out of position and was never comfortable.

The Monarchs, "fighting with their backs to the wall," wrote the *Call*, were immediately under pressure. The first batter of the game, Artie Wilson, lined a single to left field where Howard showed his inexperience. He misjudged the ball for one error, allowing Wilson to take second. Howard quickly retrieved the ball behind him and rushed his throw to third base, but the throw sailed over Herb Souell's head, allowing Wilson to advance yet another base to third. Wilson saw the errant throw and kept coming. He popped up from his slide and raced for home. First baseman Tom Cooper fielded the ball and made another mistake. His high throw went over catcher Earl Taborn's head and dented the backstop, allowing Wilson to score on the last of three errors on the same play, giving the Black Barons a 1–0 lead. Buck O'Neil kicked the dirt. It was an embarrassment of bad baseball.

The Black Barons were threatening to score in the second inning with Joe Scott on third base and Pepper Bassett on first base and two out when Piper Davis called for an unconventional play. White folks' ball would call it despicable, but as Piper explained, "The Negro ball-player gave big league baseball the unexpected—daring." Bassett, who was slower than a dog, rumbled ahead to steal second base. Taborn threw to second, and the moment he did, Scott broke for home, the lead runner in a double-steal attempt. But Hank Thompson, showing excellent infield instincts, stepped in front of the throw. He yielded second base to Bassett and fired back to Taborn, who was waiting on Scott for the third out of the inning. Bill Greason shook his head. He could have used the run.

Greason returned to the mound and continued his mastery of the Monarchs, pitching five scoreless innings to protect the 1–0 lead. He "had the slick stuff on his curve balls during the first five frames," the *Call* acknowledged. "He allowed only four unprofitable singles and made his one-run lead look bigger and bigger as the game progressed."

But his mound opponent, Jim LaMarque, showed why his calm and his curveball made him the ace. After the Black Barons tagged him for 15 hits in ten innings in Game 1 and Zapp hit the game-winning home run off him in Game 3, LaMarque was nearly untouchable. But Greason's defense was not as precise as his pitches. He allowed a leadoff single to LaMarque in the sixth inning. LaMarque advanced to second on a controversial play in which Herb Souell was called out for catcher's interference. Kansas City's Johnny Scott, in the lineup for Curtis Roberts, dribbled a ball down the first base line that Birmingham's Joe Scott failed to field. LaMarque scored from second to tie the game, 1–1.

The Black Barons did absolutely nothing with LaMarque, who retired seventeen consecutive batters, scattered three hits, gave up one unearned run, walked one, and struck out six. He departed the game after seven and one-third innings with what the *Call* reported to be a "sore pitching finger," which was probably a blister. His most compelling pitching came against Mays, whom he held hitless in four at-bats and kept off base, likely flustering the teenager with a half dozen years of pitching savvy coded in intricate speed-changing and location-shifting sequences. Jim LaMarque was training Willie Mays how to hit in the major leagues and getting him out in the process.

But Ed Steele's minor league mistake to begin the bottom of the eighth inning doomed the Black Barons. Elston Howard lifted a high and deep fly ball to right field. The ball didn't stick in Steele's glove. He dropped it for an error and Howard was safe at first. Buck O'Neil, who loved managing because he aspired to be like Connie Mack and John McGraw, men who "fascinated me more than the ballplayers," saw his opportunity. He ordered Tom Cooper to execute a sacrifice bunt, which advanced Howard, the winning run, to second base. Greason mulled over how he wanted to pitch to the dangerous Gene Baker, a feared rookie hitter. The *Call* described Baker as a "long ball hitter" whom "Manager Johnny O'Neil predicts [will] develop into another Willie Wells." Greason walked Baker to face the less formidable Taborn, who according to his owner, Tom Baird, was "the only young catcher in the Negro American League who has major league possibilities."

Taborn foiled Greason's strategy, driving a base hit to center field. Mays charged the ball and prepared to throw home, but this time it wasn't enough. Mays had taken a gamble when he threw home instead of to third. His aggressive nature translated into baseball intellect. Mays didn't care if Baker went to third. He wanted to cut down the lead runner at home plate. When Duncan ruled Mays's throw was not on time, Baker hustled from first to third. An insurance run was ninety feet away, something that in his scouting lingo Buck O'Neil surely deemed to be "Very desirable."

Then Kansas City's home-field advantage came into play, allowing the Monarchs to break conventional baseball rules without recourse. Though LaMarque exited the game with one out in the top of eighth inning, he was still allowed to hit for himself in the bottom of the eighth. Mays's presence in center field made a routine need much more complicated. A sacrifice fly would score the "speed demon" Baker, but the left-handed-hitting LaMarque had a narrow field. This time, it wasn't a matter of waving Willie off. He was going to go get any ball he could so he could make a throw home. Everyone in the park knew it.

LaMarque showed what a smart pitcher could do with a bat in his hands. He got enough wood on Greason's pitch and skied the ball down the left-field line, wisely out of the reach of Mays, who flew across the grass to try to get under the ball. But Jimmy Zapp knew the ball had to be his. He camped under it and set his feet. He made the catch as Baker tagged up at third and easily scored ahead of Zapp's ordinary throw. Ford Smith, who had entered the game in relief, struck out two Black Barons in the ninth inning to preserve the 3–1 victory. The Monarchs were still alive.

"Here was Piper's mind-set," Bobby Veale said. "No one out there is Jesus Christ." The Black Barons were walking on water the following day in Kansas City, where the inclement weather lasted into the night at sparsely populated Blues Stadium. A thin Monday night crowd of die-hard Monarchs fans congregated in the rain, their umbrellas springing forth like mushroom fields. Alonzo Perry went to the mound for the Black Barons in Game 5 during a steady drizzle and surrendered runs in the first and third innings to fall behind, 1–0. Buck O'Neil sent Gene Collins to the mound, a promising right-hander who had established himself in June when he pitched a three-hitter at Comiskey Park to defeat the Chicago American Giants, 1–0. He led the Black Barons, 3–1, entering the top of the fifth inning. Finally the Black Barons got to him and pulled ahead when Johnny Britton tripled home Artie Wilson to give Birmingham a 4–3 lead.

The rain grew steadily worse as Perry went back to the mound in the bottom of the fifth. The Monarchs had two runners on base with one out when the drizzle became a downpour. Though the game was official because five innings had been played, the Black Barons were, after all, in Kansas City. Frank Duncan, the chief umpire, conferred with his crew, which included former Monarchs pitcher Bullet Joe Rogan. Duncan pointed to the sky and told the Black Barons they would have to wait another day to be crowned champions. "A downpour of rain made the field a lake at Blues Stadium," the *Call* reported. "The score reverted to the fifth and the 3–3 tie." Piper and his players knew they had been hosed and could do nothing about it. "I don't believe we were too pleased about that," Greason said. "We could have picked the game up the very next day, but that's how it was when you played at Kansas City."

The Black Barons doubted that the Monarchs would have erased the game if they had been winning. In Game 6, pitcher Sammy C. Williams had the Black Barons within three outs of winning the series.

Williams had scattered eight hits through eight innings and had been good enough to take Birmingham into the bottom of the ninth protecting a 4–3 lead. He struck out Gene Baker for the first out of the inning and the Black Barons sensed victory, but catcher Earl Taborn then singled to put the tying run on base. Pitcher Gene Richardson was scheduled to bat, but Buck O'Neil called on his friend the pitcher Hilton Smith to pinch-hit. "Mr. Smith was a real good pitcher," Jim LaMarque said. "And a real good hitter."

Smith wasn't an automatic out even though he came off the bench on a cold night. Williams tried to put a warm fastball past him, but Smith got around on it, clubbing a double into right field, where Ed Steele got to the ball as quickly as he could. Taborn reached third base and was temped to score, but Buck O'Neil, coaching at third, held him there as Steele's solid throw arrived safely in catcher Pepper Bassett's mitt. The Monarchs had runners on second and third, and then Williams compounded his troubles when he walked Herb Souell and loaded the bases for Hank Thompson.

Piper knew this was a bad matchup. Williams had given up two consecutive hits and a walk, sure signs his command and velocity were slipping, but Piper didn't have another option. Bill Greason had pitched several innings in the series. Jehosie Heard and Nat Pollard were hurt. Piper needed Bill Powell to pitch the next day. He needed Jimmy Newberry if Powell wasn't effective. Perry had pitched five innings the day before. So Piper jogged to the mound to give Sammy a pep talk, even though he knew that this was a duel between a fading pitcher and a hitter who feasted on fastballs. Thompson was a left-handed line-drive hitter with power to right field and a reputation for being tough in the clutch. Sammy's best bet was to get a ground ball that Artie Wilson and Piper could turn into a game-ending and series-winning double play, but he would have to force Thompson to miss the ball with the good part of the bat. Failing that, if he could get Thompson to hit the ball in the air, he had to try to get Thompson to hit it somewhere where Mays could reach it and make a throw.

Buck O'Neil called Thompson aside and made certain he was aware of Mays. Hank settled into the box and it didn't take him long to recognize that Sammy C. had nothing left. He lined an opposite-field single to left field, drilled past shortstop Artie Wilson, intentionally aimed at Jimmy Zapp, the Black Barons' weakest outfield throwing arm. Taborn scored and Buck eagerly waved Hilton Smith around third base, aggressively willing to challenge Zapp's throwing arm. Smith beat the throw and scored. The Monarchs had flustered the Barons again, handing them a painful 5–4 loss. The Black Barons walked off the field disgusted while the Monarchs celebrated narrowing Birmingham's series lead to 3–2. Game 7 would be at Blues Stadium again, and the Monarchs felt they could do no wrong, infused with the confidence that led owner Tom Baird to once write, "You know when I get to raving about the Monarchs, I can go to town."

The Black Barons would have loved to leave town after the ninth-inning loss in Game 6, a rainout they felt shouldn't have been legal in Game 5, and a sound beating under LaMarque's finger in Game 4. The Black Barons still held the series advantage, but the momentum had swung to the Monarchs, who had yet another fresh arm to throw at them in Game 7.

Connie Johnson liked to wear wide-brimmed fedoras and was so tall that when he stood on the mound it looked like the button of his hat bumped against the rain clouds. He once won eleven consecutive games, hurt his arm, then came back and won eleven more. Originally from Stone Mountain, Georgia, he learned pitching was his destiny from Sammy Haynes, the same "fine brother" who started Bill Greason. Like Greason, Johnson was long and lean, threw hard, sometimes fought his control, and was always cocky. "I wasn't nothing but skin and bones, straight up and down," Johnson said.

Johnson "had plenty of stuff on his balls but seemed to have trouble putting his pitching just where he wanted to," the *Call* reported. He knew mistake fastballs to the Black Barons could be as exciting as they were deadly. Early in the game, he made a mistake to Willie Mays, who offensively hadn't been much of a force since Game 3. But this time Mays got what he wanted, a nice hard fastball where he could reach it, and he drilled it into deep right field.

The Monarchs then watched one of the most exciting plays develop—Willie Mays running out a run-scoring triple. His hat was gone before he rounded first, running like a buck and waddling like a duck. His foot cut inside the base so sharply that he could have taken the edge off the bag. He reached second in four strides and didn't need a coach to tell him he wanted third. He stopped himself from coming home only after he saw the ball come in, jerking his body to a stop as though pulling a marionette's strings. A stopwatch might have caught Mays reaching third in ten seconds. And even then there would have been disbelief, witnessing a player who was doing things that had rarely been done before.

Johnson later made another mistake, this time to catcher Pepper Bassett, who blasted a two-run home run to give the Black Barons a 3–1 lead in the fourth inning. That was all Buck O'Neil needed to see. He removed Johnson and inserted Gene Richardson. In the sixth inning, the Black Barons loaded the bases with nobody out and Bassett due up. The veteran catcher, whose .350 average was the best of his career, had the chance to put the game out of reach and put the championship preciously close to the Black Barons. It was Pepper's most important at-bat of the season, and in hindsight, the most important moment of a career that began in 1934. "Pepper," Jimmy Zapp said. "Lord, Pepper. He was very flashy. Switch-hitter. That had to be the greatest hitting season he ever had."

Buck O'Neil went to the mound with his season in the balance. Richardson was still just a rookie with a fastball that couldn't chop wood. The fans buzzed. The Black Barons wanted blood. "The crowd got a thrill out of the big catcher's appearance at bat in the sixth," the *Call* reported. "The Monarchs held a consultation as to whether to walk to him or pitch to him."

O'Neil decided to let Richardson pitch to Bassett, who "has been supplying much of the Barons' power." But "young Richardson threw his balls," the *Call* reported. "And Bassett failed to connect for a hit; he popped up to Souell for an out." Richardson did the rest. He escaped the inning and pitched shutout baseball until the ninth. Starter Bill Powell entered the final frame protecting a 3–2 lead. The Black Barons were again three outs away from the championship, but winning in the ninth inning at Kansas City was proving to be the most difficult challenge they had faced all season. Powell lost the first two batters in the ninth and Piper had seen enough. It broke his heart to take the ball from his close friend and give it to the fireball-throwing yet entirely unpredictable Jimmy Newberry to pitch to Hank Thompson.

If Newberry wasn't hungover when he threw the first pitch to Thompson, he got drunk after the game. Newberry's first pitch was a fastball. Thompson hit a line drive that soared over right fielder Ed Steele's head until the ball landed on the hill at Blues Stadium, setting off pandemonium as the Monarchs again beat the Black Barons in agonizing fashion, this time crafting a 5–3 victory in the final at-bat. "This Herculean task by the Monarchs in winning three in a row back from the Barons was jam packed with interest, and the fans came out to watch the brilliant drama," the *Call* wrote. "The Monarchs demonstrated remarkable determination."

The Black Barons were emotionally finished in the locker room before the decisive Game 8 the following morning. They were spent and exhausted and Piper knew it. He still wanted to win, but as he walked among his players, he knew something was missing. He was one of them and he understood why they were tired. It wasn't only that they had been beaten in humiliating fashion in two games. That was only the symptom. He knew they were tired from the uncertainty of their world, tired from thousands of miles holed up in Charlie Rudd's bus, tired from days and nights where the only certainty was that this little boy in center field had to play in the major leagues. They could see his future but not their own, and as proud as they were to be a part of him, they were equally terrified that their road was over.

Piper was out of pitchers. Powell had pitched Saturday, Perry complained of a sore arm, Williams had pitched nine innings two days earlier, and Heard and Pollard were both out. Exasperated, Piper cried out, "Don't anyone want to take the ball?"

Calmly, Bill Greason spoke. He felt like he had been born for the moment. "I said, 'Give me the ball, skip,'" Greason recalled. Piper nodded at him. "Okay," he said. "You got it."

Greason applied every lesson he had learned. "Fastball, push them back off the plate," he said. "Curveball, you got him on his heels." He orchestrated every pitch. "I threw a downer that was all in that little wrist of mine," he said. "Then I'd pull a little bit and make it run like a slider." He applied everything Piper had taught him. "You had to be careful the way you brought up your arms because they'd watch your wrist," Greason said. "Piper was one of the greatest at picking pitches off from the other team so he taught you how to cover your tracks. Sometimes he'd just yell 'Alright!' for a fastball and 'Hey!' for a curveball."

Piper yelled "Hey!" many times against Jim LaMarque in Game 8. He even taught his hitters how to steal signs from unsuspecting catchers who didn't conceal their signals. The Black Barons awoke, scoring single runs in the fourth, fifth, and eighth innings, pummeling LaMarque for eleven hits in seven innings, though the *Call* couldn't stand the thought of publishing how the Black Barons scored. Piper even made his point against umpire Frank Duncan, the former Monarch who had used rain to take away Birmingham's victory in Game 5.

LaMarque was called out on a play at first base by umpire Sylvester Vaughn, but Duncan overruled Vaughn. This time, Piper was angry. He pulled his team off the field and left LaMarque standing on first base. The Black Barons were winning the championship game thanks to Greason's pitching, but Piper wanted to make the message perfectly clear to Duncan and Tom Baird. He was representing his players, the owner, and his town. In that moment, Piper Davis *was* Birmingham, sticking up for the rights of his men who were treated as though they had none. Long before the first Freedom Ride, Piper Davis protested. As he jawed with Duncan, he let it all out. Buck O'Neil stood quietly on the sidelines, safely aligned with Tom Baird.

Piper's players responded with a simultaneous *umm-hmmm*, and long before anyone from Kansas City or anywhere else gave the Birmingham Black Barons any credit for understanding what they were up against, Piper struck a chord. Baseball was the sport, but this struggle was never about the game. "All we had to do was look at Baird," Greason said. "We knew he didn't care for us." After what the *Call* described as an "atmosphere of tenseness, with players and the small crowd on edge in the crucial final game," Piper ordered his players back on the field to resume play.

Greason pitched so well that the *Call* couldn't ignore him, concluding, "Greason was the answer to the Barons' prayers." He was the answer in Game 8, but not without help from Mays. Greason intentionally tried to get Monarch batters to put the ball in the air, and this time, cries of "Come on, Willie!" were not just coming from the two corner outfielders, but from every Black Baron on the field. It was a symphony. Greason, the conductor, would throw. The Monarchs would make contact. The crack of the bat would resonate, and while Willie ran each ball down, the call went out, from the oldest veterans to the youngest rookies, "Come on, Willie!" One by one, he snapped up the Monarchs' hopes in the palm of his glove. "I've seen him catch a line drive with his bare hand and shoot the ball back in. He did some unusual things," Greason said. "Ed Steele could really throw, but couldn't throw like Mays. Guy got a single, try to go from first to third on him, ball be waitin' on him. Brit would be lookin' at the guy like he wasn't surprised. Mays made the extraordinary exquisite. I never forgot the first time Buck O'Neil saw that. He said, 'Who is that boy! Man, he has got a shotgun!'"

The Black Barons had won their confidence back and were winning on the scoreboard. They owned the Monarchs again, as evidenced by Willard Brown's surrendering body language. He was a human barometer, a Hall of Fame player when he cared, and when he didn't, he was what Al LaMacchia, who had played against him in 1943, called "just an ordinary player." The Monarchs fans hated it too, and as Greason shut Brown down, the *Call* reported that Monarchs fans "gave him the razzberry but good. He's not too popular because of his Stepin-Fechit routine."

Greason was popular with his teammates as he carved his way through the Monarchs. Finally, he finished the effort in the ninth inning. "He curve-balled the Monarchs into inefficiency," the *Call* conceded. "He was poison, he was powerful, he was superb." Jimmy Zapp claimed Greason was never better. "He manhandled Hank Thompson and Willard Brown." When Greason read the *Call* years later, he said, "I was awful!" He had pitched a complete game and struck out five for his third victory of the series, in addition to his pinch-hit single that sent Game 1 to extra innings where Mays won the game. Had there been a Most Valuable Player award, Greason would have been the winner. His victory in Game 8 to seal the championship was a win that he never forgot. The way Greason liked to tell the story, Mays caught the final out. "Tell you what," Greason said. "If I had Mays playing behind me in center field every time I pitched, I might be in the Hall of Fame right there with him."

When the final out was recorded in Birmingham's 5–1 victory on Kansas City's home field, the Black Barons were right there with Greason. He jumped into Pepper Bassett's arms, and soon Piper Davis, Artie Wilson, and Johnny Britton were jumping on Greason's back. When Mays jumped into the pile, the boy Piper had told to "run 'em to death!" was squeezed to death.

There was no champagne in the locker room when it was over, no giddy spraying of beer and booze, just the normal routine of going back to the hotel in a dirty uniform. Some of the veterans undoubtedly took advantage of Kingfish's Blue Room, the hot bar on Eighteenth and Vine, and downed kick-ya-poo until sunrise. The Black Barons had a welcome break because the Negro League World Series would begin in Kansas City against the Homestead Grays. Mays never knew what went on below him at the Street Hotel that evening while he spent time with Piper and Nat Pollard and read Johnny Britton's newspapers. His team threw a party without him, and Piper and Pollard most certainly assured Willie that sleep was more important. He had years ahead to mill around at midnight. And most importantly, he was out of the steel mill, and he was never going back.

The veterans knew their celebration was partly thanks to the kid who was too young to drink with them and couldn't keep up with them off the field the way he could on it. "He was just super," Artie Wilson said. "I seen him grow all the way up. Everything he did was super. Run, throw, hit. Super."

"I don't think Willie has ever gotten the credit for a trait he had even then," Piper said. "There has never been a player a team would rather have [up] late with the score tied. He'd find some way to score or stop the other team from scoring with his glove or arm."

The 1948 Negro American League pennant belonged to Birmingham, but the players never forgot why it was meaningful. It was the balance between baseball and humanity. Mays had made them better players and Piper had made them better people. For the rest of their lives, the 1948 Birmingham Black Barons, champions of the Negro American League, could never decide which meant more.

11

"JOSH GIBSON IS DEAD AND WE STILL CAN'T BEAT THESE GUYS"

The *Birmingham World* recognized the importance of Willie to their beloved Black Barons. "Willie Howard Mays is the find of the year, if not the rookie of the year," the *World* wrote after the Black Barons toppled the Monarchs for the Negro American League pennant. "He can hit, field, throw and deliver in the pinch. He lacks experience and has a feeble batting average. He will break up your ball games and turn hits into putouts with sensational catches." The *World* echoed Piper's sentiment that "the turning point of the season was when school was out and Willie got to play full-time." School had resumed at Fairfield Industrial, where Mays would begin his junior year, ready for the world he would have to wait for. But he didn't need trade school to learn his occupation. The Black Barons found a way for him to keep playing baseball, because they knew they needed him if they were going to beat the Homestead Grays in what became the last Negro League World Series.

The Grays played like a cabaret act more than a baseball team, where the headliners were a group of players known inside black baseball by nicknames alone. There was "Bank," who was from Birmingham, the best of five brothers if you asked. "Chinky" was a two-way player who pitched and played third base. "Swish" was just plain Swish, though sometimes he requested to be addressed as the more regal "Mr. Swish." "Luke" had a personality of which it was said that "he pinned flowers on himself," and his home run balls landed three blocks away if you didn't pitch to him carefully. Then there was "Buck." Nobody hit more home runs that were never counted than Buck Leonard.

The Grays had won the Negro National League playoffs by forfeit over the Baltimore Elite Giants. There was a time in the not-so-distant past when the Grays elicited fanciful visions of debonair ballplayers, but the Grays of 1948 were a little less splendid. They pulled knives on one another inside the team bus, liberally drank kick-ya-poo juice, and behaved like such delinquents that Leonard loathed the idea of his little brother playing for them. The Grays were still a talented team, but they had changed for the worse when Josh Gibson died in 1947, a symbol of what a tormented life inside the hot box could lead a man to consume.

Before the series, Piper Davis and Pepper Bassett called a pitcher's meeting, where it was agreed that the Black Barons were not going to pitch to Buck Leonard in any situation where he could beat them. Leonard had led the Negro National League with 13 home runs. The younger sluggers, Luke Easter and Bob Thurman, "Mr. Swish," perhaps had home run power equal to Leonard. "Chinky" Wilmer Fields was more likely to beat you with a line drive than a long ball. But it was Leonard's bat speed and sense of timing that the Black Barons feared and respected. It was said that if a pitcher fired a rifle from the mound, the left-handed-hitting Buck could turn on the bullet and pull it down the right-field line. He was always placid. His power in tense situations surfaced when nibbling pitchers fell behind in the count and were forced to challenge him. "Buck Leonard was one of the best fastball hitters you ever wanted to see," Piper said. The Black Barons decided not to mess with Leonard, who after fifteen seasons was still among the league's highest-paid players, earning close to $1,000 a month. He loved to reward the crowd on important occasions. Before the playoffs, the Grays held Buck Leonard Day at Griffith Stadium in Washington, where 6,000 fans praised him. Buck thanked them with three hits and a victory.

Jimmy Newberry pitched Game 1 in Kansas City, chewing on slippery elm and digging his fingernails into the comfortable grooves his teammates had sliced into the baseball. The Black Barons took a 1–0 lead when Joe Scott singled home Ed Steele in the second inning, but in the bottom of the inning Thurman singled.

Catcher Eudie Napier, Gibson's successor, walked to bring up Willie Pope. Pope put a charge into Newberry's pitch and drilled it beyond right fielder Steele, where the ball rattled around in the corner. Thurman and Napier scored to give the Grays a 2–1 lead. After a pair of strikeouts to the bottom of the order, Newberry was burned by the electrically charged leadoff-hitting center fielder Luis Marquez, Cool Papa Bell's replacement, who slapped a single to score Pope and give the Grays a 3–1 lead.

Newberry didn't give up a run over the final seven innings, scattering six hits with six strikeouts. He pitched more effectively than his opposite, Ted Alexander, who gave up eight hits and struck out four. But after the Black Barons trimmed the lead to 3–2 in the eighth inning, bad luck began showing up, bad things that always happened when Birmingham played the Grays in the World Series. Johnny Britton drew a walk to lead off the bottom of the eighth. Mays scorched a ground ball to shortstop Sam Bankhead, who forced Britton out at second. Bassett singled Mays to third, bringing up Piper. He had faltered against the Monarchs in certain situations and hated the feeling, but he got to Alexander this time, driving a triple to right field. Mays scored with ease to trim the lead to 3–2, but Piper, running behind Bassett, knew Pepper was in trouble when he saw Napier set up to take a throw from Thurman in right field.

Napier could hear Bassett coming as he set up to take Thurman's throw from right field. A fierce collision ensued, with about four hundred pounds of pigtail tangling in a dirt cloud. The home plate umpire, Kansas City's own Frank Duncan, ruled Bassett out. The Black Barons lost Game 1, 3–2, but finally got to go home to Birmingham, far away from where Duncan could influence the outcome. As the Black Barons longingly turned for home, they had no idea how much Monarchs owner Tom Baird had turned his nose up at them, reaching a conclusion that affected the futures of Artie Wilson, Piper Davis, Bill Greason, and, more than anyone, Willie Mays.

The Black Barons were comfortably home at Rickwood Field for Game 2. Bill Powell was slowly pitching a two-hitter, armed with a 2–0 lead gifted to him by Joe Scott's two-run double in the second inning. But Powell began running out of steam in the top of the sixth inning when he allowed a leadoff single to Marquez, a player who was gaining considerable interest from major league teams for his ability to "run like hell," according to future scout George Genovese. Then Sam Bankhead, the savvy Birmingham product of whom former Monarchs catcher Frazier Robinson wrote, "You make a mistake on him and Sam could cost you a ballgame," put the ball in the air, where Mays hauled in one of his five fly balls in the game.

Easter, whose physical stature inspired white writers to call him "mastodonic," a "slugger with the strength of Samson and the home run propensity of a half dozen Babe Ruths," was next. Born in Mississippi in 1915, he was happily telling white folks' ball, with what white writers noted as his "toothy" grin, that he was born six or seven years later, and everyone in the Negro Leagues loved being in on the joke. Powell allowed Easter a single and Marquez advanced to third, bringing the dangerous Buck Leonard to the plate.

Powell turned to Piper at second base. He walked Leonard and pitched to Wilmer Fields, a man who didn't care for traveling in the

South and didn't trust white folks' ball enough to accept a minor league offer from the Brooklyn Dodgers in 1946. The strategy seemed to work when Fields "sizzled a made-to-pattern double play" ball to Piper at second, who "hummed it to Wilson," according to the *World*. But bad luck intervened. The ball got stuck in Wilson's glove and he couldn't make his typical lightning-quick throw to first base. Rather than an inning-ending double play with the lead intact, Marquez scored to cut the lead to 2–1. Napier, a catcher who wouldn't be confused with Josh Gibson when he had a bat in his hands, singled, scoring Easter to tie the game, 2–2.

Piper sensed more trouble and gestured for Jimmy Newberry to loosen up. Pope found the pitch he wanted from Powell and hit it for a three-run home run. It was the last pitch Bill Powell threw for the 1948 Black Barons, and his slow walk off the mound was slower than any he had taken all season. Though Newberry restored order and pitched three and one-third scoreless innings, the game had changed when the ball lodged in Wilson's glove. A play he could make in his sleep would keep him awake that night.

The Black Barons mounted a one-out rally in the ninth inning against relief pitcher Thurman, who was born in Kansas and would have a job waiting for him with the Monarchs after the season. Like every other ballplayer, he was lying about his age. "My age was put back several times, so much that I used the baseball age constantly," he said. Thurman thought of himself as an everyday hitter who just happened to be able to pitch, but he was making the Black Barons feel old. He had pitched well before Jimmy Zapp singled and Joe Scott walked. With Newberry's spot in the order due, Piper asked Herman Bell to pinch-hit, representing the tying run. Bell had a reputation as a light hitter, but as Bobby Veale observed, he could crush a fastball. That's what Thurman threw and that's what Bell hit for an RBI double to score Zapp and trim the lead to 5–3. It was the biggest hit in Bell's career, and it gave Artie Wilson a chance to sleep better at night if he could connect against Thurman.

Piper pulled the lumber-legged Bell out of the game and inserted pitcher Jehosie Heard as a pinch runner at second base. Wilson, who had one hit in four attempts against Thurman, wanted to make amends. If he could reach base, Johnny Britton would be next. After that, Willie Mays was due up. Nobody considered Willie a kid when he batted in a man's situation.

So Artie settled in. Thurman, however, knew how to get Artie Wilson out. Thurman cut him off with high fastballs, exposing his greatest weakness. Wilson struck out and the Black Barons were down to the last out. Britton couldn't get the Black Barons to Mays either. He grounded out to end the game and the Homestead Grays had a 5–3 victory in Game 2 and a commanding 2–0 lead in the World Series. Willie Mays, who was left standing on deck waving three bats at once, would have to wait for tomorrow. He hated waiting for tomorrow.

Winning a World Series game against the Grays in Birmingham meant everything to the Black Barons. Suddenly, Mays represented their hope. For the first time, he experienced the expectations that accompany celebrity. Everybody seemed to know him now. Men he never remembered playing against suddenly claimed they taught him everything he knew. Folks came out of the woodwork, stories from the mill surfaced, and gossip about his family circulated. "It was a strange situation there," Bobby Veale said. "I never did get into it." Mays was a star in black Birmingham long before he was a star in black and white America. "Mays got famous quick," Veale said. "First he got famous here. Then he got famous there."

Mays made himself famous in the minds of the Grays in Game 3. For the first time in a meaningful game, he put all of his fantastic skills together at once, proving that he could beat you with his speed, his defense, his throwing, and when it mattered most, his hitting. And there was something else about him. The old-timers could tell the difference. Willie didn't just want to win. He wanted to break the other guy's spirit.

With starting pitcher Alonzo Perry dueling Ted Alexander through three scoreless innings, Bob Thurman, the left-handed power hitter, who said he "could hit a ball nine miles" as a young man, launched one toward center field. Mays turned his back and started running. Thurman thought he had a double for sure. Perry helplessly watched

Willie's Boys: the 1948 Negro American League champion Birmingham Black Barons. Bottom, from left: Willie Mays, CF; Bill Greason, RHP; Roosevelt Atkins, trainer; Jimmy Newberry, RHP; Joe Scott, 1B. Middle row, from left: Artie Wilson, SS; Johnny Britton, 3B; Nat Pollard, RHP; Jehosie Heard, LHP; Wiley Griggs, utility; Piper Davis, 2B-manager. Top row, from left: Sammy C. Williams, RHP; Pepper Bassett, C; Jimmy Zapp, OF; Alonzo Perry, RHP-1B; Bill Powell, RHP; Bobby Robinson, OF; Herman Bell, C; Ed Steele, OF.

as Mays kept running. All he could see was the number 8 on Mays's back. As Thurman came into second base, Artie Wilson was waiting with words he had uttered countless times before: "The center fielder's got it." Thurman thought the ball would land in the trees, not in a teenager's glove. "Mays starred in the outfield when he pulled down Thurman's fly against the center field fence in the fourth," the *World* reported. The crowd approved. Some fans came just to see him make a play like that.

Perry helped himself with an RBI double in the fifth inning to give the Black Barons a 1–0 lead. In the top of the sixth, Buck Leonard was on first base. He had seen Mays play two games but never watched him throw. Leonard was running at the crack of the bat when the following hitter singled to center field. Leonard thought going from first to third would be routine, but then he saw a throw that defied anything else he had ever witnessed. As he rumbled between second and third base, the ball buzzed over his head like a wasp and snapped into third baseman Johnny Britton's mitt. Brit was waiting on Buck, who was out from Washington, D.C., to Birmingham. "I said to myself, 'That young boy's out there and he ain't gonna throw true to third base,'" Leonard wrote in his self-titled autobiography. "And I went to third base and he threw me out. He still remembers that and he talks about it even now."

The Black Barons took a 3–1 lead in the sixth inning when Piper singled and Pepper scored on a wild pitch, but the persistent Grays rallied in the eighth inning when Sam Bankhead doubled and Luke Easter walked. Perry induced Leonard to ground out for the second out, but Thurman hit this one where Mays couldn't reach it. His double scored Bankhead and Easter to tie the score, 3–3. Piper removed Perry and inserted Bill Greason, who got a strikeout for the final out of the inning.

The final victory for the 1948 Birmingham Black Barons would come in the last at-bat, courtesy of the last player to join the team. Greason, who had proven that he could swing the bat, lined a leadoff single in the ninth inning. Artie Wilson flew out and Johnny Britton walked. That brought up Mays, with Greason, the winning run, at second base. Mays wasted no time. He smoked a ball right back at the pitcher, and before Ted Alexander could look down, the ball had ripped through his legs and into center field. The good news for Alexander was he could still father children. The bad news was that Greason never stopped running. Whereas Mays was Birmingham's best outfield arm, Luis Marquez, Homestead's center fielder, had his team's inferior outfield arm. Greason scored without a play and the Black Barons beat the Grays, 4–3. It was the moment made for Mays. He had beaten the Grays with his legs, his glove, his arm, and his bat. Everybody who came to the park saw him do something special. "Here we thought we was the ones makin' him better, but it was the other way around," Jimmy Zapp said. One moment stayed with Mays, though. It was the hug Piper Davis gave him at the end of the game.

• • •

The Black Barons were an emotionally drained team by the time they arrived in New Orleans. They had beaten the Monarchs in a grueling series and played the Grays close for three consecutive games. With the Black Barons' major goals fulfilled, the Grays hammered Birmingham, 14–1, in New Orleans in Game 4. The demoralizing moment came when Jehosie Heard threw a pitch that was never seen again. "I didn't see Luke Easter's ball land," Piper said of the grand slam Easter hit in the fourth inning. Grays pitcher Wilmer Fields had to drive twenty-five straight hours to get to the game because he didn't learn the location had been changed until he returned home to Virginia. He drove to New Orleans, carefully watching his back in Mississippi, where he stopped to nap on the side of the road. When he arrived, "I was in such bad shape I was shaking," he said.

The Black Barons, equally tired, couldn't do anything with him, collecting only seven hits. He struck out Artie Wilson three times. "I was confused, I was disoriented," Fields said. "The fastball wouldn't go straight. It would go the other way. I never threw a running fastball before in my life." But Fields did discover his slider. Artie came up to him after the game and said, "Fields, I didn't know you could pitch like that." Fields shrugged. "Neither did I," he said.

Dizzy Dismukes was in New Orleans covering the games for the *Chicago Defender* and scouting, unbeknownst to the Black Barons, for both the Kansas City Monarchs and the New York Yankees. He took great delight in describing Birmingham's demise, happily willing to show where his loyalties resided. The Grays "hammered everything the four Birmingham Black Barons pitchers dished up" and "slaughtered the Negro American League champions, who, evidently, wore themselves out in the playoff for the league championship with the Kansas City Monarchs," Dismukes gloated in the *Defender*.

The teams drove back to Birmingham for Game 5. The Black Barons tied the score, 6–6, midway through the game, but, "not that there was any doubt about it from the beginning," Dismukes insisted, the Grays pulled away for a 10–6 victory. Details were scant in papers around the country, as black newspapers dedicated their space to the major league World Series, where the Larry Doby– and Satchel

Paige–led Cleveland Indians were playing the Boston Braves, a team that had quietly started encouraging its scouts to turn in the names of promising young black players in the South. But when the final out was recorded in Birmingham, the Homestead Grays were the last Negro League World Series champions.

The loss held mixed emotions for the Black Barons. "I remember when it was over," Sammy C. Williams said. "Jimmy Newberry said, 'Josh Gibson is dead and we still can't beat these guys.'" Wiley Griggs called the Grays a team that "could play anyone in the majors and beat them." Yet the Black Barons took great pride in their accomplishments. They had defeated the Monarchs and started Willie Mays on his baseball career. "We didn't feel too bad," Bill Greason said. "We had a great season. We had a great series against the Monarchs and played three real close games with the Grays. Everyone had a great year."

The Homestead Grays became the sad symbol of a sorrowful decline. They went from being Negro League champions in 1948 to a team that no longer existed after 1950. The Negro National League folded at the end of 1948 when the surviving teams, including Alex Pompez's New York Cubans, reshuffled into the newly formed Negro American League's Eastern Division. Pompez took a new leadership role and worked with fervor to get as many players out of the Negro American League and into white folks' ball as he could.

Though he was bleeding money, Pompez's ambition and creativity soared. He viewed helping the Negro American League survive and assisting black and Latin players as the same mission, believing that black baseball could do what white baseball couldn't—find and develop black players. Pompez wanted to find a way for it to work without putting black teams out of business, and he had faith that Negro baseball could survive with the cooperation of the major leagues, but only if the major leagues were willing to acknowledge the credibility of the black teams as minor league farm clubs. He was certain he could convince major league baseball teams to work with the Negro American League, so in 1949 and 1950 he would lead by example. Instead of white teams raiding black teams for a pittance, he would use his team as a showcase for black players, even if those players did not always play for his team.

Pompez envisioned a cooperative spirit where white folks' ball accepted that individual operators, such as himself and Black Barons owner Tom Hayes, were creditable individuals preparing players to be sold for respectable compensation, just as independent white minor league teams had the right to auction off their players and be fairly compensated for their property. The strategy harkened back to his Harlem lottery, and everyone was a winner in Pompez's imagination. The white teams would purchase black talent for modest fees, even if at auction. The black owners would make enough to keep running their teams and finding the next generation of players to be sold. Black communities would have local teams to call their own and root for their graduates in the major leagues.

He dreamed of a new era of cooperation, where white, black, and Latin players, scouts, and management shared mutual respect and opportunity. He aspired to help create a steady stream of black and Latin talent that would last for decades and keep the number of minorities in baseball at a relevant level. He hoped to make baseball a microcosm of the Harlem melting pot, infused with Birmingham work ethic, but he knew black baseball would have to earn it.

Pompez soon appreciated that instead of fighting Dutch Schultz he was struggling against men like Dan Topping, the president of the New York Yankees, whose organization's most prized source of information from the Negro Leagues was Tom Baird of the Kansas City Monarchs. Pompez's days of bootlegging and numbers running were supposed to be over, and if he couldn't have his dream, he would do things the Harlem way. The Birmingham Black Barons had attracted 168,000 fans in 1948 and Hayes, like Pompez, wanted respect for his economic power. If that day never arrived, then Pompez's background was perfectly suited for the human trafficking of professional baseball players, the delicate dance between buyers and sellers, where the middleman left no footprints.

When the Grays formally disbanded during the collapse of the Negro National League after the 1948 World Series, all the team's players were redistributed among the remaining Negro American League teams. One player Pompez purchased was infielder Howard Easterling, who had jumped the Grays to play in the Mexican League. Pompez also purchased free agent Ray Dandridge, who also elected to return to the Negro League from the Mexican League. Dandridge became Pompez's player-manager for the 1949 New York Cubans. Easterling's addition to the Cubans strengthened Piper's connections with Pompez. The two had played together on Willie Foster's Yakima Browns more than a decade earlier.

Grays outfielders Bob Thurman signed with the Monarchs and Luke Easter signed with the Indians, but there was no future for the venerable Buck Leonard, who played with the Grays until their bitter end as a freelance travel team in 1950. The man who hit so many home runs that he said he couldn't count them all fled to the Mexican League for a time before playing ten games in an undignified Class B minor league stint in 1953. The "Black Lou Gehrig" never hit a home run in white folks' ball.

Leonard always remembered the 1948 Negro League World Series, when he saw the end of one era and the start of another. The Negro Leagues as he had known them were over. He was a bridge between Josh Gibson and Willie Mays. Never did a more famous player with the first name of Buck play in the Negro Leagues, but Buck Leonard felt privileged to have witnessed Buck Duck play center field for the 1948 Birmingham Black Barons. "I think Birmingham had their best team that year," he wrote.

When Mays grew up in the next few years, he understood more than he showed. He knew that the men he loved, his 1948 Black Barons, the players who treated him like a little brother and an only child, had watched their careers slip into oblivion. Mays became a businessman after the 1948 season, and though he was still maturing, he knew he had to get out of the Negro Leagues if he wanted to survive. He seemed never to have found such camaraderie again. When Cat saw Piper after the 1948 season, he thanked him for taking care of his boy for him. What few realized was that the events that led Mays from Birmingham to the New York Giants had already been set in motion.

Piper, Artie, and Alonzo Perry were hired to play winter ball in Puerto Rico in 1948–1949. But before Piper left, he made sure that Willie got to do something he never imagined would happen. Piper saw to it that two of his closest friends from his earlier seasons on the Black Barons, Lyman Bostock and Winfield Welch, let Mays play with the Black Barons in Birmingham for one night against Jackie Robinson's All-Stars.

The tour was a racket, of course, pure cash cow games. It was Alex Pompez's baby. He asked Robinson and Roy Campanella to play for him. Their price was $2,500 each, enough to compensate for the Dodgers missing out on World Series money that October. Robinson and Campanella recruited other star black players and Pompez hired Welch to assemble the travel team that would compete with the all-stars. Welch found willing players. He stacked his roster with current and former Black Barons, including Bostock, Lester Lockett, Jimmy Newberry, Ed Steele, and others. The game was set for October 12 at Rickwood Field. Piper knew that Willie, who couldn't travel with the tour because he had to go back to school, would be in good hands. The tour began on October 11 in Atlanta, the same night Larry Doby helped the Cleveland Indians defeat the Boston Braves, 4–3, in Game 6 of the World Series. The Indians claimed the first championship in American professional sports history won with an integrated team.

The following night at Rickwood Field, a less known but equally significant piece of history occurred when Willie Mays played against Jackie Robinson for the first time. Tuesday, October 12, was a school day at Fairfield Industrial High, but Mays would never have been able to keep his mind on learning his trade. "Jackie Robinson whiffed, singled, stole home and fielded flawlessly to the delight of the estimated 7,000 fans," according to the *World*. The fans watched Newberry show his major league stuff when he struck out Robinson and Campanella, but he made two throwing errors to lose the game, 3–0. Winfield Welch's team had only two hits, but the center fielder got one of them: "Rookie Willie Mays made a two-bagger," the *World* noted. On a field with Jackie Robinson and Roy Campanella, the best player was a high school junior.

Mays and Pompez met for the first time after the game when Pompez, who traveled with the all-stars, paid the Birmingham players. "When you played for Pompez," said Birmingham outfielder Jessie Mitchell, who played for Pompez in the winter of 1956, "you always got cash after the game. He'd just take the gate money, peel off what he owed you, and say, 'Thank you very much.' I always said, 'Thank you, too.'" Mays got in line with Newberry and the rest of Welch's players, who according to the *World* "made $105 apiece as their share of the melon in the Jackie Robinson All-Star Game."

Mays believed he was the best player who was not in the big leagues, and he was probably right. He had just proven himself against Robinson and Campanella. His performance was worthy of grander stages than Birmingham, but Pompez wasn't the kind of man to steal a player for the sake of stealing him. If he was, he surely would have tried everything in his power to make sure that Willie Mays played for the New York Cubans in 1949, not the Birmingham Black Barons. While Pompez was ambitious, he was also remarkably human, which made him, like Piper Davis, a strong person in a tumultuous time, and a pivotal man in the direction of young Willie's life. "He was a businessman and an entrepreneur," George Genovese said. "But Pompez was also a very nice, soft-spoken gentleman, very dignified."

When Pompez's tour bus rolled away from Rickwood Field en route to Memphis's Martin Stadium for an October 13 date, Willie Mays went home to his aunt Sarah's house and dreamt of bigger things. As Alex Pompez tried to sleep in the bus, he too had similar visions, best expressed by the *World*: "Sensation of the Year: Willie Howard Mays, the Black Barons outfielder, is not old enough to register for the draft. He is the wonder kid of the Negro American League. Nobody has voted him the find of the year, rookie of the year or most valuable player. He may not be anything of this. But in my book, he is the most promising youngster to play baseball at Rickwood Field since I've been around."

12

SOMEBODY IS ALWAYS WATCHING

One Sunday night on Negro Avenue, Willie Mays was engrossed in a heated game of pool. He was hustling a few doors down from Bob's Savoy where Charlie Rudd's bus was warming up for a red-eye jump to St. Louis. Mays lost himself with the pool cue in his hands, lining up and knocking down trick shots that Cat and his uncles had taught him over the years. He could curve his shot the way he sliced his body to make an unusual catch in the outfield. When he nailed the cue ball just right, he could sock balls into the pockets like he was throwing out greedy base runners. He beamed when the shots fell; he loved looking good.

But Mays got too greedy. It was 1949 and he was no longer a rookie, but hustling was a rookie mistake. The Black Barons had played a day game that afternoon at Rickwood Field against the

New York Cubans and were scheduled to start a tour with the Cubans on June 11 with a double-header Monday night at Sportsman's Park in St. Louis. Mays was shedding the reputation as a great fielder who threw bullets but couldn't hit them. He entered the game Sunday afternoon hitting .413 with two home runs. In the game, he awed the Rickwood crowd when he made a catch in deep center field and then uncorked a powerful throw to home plate to nail a runner trying to score on a sacrifice fly, helping the Black Barons preserve the win.

Piper, in his second season as Black Barons manager, gave his players a few hours after the game to eat dinner and relax before the long trip. When it was time to leave, he kissed his wife, Laura, good-bye, and told his "crumb snatchers" to go to sleep. He was waiting in his customary seat on the bus when his players started boarding. He counted them, but one was missing. Everyone knew who it was, but Piper didn't say anything. He pointed his finger at the road. Charlie Rudd reluctantly closed the doors, stepped on the gas, and drove off.

The Black Barons knew exactly what was going on. Bill Greason wisecracked, "Hey, Skip! Can I play center?" Rudd kept driving through downtown Birmingham, though he flashed a worried look at Piper, who did not budge. After a few more miles, the players saw headlights racing to catch up with the bus. Rudd asked if he should stop. "Keep driving," Piper said. His face was stoic.

The taxi pulled alongside the bus and the driver honked his horn. Willie stuck his head out the window, waving his arms wildly in the dark, shouting and begging in his high-pitched voice for Rudd to stop the bus. The amused Black Barons caught a glimpse of their young center fielder hanging his torso out of the cab, as if he were straining himself to make some crazy shot. The veterans knew Piper was making a point. "He was screamin' like a bird," Piper remembered.

Finally, Piper put Willie out of his misery. He told Rudd to pull over. The cab pulled over and Willie fished money out of his pocket. Piper gave him the stern look: If you got money to gamble, you got money for fare. Willie paid the driver, flipped his bat over his shoulder like a hobo bumming a ride to his next ball game, and found Piper waiting for him on the top step of the bus.

"What you gonna do?" Willie shrieked. "You gonna leave me? I'm a pro ballplayer here! You can't leave me!"

Oh, but Piper could leave Willie behind. His players couldn't hear his words, but they knew what he said. "He would leave you behind in a heartbeat," Bobby Veale said. "Didn't care who you were. He had that big 'A'—authority—in front of his name. That was a full-time job. As a manager, that's all he wanted—the best out of everyone. Carry your own burden, and if possible, help out your fellow man."

Piper knew there was little else he could teach Mays about playing baseball, but Mays had much to learn about how to be a professional baseball player. He was no secret now. Scouts were positioning themselves to sign him. Owners maneuvered to steal him from the Black Barons. Piper never lost sight of the most important job he never took credit for. He allowed Willie to step back on the bus to help fulfill this journey, though he told Willie that his punishment was to stand next to Rudd all night and talk to him to keep him awake. Piper slept with a sliver of his eye open. As he often told Mays, somebody was always watching.

The *Birmingham World* couldn't come up with superlatives fast enough to keep up with Mays's growing fame. He followed the same ground rules in 1949 that he had in 1948, playing with the Black Barons during the weekends before joining the team full-time during summer vacation. Mays was supposed to have lost his amateur status after his sophomore season at Fairfield Industrial, which would have meant he couldn't play high school football after helping the Black Barons reach the Negro League World Series, but that was nothing that a phony name and a different jersey number couldn't fix. His high school football coach, a gruff fellow known only by his last name of McWilliams, envisioned Willie as a college quarterback because of his speed and his arm. "Did Willie Mays, Fairfield Industrial High professional baseball player, pitch a 50-yard touchdown pass against Booker T. Washington of Pensacola, Fla., in a game there November 24?" the *World* asked. This was right out of the football coach's handbook—if you're going to use an illegal player, don't call the newspaper to report he threw a fifty-yard touchdown pass. Mays knew he could play football, but he was also practical. "At that particular time," he said, "they didn't have black quarterbacks."

So Mays's choice was made for him, though he insisted football was his "first" sport and "baseball was my last sport." Though his eighteenth birthday was almost two months away when the Black Barons resumed playing in April 1949, his weekend cameos at Rickwood Field generated passionate interest. The *World* called him "arrow-armed" Willie Mays, "sparkplug of the ginger-skinned Barons."

There were a few important changes on the 1949 Black Barons. First, shortstop Artie Wilson had been sold to the Cleveland Indians in the winter and then awarded to the New York Yankees in a controversial deal in which the Black Barons, Monarchs, Yankees, and Indians all sparred over who really owned him. The deal would prove to carry ramifications for Wilson, Piper, Bill Greason, and Willie Mays in 1949 and 1950.

Mays began the season as the permanent starting center fielder, displacing Bobby Robinson, who relocated to left field to replace Jimmy Zapp. Zapp had quit the Black Barons after the 1948 season because he resented being excluded from the Birmingham barnstorming team that traveled with Jackie Robinson's All-Stars. "I got very upset about that," Zapp said. "I did something in the spur of the moment that I should have never done. I told Tom Hayes to give me my release."

Hayes never forgave players who defied him. He suspended Zapp from the Negro American League, effectively blacklisting him. "Piper always used to say I was the biggest fool he had ever seen," Zapp said. "He said, 'You quit a championship team over a few dollars.'"

With Zapp gone, Mays would play center every day, between Robinson in left and Ed Steele in right. "One of the most improved players on the team is Willie Mays, shifted from left field to center field," the *World* reported. "He covers space like a tent and has a rifle arm." But Piper worried more about Mays's efforts to look good off the field.

He had the physical skills of a man, but soaked up the adulation like an ordinary teenage boy. "I didn't have many girls," Mays said of his rookie year, "but I got a lot of sleep."

Mays set out to change that in 1949, but he still had a lot to learn. Indianapolis Clowns pitcher Raydell Maddix remembered how he took two notes from two different girls, kept the name of the prettier one, and gave the other note to Mays, who was stunned to learn the lesser player had the hotter girl. But while Mays's eyes strayed, Piper's never did. He told Mays never to let off-the-field distractions interfere with his baseball career.

Mays kept doing his part on the field. When the Black Barons played the Louisville Buckeyes, the travel team formerly based in Cleveland, in April, "Willie Mays made two spectacular catches and scored a run after hammering a triple," the *World* wrote of a 7–4 loss in which Piper used four rookie pitchers and didn't trust any of them.

Piper knew he could trust his quarterback in center field. On Easter Sunday, April 17, the Black Barons joined a large contingent of Birmingham fans at Ponce de Leon Park in Atlanta to watch the Brooklyn Dodgers play an exhibition game against the Double-A Atlanta Crackers of the Southern Association. Mays was among the 25,221 fans who watched the Dodgers lose. When Jackie Robinson and the Dodgers were finished playing and left the field, so did most of the fans. The Black Barons and the Indianapolis Clowns played immediately afterward in front of only 5,000 fans, mostly locals from Birmingham. The stark contrast of interest and attendance demonstrated that things were already worse in 1949 than they had been in 1948.

When the Black Barons returned to Rickwood Field on April 30 to host their Negro American League home opener against the Houston Eagles, the Eagles provided another reminder of what was happening. Mays wouldn't turn eighteen for another week, but his future was much brighter than the league's. The Houston Eagles were formerly the Newark Eagles, the displaced franchise from the defunct Negro National League. But celebrating Mays was a happy diversion. He was summoned to participate in the first of hundreds of pregame

An emerging star at age eighteen, Willie Mays, with his combination of superior throwing, running, and quickly developing hitting skills, became a commodity among major league teams willing to sign a black player.

ceremonies in his career. "This event will see Fairfield I.H.S. honoring center fielder Willie Mays, one of their own products," the *World* reported. "He starred as a three-way letterman at FIHS and was selected by sportswriters as the Rookie of the Year for 1948." Mays was soaking up the adulation, and in the game against the Eagles, the *World* reported, "Mays made two great running catches."

Piper was right when he told Mays that people were watching. Boston Braves scout Bill Maughn became the first scout from white folks' ball to seriously understand how good Mays was. He saw the two catches the *World* referred to and never forgot the first great play he saw Mays make. "The left fielder [Bobby Robinson] for Birmingham couldn't throw," Maughn said. "[Houston] had runners on first and second and it was the second inning. The next batter hit the ball off the scoreboard and the left fielder got to it. The center fielder came running over yelling, 'Give it to me, give it to me,' and be-doggoned if the left fielder didn't shovel pass to him like a football player. The center fielder threw out the runner trying to go from first to third."

Maughn was amazed. He had never scouted a Black Barons game because his team, the Braves, had only recently started seeking black players. In October 1948, *New York Age* reporter Buster Miller had coaxed a confession from Boston Braves publicity director Bill Sullivan, who said the Braves were seriously looking at black players. "We have had standing instructions to our scouts for the past three years to be on the watch for Negro players," Sullivan said. "There is no club in either league more anxious to obtain some good Negro players than we are."

The Braves had signed their first black minor leaguer in 1947, California pitcher Nate Moreland, who the team called "a little too old" to bring up, despite his winning 20 games in the lower minors. In December 1948, the Braves signed their first black minor league position player, second baseman Waldon Williams, nineteen, who was born in Chicago and never played Negro League baseball, but played the jazz saxophone and took boxing lessons from Joe Louis in Harlem.

The Braves tried to buy Jackie Robinson or Roy Campanella from the Dodgers in the winter of 1948, but when Branch Rickey rebuffed their efforts, the Braves insisted that their most significant black player would not be purchased from the Dodgers, but would instead be discovered and signed by one of their own scouts.

"Sullivan also revealed that the Braves have their eye on at least two Negro players now but declined to give their names or identify their clubs for fear the information would send other major league clubs scurrying after them," the *Age* had reported late in 1948, noting that Sullivan said the Braves were interested in black players who played any position except first base, shortstop, and third base. Center field was deemed a position of need.

Maughn felt he had the answer in Mays, a player who would be as important to the Boston Braves as he would be to Maughn's career. Maughn had moved from scouting near his home in Ohio to the Deep South, which was a difficult job for any white scout. He had a built-in advantage because his new home in Cullman was only sixty miles away from Rickwood Field. Maughn wanted to spend the rest of his working life in baseball and knew that signing a player like Mays was a once-in-a-lifetime opportunity to catch the big fish, a player who would provide his reputation with unsurpassed collateral.

So Maughn knew he had to make noise without being loud, had to move without being seen, and had to develop a sense of timing for something he had never timed. He used his location to his advantage, paving a trail from his doorstep in Cullman to Mays's aunt Sarah's home outside Birmingham. He watched Mays play several times and hid on the roof of the press box where he thought he wouldn't be detected. "Not another scout was watching him," Maughn said. "I'd stand on the roof at Rickwood Field and I knew this guy was mine."

Maughn was the first white scout to learn the ground rules of signing Willie Mays. The main condition was that Mays was going to have to graduate from high school whether he liked it or not. Cat insisted on that, and Piper enforced that requirement. Maughn knew it made signing Mays more difficult, so he decided he would try to get around it the best he could. He began investigating and learned that Tom Hayes had set an asking price of $15,000 for his teenage center fielder. Maughn got permission from the Braves front office to offer $7,500 for Mays and another $7,500 if he remained with the organization after a specified date. Maughn made the offer early in the 1949 season, but Hayes told him he would get back to him.

"If Maughn had been given the opportunity to sign Mays in 1949," said Al LaMacchia, who was still pitching for the white Barons in 1949 but had struck up friendships with several scouts, including Maughn, "he would have been his."

Disappointed, Maughn told Mays that Hayes wouldn't let him go. Mays was disenchanted. If it had been up to him, he would have signed long before he graduated from high school. It was illegal for a scout to sign a white player before he graduated from high school, but no one had ever pressed the rules with a black player. Though black players considered the Negro American League a professional circuit, major league teams did not recognize it as such. Therefore, Maughn was in uncharted territory and was willing to discard the rules to sign the amateur Mays. "All he ever thought about was playing ball," Maughn said. "He was pleading with me to sign him."

Maughn was convinced that he was the only scout on Mays, but his assumption was far from the truth. Whenever he climbed the ladder to the top of the press box roof, he inevitably ran into Barons general manager Eddie Glennon, who quickly realized why Maughn was closely watching the Black Barons. Glennon respected Maughn, but he also didn't want him to sign Mays. Glennon felt that it was his responsibility to see to it that the Boston Red Sox, not the Braves, acquired Mays. Bob Scranton said, "Glennon used to give Maughn hell and say, 'The Red Sox are gonna sign him if you don't get your ass down there and sign him!' Maughn was convinced he had Mays for the Braves."

Glennon hadn't given up on Mays, but he had given up on trying to get Boston general manager Joe Cronin to pay attention to him. Glennon couldn't solve Cronin. He thought he had an amicable relationship stemming from the face-to-face deal he made with Cronin at the 1947 winter meetings to sign Birmingham's affiliation agreement with the Red Sox, but he had never heard from him again. Cronin was a pale ghost, who lived on his reputation as street-smart San Francisco kid turned all-star American League shortstop. He became general manager of the Red Sox before the 1948 season, but rarely left New England. He stayed holed up in his office at Fenway Park, gained a reputation as an executive who did not travel to see prospects, and failed to communicate with his scouts and minor league executives. He seemed to only trust his inner circle, which included special assignment scouts Larry Woodall and Hugh Duffy, farm director Johnny Murphy, and Pinky Higgins, the manager of the 1949 Barons.

Glennon knew that telling Higgins about Mays was a complete waste of time. A roughneck from Red Oak, Texas, Higgins wasn't shy about hiding his disdain for blacks. When he managed the Red Sox from 1955 to 1962, he famously barked, "There'll be no niggers on this ball club as long as I have anything to say about it."

So Glennon waited until George Digby arrived. Digby was a lowly territory scout based in New Orleans who had never played professional baseball and had only become a scout in 1945. He did not come to town specifically to see Mays, but to cover the white Barons as part of his assigned coverage of the Southern Association. As soon as Digby walked into Rickwood Field, Glennon was on top of him. "Glennon told me, 'The black club is coming in tomorrow and they have a player I'd like you to see.'"

Digby hesitated, but he couldn't resist Glennon's enthusiasm. He had no idea who Willie Mays was, but he couldn't believe what he saw. He broke the rules to watch two games and evaluated Mays with the era's standard alphabet scouting scale, formulating one grade for present skills and the other for future skills:

Willie Mays, CF, May, 1949
Birmingham Black Barons (colored leagues)
Scout: Digby
Games Seen: 2 (Birmingham)
Innings: 18
Body Type: Lean, athletic, muscular
Injuries: None
Glasses: No
Hit: A/A+
Power: A/A+
Run: A+/A+
Throw: A/A+
Field: A/A+
Major League Prospect: Yes
Recommended Signing Price: $4,000

Digby never filled out another report like it again. An A+ grade was never assigned because a scout could hang himself with such bravado. But Digby's confidence never wavered. He reported what a typical scouting manual said an A+ player should be: "This prospect will be a superstar, a very special player, consistent MVP candidate and the best at his respective position in the major leagues."

"He was developing things other players didn't have to develop," Digby said. Convinced he wanted Mays, he did further investigation, with Glennon as his guide. He spoke with Tom Hayes and didn't waste any time. "I said, 'How much will you take for Willie Mays?'" Digby, who said that he didn't know that the Braves had made an offer, reported that Hayes set the asking price for Mays at $4,000. It was substantially lower than the $15,000 offer Maughn had made and lower than the $10,000 asking price Hayes put on shortstop Artie Wilson after the 1948 season. Digby didn't know why the price was only $4,000, but he didn't ask any questions.

Yet Digby feared asking Cronin if he could sign Mays. Although Digby knew that Mays was a vastly superior player to popular Red Sox center fielder Dom DiMaggio, he wondered if he would be fired for turning in a black player. "When you're working for a ball club, you hear what the big guys had to say," Digby said. "It trickled down to everyone. They never came out and said, 'Don't sign any black players,' but the talk was that you had better not sign any."

Digby had seen baseball's Mozart, but Mozart wasn't supposed to be black. Digby decided that Mays was worth risking his job. He typed his report, put a copy in the mail, and called Fenway Park. He got Cronin on the line. He could feel the cold wind radiating from Boston. Digby took a deep breath and spoke up. "I can break the color line," he said.

Silence.

Digby wasn't sure how to proceed. He began describing Mays. "He was just a skinny kid, but he could do everything," he said. "He could catch the ball, he could throw the ball and he could hit. He looked like he had some power. I wanted him."

Digby said Cronin "was kind of aloof." He sensed he had crossed the line and that Cronin was deciding his fate. But he kept pressing. He went for broke. He asked for permission to sign Mays, but Cronin shot him down. Digby hid his devastation. "He said, 'No, no, no, don't do anything like that. I'll send somebody to look at him.'"

Digby pressed again, pushing Cronin's patience. But instead of thanking his scout for sending him arguably the most talented player of his generation, Cronin demolished Digby for asking to sign a black player. He abruptly ended the conversation, telling Digby to resume his minor league coverage. "You're scouting the Southern Association," Cronin said. "I'll send Larry Woodall down there."

"That's what he told me," Digby said. "I know $4,000 was a lot of money for a player coming out of the colored leagues, but it was a very reasonable amount for a white player. Mays was so quick with the bat. I saw him hit balls to left-center field. You should have seen him at that age. He developed just like I thought he would."

Digby told Glennon that Cronin wouldn't let him sign Mays. The experience left a bitter taste in Digby's mouth. He didn't care if Mays was black. He thought it shouldn't have mattered. He thought Mays could play and that's all that should matter. "After what they did to me with Mays, I didn't look to scout black players because I knew the Red Sox didn't want them," he said.

Glennon thought the Red Sox were finished with looking at Mays, but he didn't know that Cronin was thinking and planning. As Digby left the ballpark, Bill Maughn thought that if Glennon couldn't get the Red Sox to bite, then Mays was going to go from the Birmingham Black Barons to the Boston Braves in 1950. He continued to watch Mays, convinced that he was the only scout sitting on Willie Mays in 1949. Maughn was right in one respect. He was the only white scout tailing Mays.

There were only a handful of white teams in 1949 that realized that if they wanted to effectively scout the Negro Leagues, they needed to hire black scouts. Among them were Chuck Esmoke of the Browns, Elwood Parsons of the Dodgers, and Dizzy Dismukes, the Kansas City Monarchs traveling secretary who earned an annual salary of $250 from the New York Yankees to be a part-time scout. The job was arranged for him by Tom Baird, who promised Yankees junior executive Lee MacPhail that "Dizzy is not the type of fellow that would try to get you to take every player he has heard of."

There was a time when everyone had heard of John Donaldson, whom the Chicago White Sox had hired as baseball's first full-time black scout on June 29, 1949. Sitting among the gamblers and the garbage men, the preachers and the petty thieves, arm in arm with everyday black folks who naturally assumed he was from Birmingham, was the former pitcher whose talents were once unmatched. Donaldson was Satchel Paige before Satchel Paige, only he was left-handed instead of right-handed, and as modest as Paige was extravagant. Tattered box scores from three decades of forgotten barnstorming games around the country indicate that he recorded at least 300 victories and struck out at least 5,000 batters. Legend had it that Ty Cobb said Donaldson threw the best left-handed curveball he had ever seen. New York Giants manager John McGraw claimed Donaldson would have been worth $50,000 if he were a white pitcher. Many speculated it was McGraw who had offered Donaldson thousands of dollars if he would agree to be smuggled through Cuba to New York on the condition that he shed his identity, but Donaldson would not compromise his color. "I am not ashamed," he said. "It would have meant renouncing my family. I was never again to visit my mother or have anything to do with colored people. I refused."

Instead, Donaldson pitched gate games for as long as he could throw the ball over the plate. After his pitching career, he vanished from baseball for about a decade, working for the Chicago post office before he surfaced in 1948 as a scout covering the Negro Leagues for the White Sox. He was the first former Negro League star player to try to build his career inside a white front office. Donaldson had to scrape by on year-to-year contracts with the White Sox, who he suspected were using him more for show than scouting.

He learned he would have a much harder time acquiring the top black players than white scouts had signing top white players, so he needed to be very selective, turning in only players he was certain could play well in the majors. He had to succeed because there was nothing left for him in Negro baseball. He lived the good years of the Negro Leagues and fled in the final years. "Take 30 years off Donaldson's age," the *Chicago Defender* wrote, "and he could sign with the White Sox as a starting pitcher."

Donaldson naturally had an eye for pitchers. He compiled a follow list, starting with right-handers Bill Powell and Bill Greason of the Black Barons. He also liked Monarchs right-hander Connie Johnson. Donaldson was a gifted hitter who had played the outfield when he wasn't pitching, so his scouting eye wasn't limited to the mound. He liked Sam Hairston, the former Black Barons and ACIPCO catcher who was playing for the Indianapolis Clowns. He liked another catcher, Bill Cash, of the Philadelphia Stars. He thought Bob Boyd of the Memphis Red Sox and Bob Wilson of the Houston Eagles were the best infielders. He liked Monarchs outfielders Elston Howard and Bob Thurman, and he already knew about teenage shortstop Ernie Banks, whom the Monarchs were hiding on lower-level teams. But more than any other black player, even more than Banks, John Donaldson wanted Willie Mays, the player who could give him more credibility than all the strikeouts in the world.

A few weeks before the Black Barons struck out on the first road jump of the summer of 1949, Piper had a visitor. It was to be the first trip in which Willie Mays would accompany the team on its annual East Coast trip that included stops at the Polo Grounds in New York City to play the Cubans; Brooklyn to play the semipro Bushwicks within walking distance of the home of the Dodgers, Ebbets Field; Philadelphia to play the Baltimore Elite Giants; and finally the heart of Red Sox territory, West Haven, Connecticut, to play a semipro team called the Erie Sailors.

The rain wouldn't let up on Sunday, May 14, but the Black Barons and Chicago American Giants played through it. Money was tight, so neither team could afford to sit. Mays collected three hits and threw out a runner at home plate with a heavy waterlogged ball. After the game, Red Sox scout Larry Woodall asked Piper for the team's schedule, which included the game in West Haven.

Woodall had seen Mays on a good day, throwing the ball so sharply that he could make it drip dry. He had seen Mays hit and confirmed Digby's observations. Eddie Glennon could surely inform him that Mays was untouchable until May 1950. There was nothing else Woodall needed to see, yet despite Piper confirming that Woodall asked him for the Black Barons schedule, Woodall claimed he had never seen Mays. Born was the long-standing fable that the Red Sox missed Willie Mays because the game Woodall scouted was rained out. "When he came home, he still hadn't seen Mays in action," Boston sportswriter Al Hirshberg wrote.

Piper didn't think too much of a scout asking him for the team's schedule. Every chance for the Black Barons to be seen, even if they were only coming to see Mays, was precious. Woodall was acting on Cronin's orders, completely independent from George Digby. Piper thought the Red Sox were more interested in Mays than they were in him.

Mays could play in the big leagues, and now. The Red Sox knew it; so did the Boston Braves and the Chicago White Sox. What no other team knew was that the way to get him did not necessarily run through Rickwood Field. It ran through the Polo Grounds in New York City, where Mays was about to play for the first time when the Black Barons left town for their annual East Coast summer jump.

THE GOOSE SHOOTER

Center field at the Polo Grounds was wide and intimidating, a place few outfielders could reach and where fewer lingered. The first time that Willie Mays stood on the green-and-brown grass on May 29, 1949, he took one look around the empty outfield and thought he would have no problem covering such a great amount of ground. He was playing center field for the Black Barons against the New York Cubans only a few weeks after his eighteenth birthday, and it never occurred to him who might be watching.

In the first inning, Mays intently watched Cubans infielder Ray Dandridge at the plate, unaware that the New York Giants officials who were in the ballpark to scout Dandridge were also there to see him play. Dandridge longed to play in the big leagues. Black players considered him the best third baseman of his generation, a bowlegged little man who scraped six feet tall in a good pair of spikes. Offensively, Dandridge could murder you with searing line drives that banged against the outfield walls if they didn't clear the fence. He had made

$10,000 playing for Vera Cruz in the Mexican League during the 1947 season and then turned down overtures from Bill Veeck to sign with the Cleveland Indians when he learned there was no bonus money involved.

It was Negro American League opening day for the Cubans, and though he had played in more opening days in more countries than he could remember, Dandridge knew this double-header was monumentally important. This was an arranged audition, orchestrated by Alex Pompez for Carl Hubbell, and in his office overlooking center field sat Giants owner Horace Stoneham. Dandridge rubbed dirt on his hands, shaved five years off his age, gripped his bat, and ripped Jimmy Newberry and Bill Greason. His line drives kept Mays sprinting across the outfield grass. In front of a crowd of 7,500 fans, Dandridge went 2-for-3 against Newberry and tripled in Birmingham's 8–4 win, then found Greason and Alonzo Perry to his liking in the second game, going 3-for-5 with another triple. "Man, that boy could swing a bat," Greason said. "We could not get him out."

Dandridge was as smooth with the glove as he was with the bat, turning a graceful double play at second base. He believed he had many more good years left and prayed for a shot. *New York Age* columnist Dan Burley, whose influential public campaign helped pressure the Giants into signing black players, noted the energy in the air. "There was teeming anticipation in the ballpark," he wrote. "There was a definite interest in what was going on."

The Black Barons knew something was happening when hard-throwing right-handed pitcher Dave Barnhill was held out of both games. It was a sure sign that a sale was imminent. After the double-header, Dandridge and Barnhill were summoned to Stoneham's office where Pompez and Hubbell waited. The Giants purchased both players for $7,500 and assigned their contracts to Class B Trenton. Barnhill wished he could have received a percentage of his sales price, but Dandridge didn't argue this time. He let Pompez pocket all of the money because he knew time was running out. "I just wanted to put my left foot in there," Dandridge said of playing in the majors. When secretary Jack Schwarz slid the contract across the table, Dandridge turned up his nose at nature. "I lied," he said. "I told them I was 30."

Age was the issue for black players as far as Hubbell was concerned. He felt he couldn't take them at their word, so he relied on his eyes. The Giants had purchased outfielders Monte Irvin from the Newark Eagles and Hank Thompson from Tom Baird and the Kansas City Monarchs after the 1948 season. Hubbell thought both players were safe bets. They debuted with the Giants in early July, but the public was hungry for more, clamoring as a black fan named Scotty wrote to the *Age* in 1948:

> You would think I would have fallen in with the crowds when Jackie came to the Dodgers (Dem Bums, I mean), but no, I remained a real, true, dyed in the wool Giant fan of the Right Field Bleacher Corporation in good standing. And what has it gotten me? Heartaches, frustration, disillusion. I dash to pick up my morning newspaper only to see 'Giants buy two Negroes for tryouts,' but as usual, it's the same old headline: "Jackie wins game with steal of home." Why, why, why was I born in Harlem? But with the way times are changing so fast, we Giants and Yankee fans haven't got to wait long before we'll be seeing a dashing brown, black or high-yaller figure chasing a fly ball out there on the field.

Mays had his youth, which is what every talented black player wished for, on display in both games of the double-header that the teams split by identical 8–4 scores. Mays showed the Giants he was ready a year before they could sign him. The true selling point was the bat. He went 0-for-3 in the first game, but found his stroke in the second game when he went 2-for-4 with two runs batted in and a solo home run in the ninth inning. The tantalizing combination of speed, arm, and power was too much to ignore. "One thing you cannot erase from a ballplayer is hitting for power," scout George Genovese said. "You can't give power to somebody that doesn't have power. That's a natural thing, like a great arm or great speed."

Hubbell saw that Mays had power, but he didn't want to talk to him yet. He learned the details from Pompez, who related that Tom Hayes only wished to deal directly with team executives rather than scouts because of the way he had been treated by other major league teams, most notably the New York Yankees over Artie Wilson. Hubbell didn't want to lose Mays to the hated Yankees, who needed a replacement for DiMaggio, so he kept a low profile, knowing he needed to win Hayes's trust. Hubbell stayed in touch with Pompez during the season, and through Pompez he had indirect communication with Hayes.

Hubbell knew the rules had been established that Mays could not sign until after he graduated in 1950. But now Hubbell had seen Mays play a full year before the Giants could actually sign him. Piper remained the go-between, the protector, and the mentor. "If the scouts were in the stands," Greason said, "Piper spoke to them in a discreet way."

Most importantly, Horace Stoneham himself was now aware of Willie Mays. "Stoneham doesn't need the reports of scouts," Burley wrote. "He can see star Negro players from his own lounge and office in centerfield at the Polo Grounds."

The Brooklyn Dodgers were playing the Boston Braves at Ebbets Field the day Mays played center field in the double-header at the Polo Grounds. Harlem fans held transistor radios to their ears to hear Red Barber describe Jackie Robinson's two-run single in the seventh inning against left-hander Warren Spahn to lead the Dodgers to a 3–2 victory before 24,249 fans. The Dodger fans weren't aware that Mays had already played against Robinson in Birmingham in 1948. They would have been stunned to learn that the Dodgers missed detecting Mays when he was only a few blocks away from Ebbets Field a day after he played at the Polo Grounds.

Mays and the Black Barons arrived in Brooklyn to play the Bushwicks, a motley collection of former minor leaguers who played baseball with the reckless passion of bandits who didn't care if they were washed up. The configuration of their field was strange, as were the attitudes of the white ballplayers. "We had played in a lot of ball-parks, but I think the strangest one, rather than the Polo Grounds, was over in Brooklyn, called the Bushwick," Mays said. "Now that was strange, more so than the Polo Grounds, because they had all these ex-players over there."

The Bushwicks were in Dodger territory, and though general manager Joe Press's loyalty rested with the Yankees, they were testing his patience. Many of the Bushwicks' best players were former Yankee minor leaguers who had been released. Yankees chief scout Paul Krichell sent Press secondhand talent on the condition that Press hide prospects when he was asked to. When the Yankees wanted to sign an amateur prospect before he graduated, the player might turn up with the Bushwicks, where Press would give him a false identity to throw competing scouts off the trail. It wasn't uncommon. Genovese, an infielder who grew up on Staten Island, was discovered by Washington Senators scout Joe Cambria, who offered him a minor league contract on the condition that he sign it before graduation and not tell his parents.

Krichell was a master at hiding talented ballplayers. He buried Lou Gehrig in the bush leagues under false names before signing him in 1921 out of Columbia University. That's why Mays was correct when he thought the Bushwicks had a strange feel. Nobody knew anybody's real name.

When Press saw Mays, he made sure to get his name correct. While Joe DiMaggio's body was breaking down in 1949, every Yankee scout clamored to be the savior who replaced the savior. But Press knew the Yankees were resisting signing black players. While Mays watched Ebbets Field vanish from sight as Charlie Rudd's bus passed through Brooklyn on the way to Baltimore, the Dodgers weren't the only team in New York who had missed their first shot at Willie Mays. So had the Yankees.

"It is quite hard for me to understand your complete turnaround as far as the Negro baseball players are concerned," Press wrote to Krichell. "Within the past two years I have given you reports on practically every player, with the exception of a very few, who have since signed with other teams. You could have had practically all of them, just for the asking. A few of those I mentioned to you were Art Wilson and Orestes Minoso and there are still more of these, whom, in my opinion, would fit in Organized Baseball without any trouble. They are Piper Davis, infielder, and Mays, outfielder, both of the Birmingham Black Barons."

It wasn't the first time the Yankees had rejected Birmingham players, an attitude that was reflected in an anonymous 1948 scouting report. The report called Piper Davis "a good ballplayer," but concluded, "If he wasn't good enough for the Browns two years ago, I don't believe he could make it with the Yankees now."

The report showed the scout catering to the Yankees' institutional racism. "There isn't an outstanding Negro player that anybody could recommend to step into the big leagues and hold down a regular job," the scout concluded. "The better players in Negro baseball are past the age for the big leagues. Several years ago I could have named several players that could more than hold their own in the big leagues. Several of them would have been stars, but now I know of not one that would stick."

Pitches crushed into the deepest part of the outfield had a way of sticking in Mays's glove. A few days later in Philadelphia, where the Black Barons played the Baltimore Elite Giants in a Sunday double-header and in a Monday night game, pitcher Joe Black couldn't wait to take his best rip against Bill Greason. The two had an amicable trash-talking relationship and vowed to throw nothing but their hardest fastballs against each other. Greason humped up and his heater flattened out, much to Black's liking, who drove the pitch deep to center field. "I had given the ball a ride," Black wrote. "While running to first base I glanced at the ball in flight and noticed an outfielder racing toward the fence in left center field. I laughed to myself because I knew that I had a double or a triple, but when I rounded first base my grin turned to chagrin. The outfielder had caught my long drive and was throwing the ball to an infielder. While trotting back to our dugout, I mumbled some unprintable words." Black sat next to second baseman Jim Gilliam. Before Black asked the question, Gilliam was ready with the answer: "That's Willie Mays, a young high school boy."

If Boston Red Sox scout Larry Woodall was following normal procedures, there's a good chance that he was watching the games Sunday and Monday. He would have seen Mays make the outstanding catch, and he also would have seen Black strike out Piper in a crucial situation, then let his emotions get the better of him when he directed an unsportsmanlike gesture at Piper. Monday night, Piper got his revenge, showing his talent and his instincts. Black hurriedly warmed up and entered the game with the bases loaded in the eighth inning of a tied game specifically to pitch to Piper, who hadn't forgotten Black's gesture. "He threw me a fastball and I missed," Piper said. "Then he came back with that curveball. BAM! Now I'm runnin' like the devil. When I made my turn, I saw the umpire call it a home run. When I got to second base, I looked for Black, and I done him like he done me."

The following night, the Black Barons were in East Haven, Connecticut, to play the semipro West Haven Sailors. Woodall followed the Black Barons in, and this time he had company. Piper remembered two Red Sox scouts watching the Black Barons. One of the scouts talked to Nat Pollard, the sore-armed pitcher who was the team's road secretary in 1949. Piper distinctly remembered Pollard saying, "Hey, some scouts out here want to see you."

The second scout was most likely Hugh Duffy or farm director Johnny Murphy, both Cronin's senior advisors. Al Hirshberg later wrote that the older scouts were responsible for not signing Mays. "It was these men, really, the older scouts, who can be blamed for the club's failure to get a top black player when plenty of good ones were available." But Hirshberg, Boston's unofficial revisionist historian, didn't know the entire story. If George Digby didn't consider Piper a Red Sox type of player, Woodall and his associate certainly did not either. But they had seen Mays now, and if they had inquired about him, they would have learned that Tom Hayes was not considering selling him until after his graduation in May 1950. The Red Sox had never seriously considered signing a black player, but Mays's talent forced the front office to question their policy. If they signed Mays, they knew public opinion in Boston might not be immediately favorable. Before they signed Mays, the Red Sox would need to condition their fan base and also have a minor-league roommate arranged for him.

There was an ulterior benefit to signing Piper Davis for the Red Sox. It was an old, dirty scouting trick Branch Rickey called "the goose shooter method." It was often employed with brothers. If a team considered a younger brother a prospect and an older brother a non-prospect, it would sign the older brother to entice the younger brother to sign with the team that had so kindly brought aboard his big brother. Then the younger brother would go off to the minor leagues, often to be teammates with his older brother during his first summer. The older brother would provide companionship and encouragement for his kid brother, but once the younger brother learned to walk on his own, the goose shooter was almost always discarded.

When Piper walked out of the dressing room, he recognized Woodall, who had asked for his schedule back in Birmingham. Piper remembered how impatient and nearly condescending Woodall acted. He was told that the Red Sox had come specifically for him. He said his luggage was at the hotel in New York and that he only had his shaving kit and his street clothes. Woodall told him it was enough. Piper hated the idea of jumping the Black Barons, detested the idea of becoming a mercenary, but he had no choice. "I knew what I wanted," he said. "To educate my kids."

So Piper turned the team over to Pepper Bassett and went with the two scouts to Boston, where they arrived in the middle of the night and checked him into a downtown hotel. Woodall dismissed Piper with a curt order to call down for his breakfast in the morning and to wait for Joe Cronin in the lobby. The two scouts departed and Piper never saw them again.

In the morning, Piper ate breakfast and waited in the lobby. Finally, Cronin, wearing his omnipresent double-breasted suit with his blond hair slicked back, strode into the lobby. He possessed the stocky physique of a former ballplayer who had put on a few extra pounds. If you caught him in the correct profile, he might resemble comedian Bob Hope, but his personality was terse and distant. Proud and Irish, a seven-time American League All-Star, Cronin was described by George Digby as a man "who didn't go out on ballplayers." Both Piper and Cronin were player-managers and top infielders in their respective leagues, but Cronin did not see Piper at a level perspective. He never called him by his name, only by the obtuse and generic nickname "Slugger."

Cronin told his black slugger he wanted to sign him. "You have to buy my contract from Tom Hayes," Piper dutifully replied. He told

Cronin that after the Browns lowballed him in 1947, he and Hayes had agreed that he would receive a cut of his sale to white folks' ball. White teams hated that. It automatically made the price of Hayes's players steeper than white teams felt obligated to play. Cronin seemed surprised. Piper remembered the conversation very well.

"How much will he give you out of $7,500?" asked Cronin.

"Maybe $1,500 or better," said Piper.

"How much will he give you out of $10,000?" asked Cronin.

"Maybe $2,000 or better," said Piper.

"How much will he give you out of $15,000?" Cronin suggested.

Cronin was talking about a lot of money. Piper thought white teams only paid major league money for major league players. He thought that boded well for him. He never thought for a moment that he was the goose shooter. Cronin noticed the silence after Piper's normally quick replies.

"I tell you what we'll do. We'll give Tom Hayes $7,500 and if you're with our organization after May 15, 1950, we'll give you another $7,500."

Piper called Hayes. He quickly made a deal in which Hayes would pay Piper $1,800 of the first $7,500 and Hayes and Piper would split the other $7,500 in half. Piper told Hayes to call the Red Sox and accept the deal. "Get on the phone," he said.

It was unspoken between Cronin and Piper that the deal was to remain a secret. Cronin didn't want to notify any of his minor league clubs that he was sending them a black player until he absolutely needed to. Piper would finish the 1949 season with the Black Barons, including his last East-West All-Star game at Chicago's Comiskey Park. He would then go to minor league spring training in 1950 as the first Negro player signed by the Boston Red Sox. The dates never crossed Piper's mind, but the timing of the goose shooter was enormous. The Red Sox knew roughly when Mays would become eligible to sign. The May 15 option date was ten days away from Mays's May 25 high school graduation. It should have been close enough. If the Red Sox kept Piper for an extra $7,500, they would have the perfect minor league roommate for Willie Mays.

Mays observed what was occurring around him. "We had to create different things among ourselves," he said. "When you bought a car, you had to buy it from the right guy." Buying ballplayers from the right guy was no different. The 1949 East-West All-Star Game promised to be Negro baseball's last great used car sale. Piper rejoined his team and a few weeks later took Bill Greason, Herman Bell, and shortstop Jose Burgos with him from the Black Barons to play in the game. Burgos was Artie Wilson's replacement, a Puerto Rican player supplied to Hayes by Alex Pompez. Wilson's transaction was still being resolved when Hayes received a letter dated August 13 from a minor league general manager confirming the Red Sox's purchase of Piper:

Dear Mr. Hayes:

Mr. Joseph Cronin, General Manager of the Red Sox, called me today to tell me that he arranged for the Scranton Club to purchase the contract of Lorenzo Piper Davis. Enclosed you will find our check for $7,500 which is the amount Mr. Cronin says was agreed upon. Will you please send us the necessary papers stating that he purchased player Davis for the sum stipulated on the enclosed check?

James F. Murray
President
Scranton Electric City Baseball Club

Hayes immediately thought the Red Sox were trying to get Piper for less than they promised. He was angry that the letter said nothing of the back end of the deal in which the Red Sox would owe another $7,500 after May 15, 1950. He tussled right back, but he had the term dates of the agreement incorrect, confusing May with March in his August 23 reply:

I am in receipt of your check for $7,500 on the purchase price of Lorenzo "Piper" Davis. It was agreed with Mr. Joseph Cronin of the Boston Red Sox that I should receive this $7,500 as paid and the balance of $7,500 when Davis reported in March 1950. The total price agreed upon was $15,000. Your letter does not make the total purchase price clear nor does the date the balance is to be paid. I am holding your check for reply.

Hayes was holding the futures of Piper and Mays in his hands. He had two things to gain from selling Piper to the Red Sox. If he could sell them Piper, he could sell them Mays and could try to become a black farm club for the Red Sox. Such a deal would provide a much-needed financial windfall for a team that was struggling so mightily that Hayes could only find crowds in small towns where Negro baseball was still a novelty, compelling the *World* to report in summer 1949, "The Birmingham Black Barons are touring tank towns and drawing crowds. Some of those cities the club recently played in Mississippi couldn't be found on a relief map." Things had deteriorated so much that in August when the team returned to Rickwood Field after a road trip, the deputy sheriff arrested pitcher Sammy C. Williams for skipping out on a $22.43 grocery bill and trainer Roosevelt Atkins on a $37.22 bill at another grocery store. Hayes was ordered to court to settle the debts. Money was tight, but so was the comparatively wealthy Hayes. The desperate signs should have been impossible to miss. While Hayes was holding a $7,500 check, his Black Barons were stealing groceries to eat.

When Piper, Greason, Bell, and Burgos arrived at the all-star game in Chicago, there were two players noticeably missing: Willie Mays from the Black Barons and Elston Howard from the Kansas City Monarchs. They were the two best young players in the Negro American League. The East-West game was still considered an event where a black player could be seen and signed. *Pittsburgh Courier* columnist Wendell Smith wrote that players were "especially anxious because no less than eight major league scouts have already notified league headquarters that they will be on hand to see the fray." Just as Hank Thompson had been left off both 1948 All-Star Game rosters before he was signed by the Giants, the absence of Mays and Howard indicated that Tom Hayes and Tom Baird were both hiding their best players, fearful that exposing them to other clubs would jeopardize the fragile under-the-table agreements they thought they had working with other teams. In the case of Hayes, he knew he had Pompez and the Giants eager to take Mays, and was well aware that White Sox scout John Donaldson would be at Comiskey Park. He also wanted to see if his contact with the Boston Braves or Boston Red Sox would drive up Mays's price. Baird, for his part, already had aspirations of selling Howard to the New York Yankees.

This East-West game had more tension, because in the stands was Commissioner A. B. "Happy" Chandler and his aide, Dick Butler. This was a show of force on Chandler's behalf to major league teams not to raid Negro League teams without gaining proper authorization from organized baseball. Also lingering in the crowd was Yankee scout Tom Greenwade, who only two weeks before had purchased Bob Thurman and Earl Taborn for $7,500 from Baird's Monarchs. Greenwade boasted that "I'm still a busher," though his minor league pitching career is suspect and his on-the-field talents paled in comparison to those of the extremely humble Donaldson, who was there to see Bill Greason pitch. Greason was Donaldson's goose shooter to get Willie Mays, though Donaldson really did consider Greason a major league prospect. Donaldson and the other scouts settled in to watch a game in which eight Negro League All-Stars who participated eventually reached the majors.

A crowd of 26,967 came to the game, a strong showing but a substantial drop-off from the attendance of 50,000 during the war years. Piper was the manager of the West team and some members of the black press thought he would start Greason over Kansas City's Gene Richardson based on the animosity between the two teams. But Piper didn't play such games. He wanted Richardson to start the game because his 11–4 record was superior, but Richardson gave up two runs and four hits in three innings, and Piper called on Greason.

Greason took the ball and began pumping strikes, throwing three scoreless innings in what he called one of the highlights of his career. John Donaldson watched him pitch with his superiors, John Rigney and George Toporczer. "After the game, the men from the White Sox wanted to see me," Greason said. When he was informed that the

White Sox wanted to purchase him, he dutifully informed them that they had to speak to Hayes, who was at the game. Donaldson told Hayes the White Sox wanted two of his players: Greason and Willie Mays.

Hayes liked Donaldson's gentlemanly nature enough to give him his office address in Memphis, but he also received him apprehensively because of his pitching pedigree. Donaldson had won his fame as a pitcher for the All-Nations team, which was operated by J. L. Wilkinson, a Kansas City baseball man. "Donaldson suggested the name, 'Monarchs,'" Wilkinson told the *Kansas City Call* in 1948. "Right away, the name sounded good." Though Donaldson considered his association with the Monarchs long over, it was difficult for Hayes to trust one because of the other.

If Hayes was asked about Mays, he kept his mouth shut. But he couldn't do the same about Piper. Despite the fact that the Red Sox wanted the deal done quietly, Wendell Smith heard the rumors and asked Piper if it was true. "No one had told me anything about it," he told the *Courier*. Smith didn't believe him. He sought out the reclusive Hayes and pressed him. Hayes relented, confirming to Smith that Piper was sold to the Red Sox and would report next spring. Privately, Piper was infuriated. He didn't want Joe Cronin to think he had violated his trust. Smith's scoop made national news, but Cronin refused immediate comment. The *Chicago Defender* did not quote Piper, Hayes, or Cronin, but curiously mentioned that the New York Giants had also been interested in Piper. The *Birmingham World*, however, knew something didn't add up about Boston's interest in Piper, because they knew he wasn't the best player anymore.

"Local fans of the Magic City direct their eyes upon Willie Mays, sensational ball-hitting centerfielder of the Birmingham Black Barons," the *World* wrote. "Sonny boy Mays, the youthful spitfire from Fairfield, from an age point of view has the advantage over many of the players from the Negro American League. Davis is around the 30-year mark and the question is: Could he last four or five more years in the majors?"

The *World* loved Piper, but it was a fair question. Why had the Red Sox signed the older Piper instead of the younger Mays?

Perhaps it was best that Mays had stayed in Birmingham that weekend, where the Black Barons played the Chicago American Giants and old friends Lyman Bostock and Tommy Sampson. A few weeks later, on August 27, *Chicago Defender* sportswriter Russ J. Cowans published the first national profile of Mays, complete with a posed publicity shot, the first famous photograph of his baseball career. Cowans wrote the first words of the Mays legend, recounting his three-sport success at Fairfield High while omitting that Mays was raised by his aunt and didn't live with his parents. He regaled his audience about Mays's stubborn slump to start the 1948 season, but how under the wise guidance of fatherly Piper Davis he found his swing and led the Barons to the Negro World Series with a dramatic playoff victory over the Kansas City Monarchs. The headline offered a tantalizing glimpse of the future and a dire warning to older players trapped in the hot box: "Move Over You Vets! Willie Mays Is Coming Up Like a Prairie Fire."

Mays's powerful throwing arm was well known around the Negro American League. Veteran catcher Pepper Bassett's praise offered validity. "The base runners don't take any liberties with Willie's arm," Bassett said. "He has one of the best arms in the game." Tom Hayes made it clear that he understood that Willie was a valuable commodity. "That kid looks good to me," he said. "Already, some of the major league scouts have been looking him over, but he'll cost a lot of money."

Hayes believed that Mays would become the best professional baseball player to ever rise from Birmingham. "I think Willie will be the best player ever developed by the Barons," he said. "That's a big statement, particularly when I recall men like Satchel Paige, Mule Suttles, Harry Salmon, Piper Davis, and many others who have won fame in Birmingham uniforms."

Mays continued to win fame during the 1949 season, when despite Birmingham's nomadic, slumming existence, his talent was impossible to hide. There were more glaring moments that indicated Mays's brilliance, moments that occurred with little attention. Among them was the game in July at Rickwood Field against the Philadelphia Stars, whose manager, Oscar Charleston, before Mays was considered the best center fielder in Negro League history. Mays obliged his gifted predecessor when he went 5-for-6 against the Stars. Charleston, his muscular torso having surrendered to a soft belly and his once nimble legs needing every inch of his baggy uniform pants, waved his hat in appreciation.

The Black Barons played a series against the Monarchs in late August, where Mays showed the Monarchs—and by association, the New York Yankees—what he could do one last time. In one game, manager Buck O'Neil told his pitchers to walk Mays three times. In another game, Mays belted a 387-foot home run, further proof that his home run power was coming in like wisdom teeth. Finally, in a 3–2 victory in fifteen innings in Montgomery, Mays made a throw O'Neil never bothered to mention. "Willie Mays picked up a drive against the left centerfield wall and threw a perfect strike to third base to nip the base runner in the seventh. The ball carried the distance in the air," the *Montgomery Advertiser* reported. The Monarchs never went after a black player from Birmingham until 1954, when O'Neil found a young left-handed pitcher that the Kansas City Monarchs absolutely had to own.

After the season, Piper made plans to play winter ball so he could arrive at spring training in top shape for the Red Sox. Alex Pompez organized another barnstorming tour, again securing Jackie Robinson and Roy Campanella. Mays was again invited to play for the Black Barons when the team came to Birmingham. Winfield Welch reprised his role as travel team manager. Abe Saperstein wrote to Tom Hayes, informing him that Welch had successfully recruited Artie Wilson to play for the Black Barons against the Robinson All-Stars for the game at Rickwood Field before Wilson went to winter ball. "This will be a lineup that will include many outstanding names and certainly 1,001 publicity angles," Saperstein wrote.

But when the 15,721 fans piled into Rickwood Field on an October night, it wasn't Robinson, Campanella, Larry Doby, or Don Newcombe they remembered so well. It wasn't even hometown hero Artie Wilson, who doffed his hat to his loving fans, nor was it the Robinson All-Stars' 9–3 victory over the Black Barons. It was Willie Mays, a high school senior, who was the best player on a field of big league all-stars.

"This kid was playing center field," Campanella wrote in his 1959 autobiography *It's Good to Be Alive*. "We had Larry Doby on third base and Larry was a real speed demon in those days. Somebody hit a fly ball to center field. The kid caught the ball, making that fancy bread-basket catch of his, and threw Doby out at the plate. I didn't believe it. I can't recall what he did at the plate. All I remember is that throw and what a beauty it was."

Campanella, who had once tried to get the Dodgers to sign Black Barons pitcher Bill Powell, couldn't resist. He dropped a dime in a pay phone and called Brooklyn general manager Branch Rickey, urging the Dodgers to send a scout to see Mays. Rickey sent Wid Matthews, the same southern scout who had dismissed Piper Davis in 1945. It was the wrong scout for the wrong assignment. Matthews claimed that Mays couldn't hit, though Mays was credited with a .311 batting average for 1949. When Rickey left the Dodgers for the Pirates in September 1950, Matthews fled to the Chicago Cubs, where he became scouting and minor league director. He formed a close relationship with Monarchs owner Tom Baird, writing to him in 1956 that "it is fellows like you we should not lose."

When Pompez left town with Jackie Robinson and his barnstorming team, Mays put his money in his pocket and returned to his mundane life as a high school student. It was no fun. He longed for 1950 to begin, when he would finish out his career as a Black Baron in the spring before he hopefully signed a contract with a white folks' ball team after graduation. Still, so much was uncertain. Scouts had seen and loved him, but he felt blocked, constricted by rules and owners. He had no idea how important Pompez was going to be to his career in 1950, or how Artie Wilson was trying to get him to California long before he ever dreamed he would play there. Wid Matthews had thought Baird was the kind of person baseball should not lose. Funny. The same could have been said of Willie Mays.

"WAIT UNTIL YOU SEE MAYS"

Artie Wilson was Oakland's coolest cat. When he wasn't playing shortstop, he was nattily attired in a sport coat, slacks, and loafers with matching socks, topped off by his trademark bebop cap. Artie wore a different cap every day of the week, always in vibrant colors that matched his glowing mood. His hats wouldn't work for everyone but they did for him. He loved the relative tranquillity of playing baseball in Oakland, and the fans, both black and white, loved him right back.

Oakland was growing richly diverse, infused with southern blacks who had migrated for industry jobs during the war years. Whatever discrimination Artie encountered was easier to handle than it had been in Birmingham. The Pacific Coast League, home to the Oaks, was generally more accepting of Negro players than any other white league in organized baseball, and Artie was Oakland's first black ballplayer.

There was a fan in Sacramento who used to lean over the dugout railing and wail at Artie, who said, "He called me names I never even heard." Artie flashed a smile and asked the fan his name. What worked for Artie didn't work for everyone. "That fella got to be my best friend when he saw he didn't get me all riled up," he said.

Artie's personality could soften the toughest soul. He even melted his new double-play partner, the young second baseman Billy Martin, a don't-mess-with-me Italian kid from the Berkeley projects who grew up picking fights with guys twice his size.

Artie wore Oakland like a tailored wardrobe. Many newly rooted southern black fans remembered him well from his winning four Negro American League batting titles for the Black Barons. Artie joined the Oaks on May 22, 1949, cast off by the New York Yankees, who fought for him for months and then sold him within minutes. The Oaks were an independent team owned by Brick Laws and managed by Charlie Dressen, who immediately installed Wilson as his starting shortstop.

Dressen worked with Artie to hit the ball to right field and to smooth out his defense. He helped Artie learn how white folks' ball was different from Negro baseball, and Artie helped Dressen understand that black players were distinctive individuals learning to play with white players who had all been trained the same way. Playing every day did wonders for Artie's confidence, and being cool helped him keep his color.

But while he played in Oakland in the summer of 1949, his heart was still in Birmingham, hearing new stories about the amazing Willie Mays, whom Artie had known since Willie was old enough to walk. The Oaks had signed a black teammate, Parnell Woods, who had once played for the Black Barons. Artie, who bought a house in Oakland with his wife, Dorothy, didn't need a teammate. He was perfectly happy, but his newfound success in white folks' ball had earned him credibility, so he thought.

He strode into a meeting with Laws and flashed a smile so bright that you could play a double-header at midnight. He told Laws he knew of a ballplayer back home in Birmingham who could make him a hell of a lot of money. Artie thought his word was enough, but Laws

In his first year in white folks' ball, shortstop Artie Wilson became an immediate sensation for the Pacific Coast League's Oakland Oaks, winning the batting title with his slap-hitting, aggressive style that resulted in a .348 average.

responded like Artie didn't know what he was talking about. The Oaks already had a prized center fielder, local boy Jackie Jensen, a former All-American football player at Cal who had signed with the Oaks for $75,000. Laws loved Jensen, who was indeed destined for a solid major league career, and believed he would fetch a high price from a major league team. The press called Jensen a "husky blond," with "all the potential."

For a moment, Artie's ever-present smile faded and he lowered his soft voice as deep as he could, his words prophesizing.

"Wait until you see Mays," he said.

He left the meeting disappointed. What worked for Artie didn't always work in white folks' ball.

How Artie Wilson had left the Black Barons and arrived in Oakland started with the last person who would have cared to help any ballplayer from Birmingham: Tom Baird of the Kansas City Monarchs. And for the next two seasons, the paths of Artie and Piper would rotate tightly around Mays, like planets around the sun. Despite the interference of

Baird, who raced through their paths like an errant stone, Mays's next stop at white folks' ball was partially determined by how Artie Wilson wound up flashing smiles and slashing singles in Oakland.

In Baird's eagerness to win respect in white folks' ball, he easily sold out his Birmingham counterpart, Tom Hayes, to the completely racist New York Yankees. The Yankees may not have been aware in 1948–1950, when their correspondence with Baird was at its height, that their primary source of firsthand Negro American League information was a registered member of the Ku Klux Klan. Born in Arkansas twenty years after the Civil War, Baird found common ground with the Yankees. He was listed as "T. Baird" in the ten-page roster of the Kansas Ku Klux Klan. He bought his home from a fellow Klansman and moved in beside three Klansman neighbors. His business office, where letters from the Yankees arrived, also housed the local Klan headquarters. His family doctor was a Klansman. His insurance agent was a Klansman. The manager of his prized bowling alley was a Klansman. "Tom Baird, in other words," wrote historian Tim Rives, "fit the Klan social profile to a 'T.'"

Mays did not fit the Yankees, but they still wanted information on Negro players. In his fervor to cater to the Yankees, Baird failed to realize that the Yankees were not interested in making the Monarchs a farm team, but only in obtaining his information. The relationship worked partly because both the Yankees and the Monarchs shared distorted views. "I can't see what some clubs see in players like [Art] Pennington, Parnell Woods, [Alonzo] Perry and Piper Davis," Baird wrote to the Yankees in 1950. "I can't see any of 'em going higher than AAA."

It was Artie Wilson's talent that led the Yankees to seek Baird. The team got to know Baird because the Monarchs rented the minor league stadium in Kansas City where the Yankees' Triple-A affiliate, the Blues, played. Baird struck up a relationship with former Blues general manager Roy Hamey.

The Yankees had seen Artie play in the second 1948 East-West All-Star game, which had been held at Yankee Stadium. There were rumors that Abe Saperstein was chasing Wilson on behalf of owner Bill Veeck of the Cleveland Indians. The Yankees didn't want black players for any noble cause. They wanted to keep talented black players out of the hands of other teams, so that the very talent they shunned—"The only question is one of ability," Joe DiMaggio told the *Chicago Defender*— could not beat them. It was hypocrisy of the highest order.

When Baird received a letter from Yankee Stadium in late 1948, from Lee MacPhail, the thirty-one-year-old regional supervisor who was being groomed for a long career in the family business, MacPhail's reluctance was clear from Baird's reply: "No doubt the Negroes have been putting the pressure on the big leagues to hire the Negro players. Perhaps they will go stronger since the Negro National League folded up."

So MacPhail milked Baird. When he heard the Giants were about to sign Hank Thompson and Monte Irvin in 1948, he contacted Baird, who told him Irvin (who became a member of the Hall of Fame) was "not near the player" as his Monarch outfielder, Thompson. Baird was willing to do anything to make the Yankees happy, including reneging on his deal with Carl Hubbell to sell Thompson to the Giants if the Yankees wanted him instead. The Yankees declined Baird's invitation.

Baird became a Yankee headhunter, though he refused to recommend Mays despite all the times Buck O'Neil and Dizzy Dismukes had seen him play so admirably. When MacPhail asked Baird for information about Wilson, Baird did one better: "The Negro American League will hold their scheduled meeting in the office of Dr. J.B. Martin February 6–7 [1949]. I will be stopping at the Morrison Hotel in Chicago and since all the club owners will be present, I will be able to obtain any information you desire."

The Yankees wanted more information about Wilson. Baird wrote:

I talked with Tom Hayes Jr., owner of the Birmingham Black Barons, and was advised that he wants $10,000 for Art Wilson. Hayes said that he really did not care to sell Wilson due to the fact that he is a home town boy and very popular and if the sale of Wilson caused him to have a losing club, he would not make any money on the sale. He compared his selling [of] Wilson to Cleveland selling Boudreau. However, I personally believe that

Hayes would take less than $10,000 for Wilson. Wilson is managing the Mayaguez club in Puerto Rico, which is the leading club, and he is hitting .397.

Hayes didn't know about Baird's correspondence with the Yankees, but he knew that he could no longer keep his best veteran players for very long. "The outlook for Negro baseball is bright, although the golden age has passed," he said. "Teams that are to survive must retrench and proceed with caution. Bringing in new players will force the veterans to keep pace."

Wilson trusted Hayes more than some Black Barons did, calling him "one of the great owners," who "didn't spare any money." Bill Greason believed Hayes cared about the players who were loyal to him, but business was always first. "He was interested in protecting his property," Greason said.

Yankee scout Tom Greenwade approached Wilson in Puerto Rico. Greenwade, who lived in Willard, Missouri, where he was a wealthy landowner and banker, was one of Branch Rickey's chief Dodger scouts before he defected to the Yankees for more money.

Greenwade adhered to the Rickey way of signing players for less than they were worth, using props and philosophy. He distributed copies of the Yankees recruiting booklet, *Play Ball with the Yankees*, which enticed players with promises such as "Headlines in New York pay off richly in paid testimonials." Greenwade lived by another dirty scouting trick, taking advantage of impoverished boys, as best described by Branch's brother Frank, a former Cardinals scout: "Best time of the year to sign boys is just before Christmas. Cash is a little scarce and $100 will often go as far as $500 in the spring. A fine hunting dog or a rifle can do wonders, too."

Greenwade portrayed himself as an affable country bumpkin, but black and white players both resented his tightfisted salary talk and his elusive relationship with the truth. The most famous player he ever signed, Mickey Mantle, chided him for wearing "cardboard shoes." Black catcher Quincy Trouppe said Greenwade asked to meet him after a winter game in 1942 and never showed up. Monarchs pitcher Jim

LaMarque questioned Greenwade's integrity, claiming that Greenwade backed off signing him because he said Baird hiked the price. White third baseman Clete Boyer detested Greenwade as a freeloader, telling him, "How come you used to come to my house every day and eat dinner? You never made an offer. You just ate." Greenwade mirrored Baird, who once wrote to Wid Matthews, "I always have the players thinking they are getting a chance to make good. This way they don't expect a bonus for signing." Al LaMacchia, who later became a scout and befriended Greenwade, said that Greenwade confessed to him that he had not seen Mantle play once before he signed him in June 1949 for a $400 minor league contract and a meager $1,150 bonus. Greenwade, however, milked his Mantle claim for all it was worth.

Greenwade was a master of bait-and-switch, but his word carried enormous pull in white folks' ball. The $400 mark was a magic number for him. It was usually his first and only offer. Artie was friendly, but he was making $725 a month to play for the Black Barons. Wilson said Greenwade offered him $400 to play Triple-A ball at Newark with no signing bonus. Wilson wasn't interested, but Greenwade claimed Wilson told him, "Salary is not important—just interested in getting a chance."

"The Yankees were the first team to contact me," Artie said. "There was no question I could play with the best in the major leagues. It was just a matter of getting a chance to play, but I never signed with the Yankees."

But Greenwade claimed that Wilson had accepted. What followed was the most acrimonious transaction between white baseball and Negro baseball during the integration period. It was the word of the New York Yankees against the Birmingham Black Barons.

The Yankees claimed Hayes agreed to sell Wilson for Greenwade's terms and the $10,000 figure quoted by Baird. Hayes allegedly accepted the deal via telegram, stating on January 29, "AGREE TO ASSIGN ART WILSON TO NEWARK FOR $5,000 ON SIGNING AND $5,000 ADDITIONAL IF RETAINED JUNE 1, 1949." Hayes also allegedly sent a letter to Commissioner A. B. Chandler dated March 19 stating, "I accepted these terms on January 29." Though quoted in newspapers of the time, neither document is known to exist. Hayes kept correspondence relating to transactions of all his players, but had no such confirmation to the Yankees about Wilson. Chandler's papers were stored at Cincinnati's Crosley Field until the ballpark was demolished in 1974. His papers, and the documentation the Yankees claimed existed, were never seen again.

Wilson never saw Greenwade again and he thought the deal was over. Hayes seems to have accepted the terms on a handshake agreement, but likely got his initial information from the Yankees, who took Greenwade's word, before he clarified specifics with Wilson. When Hayes learned Wilson's story differed from Greenwade's, he changed his mind and denied he had ever accepted such terms. But the damage was done and the war for Wilson started.

"Wilson wrote to me and said that he would rather come back to Birmingham than go to Newark for less money," Hayes said. Wilson believed "everything was cancelled." Hayes later said the "Yankees did not want Wilson because they offered him much less than I was paying him," and that he "wired that the deal was off." Hayes asked, "How do they expect him to sign when no money has been posted or paid?"

When Hayes thought the deal was over, he contacted Abe Saperstein. He asked Saperstein if the Indians still wanted Wilson. He had already decided he would never deal with the Yankees again. Saperstein informed him that Bill Veeck would pay him $10,000 for Wilson and sign the shortstop for a $5,000 major league contract. It was a sweetheart sale. The $15,000 deal was an extraordinary sum, representing the highest amount any major league team had paid at one time for a Negro League player.

Veeck personally tracked Wilson down in Puerto Rico, hiring a pilot to help him scour the countryside. With one swooping major league signature, Arthur Lee Wilson had played his last game for the Birmingham Black Barons. He loved the way it sounded: Arthur Wilson, Cleveland Indians. He inhaled the salty Caribbean air and exhaled the feelings created by the hot box. "This is the greatest day of my life," he said.

When the Yankees learned that the Indians had signed Wilson, Yankees general manager George Weiss ripped Veeck. "There is no place in baseball—major league, minor league or Negro league—for tactics encountered in this case." Weiss demanded that Commissioner Chandler launch an investigation. Baird saw another opportunity to align himself with the Yankees. He taunted Saperstein in a letter: "Abe, you are a big man and shouldn't act like a schoolboy." Baird applauded when Weiss attacked Veeck. "I was glad to see Mr. Weiss blasted Bill Veeck for [the] tactics Cleveland used in the Art Wilson case," he wrote to MacPhail. "There is no question that Mr. Weiss is 100 percent correct when you are aware of the facts involved. Abe Saperstein has known Artie Wilson since he was in baseball and if he knows so much about baseball talent, why didn't he recommend Wilson before the story broke that the Yankees were about to sign him?

"The only chance you have of getting Wilson, as I see it," Baird continued, "is for Mr. Chandler to rule that Tom Hayes accepted your offer, which he did. I suggested after our meeting here Tuesday in Chicago that Tom Hayes [give] Art Wilson $500 of his $10,000. The Yankees gave him $500, which would give Wilson $500 a month, $1,000 for signing and leave Tom Hayes $9,500. Tom Hayes agreed to those terms."

Baird deeply resented that the Indians had paid Hayes $10,000 more for Wilson than they had for his own Satchel Paige. Artie was trapped in the middle. All he wanted was to play baseball. "I'll play wherever [the Indians] send me and do the best I can to make good," he said. He left Birmingham for spring training with the Indians in Tucson, Arizona, "with the best wishes of his former teammates, management and fans," the *World* wrote.

Artie never stopped to think that the Yankees would fight for him just so he could never play against them. He simply played in a time when black players had no voice. "When we signed a contract, all we wanted to do was play ball," Bill Greason said. "We didn't get anybody to examine a contract to find out what it was all about. Once we signed, we belonged to that owner. He could trade us, loan us, sell us, do whatever he wanted with us. We was his property. We couldn't go to another club. If you did, they would blackball you."

As much as white folks' ball distanced itself from Negro baseball, it operated under many of the same unwritten rules. The Yankees held considerable sway in baseball government, beating the drums louder than the Indians ever could, as best expressed by a *Los Angeles Times* headline shouting, "Veeck Pulls Fast One on Yanks."

Chandler obliged the Yankees and launched an inquiry conducted by Dick Butler, his aide-de-camp and lead investigator. Nobody in baseball knew much of anything about Butler's background, but his appearance was always dreaded. Nobody knew when he was coming or going. He never chatted. He asked questions and vanished. Butler interviewed George Weiss, Tom Greenwade, and Bill Veeck, but not Tom Hayes, Artie Wilson, or outfielder Luis Marquez, another player Greenwade claimed had agreed with the Yankees. "I am sorry I wasn't given a chance to state my case to the Commissioner," Marquez said. Wilson never got his chance, either. "I'm still waiting for a phone call," he said.

Hayes was a staunch, proud man who felt humiliated and insulted. Though Chandler presided over baseball's integration era, his support for segregationist Strom Thurmond's 1948 presidential bid had lowered his esteem in the eyes of many blacks. On May 13, Chandler ruled that Wilson was the rightful property of the Yankees. He awarded Marquez to the Indians as compensation. Artie had been sent by the Indians to the independent San Diego Padres in the Pacific Coast League after spring training, where manager Bucky Harris, the former manager of the Yankees, benched him. "Harris has certain prejudices against these ballplayers," the *Kansas City Call* wrote in 1948, citing that Harris was teammates with Jake Powell of the 1938 Washington Senators when Powell infamously blurted out on a national radio broadcast that he stayed in shape during the winter by "beating niggers over the head."

It was an unwritten rule of white baseball to black baseball: Do what we say and you won't get hurt. The sad case of Artie Wilson was extortion masquerading as integration. "Weiss doesn't want Wilson now," *New York Newsday* reported. "But George doesn't want Bill Veeck to have him either. What Wilson wants does not seem to matter, because Art is a bad boy in the Yankee book."

The Yankees were stuck with Wilson. They didn't need a shortstop because all-star Phil Rizzuto was entering his prime years. They wanted to sell Wilson, but they didn't know where. So Lee MacPhail wrote a letter to Tom Baird, who, in his fervor to disclose Negro American League baseball secrets to the Yankees, inadvertently did Artie Wilson the biggest favor of his career, writing, "Mr. Brick Laws, President of the Oakland club, told me that he was going to notify the papers that he had made an offer for [Monarchs pitcher Gene Richardson and second baseman Curtis Roberts] because they had been on him to hire a Negro."

When Baird told MacPhail Oakland was in the market, if only to satisfy public opinion, the Yankees dumped Wilson to the Oaks at a profit. The double standard galled Negro team owners. Why was the same black player sold from one white man to another worth many times more than when sold from a black man to a white man? Hayes was pleased that Artie was happy in Oakland, but was infuriated by the Yankees. He was also responsible for returning $15,000, Wilson's contract fee and signing bonus, to the Indians. Veeck made Saperstein do the dirty work. "With that being the case," Saperstein wrote to his friend, "the Cleveland Indians organization feels that the check covering this particular deal be returned to us."

Hayes told Saperstein he couldn't reimburse the Indians because the Yankees wouldn't pay him the $10,000 they owed him. "Dear Abe," he wrote on June 29, two months after Wilson was awarded to the Yankees. "What steps must I take to get the money from the Yankees for Wilson? They have not sent me one red cent."

Saperstein got the Indians to agree to allow Hayes to split the payments into two installments and pay the second half after the Yankees paid him. Hayes's rage exploded when Saperstein told him, "From what I gather, [the Yankees] must have gotten more [than $10,000] from the Oakland club for Wilson."

Finally, almost a full year after Artie played his last game in Birmingham and three months after the Yankees sold Wilson to the Oaks, Hayes received a check for $10,000 on August 31. Saperstein hated breathing down his friend's neck. "Note the long expected check from New York has finally reached you," he wrote. "I hope that you are able to clear this business up as quickly as possible as it doesn't tend to create goodwill anywhere among the major league teams."

Hayes felt disgraced. The stigma never left him or Saperstein, whose influence with the Indians declined thereafter. There once was a time in 1948 when Hayes thought Willie Mays might end up with the Cleveland Indians. That dream was gone now. In Oakland, Artie dreamed of playing with Mays once more. He was convinced Willie would love playing baseball in California, where it was always sunny, it never rained, and most people thought being black wasn't such a big deal. Laws loved the extra attendance Wilson brought through the gates, but he thought one black star player was enough.

Artie won respect with a tremendous offensive season. The Negro American League batting champion of 1948 homed in on winning the Pacific Coast League batting championship of 1949. "I'm trying very hard to win the league's batting championship this season," he told the *Oakland Tribune*. "This league is the place for Negro players to make good."

Artie helped Hayes when he suggested the Oaks sign Alonzo Perry, who joined the team for a brief and unsuccessful pitching stint and landed Hayes a much-needed $2,500 in August, which the Oaks, unlike the Yankees, promptly paid. The Black Barons smiled when they learned Artie had pulled that one off. They had him to thank for the crisp cash. Artie saw every hit as a way to help Willie's Boys. He chatted his Black Barons up to the Oaks, using his hitting as credibility. And he won the batting title with a .348 average and 211 hits. "You should see Mays." Artie had 19 doubles and 11 triples. "This boy Greason has an 'awful' fastball." Artie made the Pacific Coast League All-Star team. "I know a fine brother named Piper Davis."

Hayes, though, was forever jaded. From now on, he would proceed with such caution and suspicion that his decisions began impeding some of his players. He looked amateurish in white folks' ball, validating every stereotype white owners had about their crude counterparts. He knew he would never get another chance to fix his reputation on his own. He decided he would never sell Willie Mays to the New York

Yankees, even if they had signed a teenage center fielder from Oklahoma, Mickey Mantle, whom Greenwade bragged about. Hayes thought further about his relationship with Pompez, a man Baird completely detested, and how it might benefit him in the future.

When Hayes cooled off, he relished revenge. He loved the idea of selling Mays to play baseball in New York City, where Mays could remind the goddamned New York Yankees every single day how good he was, how much money this little black kid was worth, and how lying to Hayes about Artie Wilson, and humiliating him in the eyes of white businessmen, had cost them the best ballplayer they would ever see.

15

THE BOSTON
GOLD SOX

Amid a sea of black faces at the graduation ceremonies at Fairfield Industrial High on May 25, 1950, was a group of white businessmen dressed well above the black working-class families, even after they shed their ties for polo shirts and tried to dress down. Perhaps it was the management of the Tutwiler, downtown Birmingham's five-star hotel with redbrick architecture that hosted whites and hired blacks. Perhaps the men were scouring the graduates for new hires. Such practices were common, and despite their social status, the white men's presence wouldn't have been unusual. A black kid could graduate one day and wash dishes the next. Still more of them were trained to do laundry, and to always press and fold a man's socks.

But the men weren't from the Tutwiler. They were from the Boston Red Sox. Joe Cronin, the general manager of the major league team, had brought his entourage to Birmingham with the intention of hiring one special worker from the 1950 graduating class of Fairfield Industrial High.

The Red Sox had a nickname in white folks' ball: the Boston Gold Sox, often said jokingly and enviously, and always behind their backs. Chick Genovese played center field for four spectacular years in the 1940s for the Louisville Colonels, Boston's Triple-A team. Boston kept him from jumping to another major league organization by paying him a major league salary. "The Red Sox were always a well-paid team," Chick's brother, George, said. "When I managed against their minor league clubs, the Red Sox used to have two or three different uniform sets. They always looked immaculate. Tom Yawkey was Mr. Gold Sox. They were a wealthy organization and they wanted you to know it."

Cash was not the issue. The Red Sox had money to spend on Mays, but when they soon released Piper Davis, they killed a potential outfield of Ted Williams and Willie Mays playing together for a decade. Cronin didn't leave the office very much, but he knew how to work a prospect's high school graduation.

The Louisville Colonels had been co-owned by Frank McKinney and Red Sox owner Tom Yawkey, and when McKinney bought the Pittsburgh Pirates, he had to sell his share of Louisville. But McKinney had learned much from Yawkey and Cronin about how to sign players under the table. When left-hander Paul Pettit graduated from Narbonne High School in Los Angeles in 1949, he recalled that there were so many scouts at his graduation ceremony that he couldn't move without one of them tugging on his gown. It didn't matter. Pettit had already had an agent approach him, film producer Frederick Stephani, who had ties to Pirates co-owner Bing Crosby. Pettit signed with the agent, who sold him to the Pirates for $100,000, the most ever paid for an amateur player. The Pirates, coincidentally, also signed four goose shooters from Pettit's high school baseball team.

Other teams believed the Pirates had fixed the deal. Commissioner Chandler dispatched his investigator, Dick Butler, to interview Pettit. "I gave him all the time he asked for," Pettit recalled. Nearly sixty years later, Pettit still adhered to the code of old world scouting. "I liked the Red Sox and I liked the Yankees," he said. "But I can't remember too much."

Cronin used all the tactics he could to try to get Mays, but the Red Sox had already made a fatal mistake. Piper Davis had been released on May 15, ten days before Mays's graduation. Cronin's goose shooter was gone, though he told Piper when he released him that the Red Sox were refusing to pay the $7,500 option on his contract because of "economic conditions." Nobody believed it.

Inside Birmingham, several rumors circulated about why Piper had been released from Double-A Scranton. The Red Sox already had two first basemen, Walt Dropo and Dick Gernert, who were in the big club's plans. It forced the question: If the Red Sox didn't need Piper, why did they sign him in the first place?

The gut reaction was racism, but there was more to it. Some fans thought Tom Hayes had a deal for Mays lined up with another team, and when he refused to sell Mays to the Red Sox because of it, the Red Sox released Piper. Some conversely wondered if Mays rejected the Red Sox because they had released Piper. Cat Mays was very aware of the role his former high school teammate had taken in shaping his son's future. "Piper took so [many] pains with Willie," Cat said in 1951. Cronin was confused and frustrated. He thought the Red Sox were doing Piper a favor by releasing him so he could find a job with another team. And theoretically, they were.

But Cronin and the Red Sox didn't understand the communal nature of black baseball in Birmingham. They didn't understand that releasing Piper was like tossing one of the Molotov cocktails that were exploding with increasing frequency around Birmingham's Negro neighborhoods. The Red Sox had violated the same unwritten rule that the Yankees had: if you screw one of Willie's Boys, you ain't gettin' Willie.

But Cronin tried anyhow. He arrived in Birmingham unannounced on Thursday, May 18. Eddie Glennon, the general manager of the white Barons who had tried for two years to make the Red Sox aware of Mays, had no idea he was coming. He was shocked when Cronin arrived at Rickwood Field, announcing his presence by tossing his bowler hat into Glennon's office. In the fourteen months that the Birmingham white Barons had been the Double-A team for the Red Sox, Cronin had never visited once, not even to see the powerful 1948

Southern Association championship team. Cronin said he hadn't been to Birmingham since 1929, but the timing of this visit was impeccably precise. The 1950 white Barons were a decent ball club, but not much to look at. "Just paying Birmingham a friendly visit," Cronin told the *Birmingham News*. He was vague and impersonal. "I'm just looking over the Red Sox boys." Cronin said he was going to take farm director Johnny Murphy with him back to Boston, a curious statement, because farm directors almost always had a direct say on which black players joined a team's minor league system. Had Cronin come to Birmingham to take Murphy and Mays back with him? The last trace of Cronin, according to the timelines assembled from different parts of the *Birmingham News*, was May 23. On May 24, the Black Barons played the Houston Eagles at Rickwood Field, but Mays did not play because school was in session. On May 25, he graduated at the insistence of Cat, who Willie said often told him, "You have to have that piece of paper." Cronin had a different piece of paper. It was a Boston Red Sox contract for Willie Mays.

If Cronin had been brazen enough to go to Fairfield High's graduation, just as countless other scouts had made a last-ditch effort to sign Paul Pettit, he would have run into more than another team's grip on Mays. He would have encountered a scout's worst nightmare, a ballplayer's father, one who had known his son's mentor for years and was not oblivious to that mentor's contributions, nor his recent pain. Cronin would have ran into the fierce anger Birmingham's black baseball community felt toward the Red Sox, not about Mays, but for what they had done to Piper Davis.

Piper Davis had arrived at Red Sox spring training in Cocoa Beach, Florida, in 1950. "Boy," he said. "That's where it all started, right there. I was the only black." The Red Sox stayed in the biggest hotel in town, luxury accommodations provided by Mr. Gold Sox. But Piper had different accommodations. The Red Sox would not allow him to live in the hotel, so they bribed the headwaiter to let him stay in the hotel's servers' quarters. "He'd bring me down to the hotel around

8 a.m. and we would eat breakfast," Piper said. "I'd get on the bus and go to the ballpark."

When Piper boarded the bus, none of the white players cared who he was. There were a few murmurs. In baseball's parallel world, he was considered one of the best Negro American League players, a multiple all-star in his league, but on this jump he was an ordinary minor leaguer. When the bus arrived, Piper cautiously milled in the middle. He acted like any other ballplayer. Nothing to it, he thought. He walked into the locker room and went down one aisle of lockers, but he couldn't find his stall, so he went down the other aisle. "I went all the way around to the back by the showers, the training room, the rubdown table, the manager's office, and the equipment room. Come to the rubdown table and the trainer looked up at me," Piper said. He asked where his locker was.

Piper recalled the emotionless expression on the trainer's face. "Oh," the trainer said, "your equipment is on the other side." Piper walked out of the Red Sox dressing room. "I was on the visitor's side by myself," he said. When games started, he did his best to focus on baseball, but it wasn't easy. The verbal abuse worsened. Willie remembered how Piper had taught him, "Hey, whatever they call you, they can't touch you. Don't talk back." But though his livelihood and his family's future were at stake, Piper's temper hadn't burned like this in years. He channeled his anger onto the diamond, where he showed his versatility, playing the infield skill positions, where the Red Sox were stacked, instead of first base, his best position. Jack Burns, Scranton's manager, a lifelong Massachusetts resident born in Cambridge, played six years for the St. Louis Browns in the 1930s, where his manager in 1935 and 1936 was noted bigot Rogers Hornsby. During an exhibition game, Burns told Piper to pinch-hit. "There was two white fellas right by the dugout," Piper said. "They were sitting there with no shirts on. When I came out, one of them said, 'Well I'll be goddamned. Boston went out and got 'em a nigger.'"

Piper inhaled deeply and prayed: Lord help me hold out. "I didn't have to say it but three times," he said. "I hit me a home run. You could see it rise and it got over the fence by about two inches. I looked at the man and said, 'Take that.'"

After the games, there was no escape. When the visiting team used the other locker room, Piper wasn't allowed to use either. He was sent to the tiny umpire's room, where he showered only after the umpires finished. "It made me so mad," he said. "I stayed in the shower. I know the umpires cussed me out. Those were rough times."

When the season started in Scranton, the Double-A team where Mays would have been sent, Piper couldn't stay at the hotel where the white players stayed, so one of the bellhops told him he could rent a room in his home. Piper's salary was to be $800 a month, but on his first payday, he received only $150 instead of $400. "That ain't no money," he said.

Worried and frustrated, Piper did what he knew how to do. He played baseball. In 15 games, he had 21 hits in 63 at-bats, including three home runs and four doubles and a team-high .333 batting average. Though he had never taken a ground ball at first base during spring training, Burns told him to play first. Piper knew he wouldn't be the most physically superior player on the field, but he also didn't believe he received credit for being a technician. He believed he could be a utility player in the major leagues, an evaluation many white players who faced him agreed with.

"As a prospect he wouldn't pop your eyes out, but I would say he would have hit enough to have been an extra player in the major leagues," said former Pirates pitcher Lenny Yochim, who played against Piper in 1953. "I wouldn't say he was a power guy, but he hit a home run against me. Piper was an outstanding athlete. He was much older and wiser at the time I played him. He always adjusted to the situation. He was not a strikeout guy. He made contact and used the whole field. He hit what you gave him and was a team player with the bat, moving a runner over or hitting behind a runner. Piper knew what he was doing."

On May 15, the day when Piper's option for $7,500 had to be exercised, he practiced with the team in the morning. He felt safe in his performance and looked forward to the financial windfall of $3,750 that the option would bring him. But when he returned to his room, he was told the team had called for him. His stomach sank.

"I went back to the park," Piper said. "When I walked in [Burns's] office, [team president James Murray] was there. I said, 'I understand you called.' Burns said, 'Yeah.' They picked up the phone and called Boston. I got on with Cronin and he said, 'I got to let you go.' I said, 'For what, man?' He said, 'Economic conditions.' I'm leading the team in hitting, RBIs, home runs, and tied in stolen bases. If I had stayed past May 15, they were going to have to pay Tom Hayes $7,500 to keep me. They let me go. I forgot exactly what I said. I didn't curse. That was one of the toughest moments of my . . . career."

It was the longest night of Piper Davis's life. He couldn't get a train out until the next day. He stayed and watched the game, and when he heard that a group of black fans had come to Scranton to see him play, it broke his heart. He was an unemployed ballplayer who had to go back to the Negro American League to play for the Birmingham Black Barons. "When Boston released me," Piper said, "that took all the joy out of it."

The following morning, Piper packed and caught a train out of Scranton. When the train connected in Washington, he had to switch seats, as was the custom for black passengers headed south, "to the car right behind the engine." As he stepped out of the train, he encountered the last person he expected to see. It was Cronin, traveling south from Boston.

" 'What a coincidence,' " Piper remembered Cronin saying. "So he says, 'Sorry about the deal and all that.' I didn't ask him. I didn't even want to know." As Cronin walked to his first-class Pullman car where hot towels and hot meals were served, Piper trudged to the Negroes-only engine car, where the stench of gas and coal pervaded. Cronin still didn't call Piper by his name, though he had met him twice and knew it well enough to release him. "Where are you going, 'Slugger'?" Cronin asked. "I'm going where my money can afford," Piper said.

Before Piper and Cronin parted ways, Piper remembered being curious about why Cronin was going south the day after he had released the only black player the Red Sox had signed. "Where are you going?" he asked in passing. "Louisville," was Cronin's reply. But Cronin didn't tell Piper that he had another stop on his southern journey, a destination about which he told nobody outside of his inner circle. Joe Cronin was going to Birmingham to sign Willie Mays.

Mays's feats were now commonplace, but no less awe-inspiring. The *Birmingham World* was calling him "The Prince of Centerfield," and "The Arm." In April, the *World* reported, Mays caught a "295-foot fly" and "threw the ball the entire distance" to home plate with the bases loaded to complete an inning-ending double play. Eddie Glennon believed he would make an excellent pitcher.

Black Barons pitcher Bill Greason believed Piper's time with the Red Sox was "a token thing, you may call it." Piper was still beloved in Birmingham, and no matter how many flashy plays Mays made, Piper's place in the city's pride never diminished. He covered his pain like a ballplayer in the batter's box, scratching at the dirt with his back foot, erasing the chalk lines until they were gone. "He knew they had mistreated him," Greason said. "That's the way it was. We were just pawns in their hands. Couldn't do anything about it."

Cronin left Birmingham empty-handed. He stayed out of the Fenway Park press box on July 4, 1951, when the New York Giants played an exhibition game in Boston with their rookie center fielder in the starting lineup. "It was another case of Tom Yawkey being done dirt by the people he trusted most," Hirshberg later wrote. "I'm sure he had no prejudices, either. The same goes for Joe Cronin."

Piper had almost a week to talk to Willie before the Red Sox arrived. Piper played in his first game in 1950 with the Black Barons on May 24, the night before Mays graduated. It was the same week Mays posed for his graduation photo, fidgeting in his cap and gown, eager to leave Birmingham and never come back, aware he was destined for more than his teammates. "I believe Piper helped him a lot with making his choices," Greason said. "Piper was Willie's counselor."

Piper scratched at the batter's box for the rest of his life. When writers asked him years later, he demurred. His personality would evaporate for a split second and he would hastily say he knew nothing about Mays and the Red Sox. Then he would rebound, warm up the room and say, "I had some beautiful moments." He never criticized the team that had treated him so poorly and taken all the joy out of it, simply to try to get the boy who put all the joy into it.

Piper's daughter, Faye Davis, is a sharp woman who still resides in Birmingham. Her face expresses the happy memories of her father, and when the moment is right, she's the little girl who is thrilled when she recalls how her daddy let her ride in the front seat of Charlie Rudd's bus. But when talk turns to 1950 and the names of Joe Cronin and Tom Yawkey surface, bones that never rested rise again. The hurt and rage that Piper Davis left swirling inside his family rush forward. Piper never completely scratched those lines away. "To this day," Faye said, catching her father's good look and his pain that seethes and stirs for a split second before hurrying away, "I am still not a fan of the Boston Red Sox."

16

MIRACLE IN HARLEM

Sometimes she was cranky and sometimes she ran like a beauty. Sometimes she was bumpy and sometimes she was smooth. Sometimes she could run forever, and sometimes she wouldn't get out of bed. Her creaky engine was held together with spit and glue, with borrowed parts wound together like an elaborate ball of twine, but she never let herself be seen with her makeup mussed. She was always there for her Black Barons. They climbed into her belly, spread out their playing cards, ate their cheese sandwiches and picked at sardines, drank their beers and sucked from their flasks, and sometimes from a Coke bottle if they were lucky. They hung their laundry out her windows, sang songs, regaled her after momentous wins, and hushed her after hard losses. Safe in her berth, they dreamt and lived and worried about baseball and life. She always waited for them.

If her front lights were eyes, then she had witnessed more of America than most whites and most blacks ever would. She had seen the cities and the pastures, the skyscrapers in New York and the silos in Kansas, driven on paved streets and dirt roads, been cut off by taxicabs and waited for milk cows to cross the road. She had traversed the Brooklyn and George Washington bridges and crawled across ramshackle wooden drawbridges held together by twigs and prayers, always keeping her feet dry. Charlie Rudd's bus was home and she was the only girl on the team.

Her youngest child, Willie Mays, was nineteen now and hardly the same boy he was when he took his first jump with her in 1948. He had graduated from Fairfield Industrial High on May 25, and in the early morning hours of June 11, had yet to sign a white folks' ball contract. Mays was scared. His mind meandered as her engine droned, coughing occasionally as she sometimes did, though he was too deep in thought to notice that she sounded worse today. "I didn't think I would ever get out of Birmingham," Mays said. "I didn't think I would have a chance because of the segregation."

Mays had proven himself to be a capable hitter, but somehow the reputation that he was an inferior batter hadn't been knocked loose. How closely were the white scouts looking? "Certain sports authorities say if Black Barons center fielder Willie Mays were sold to another team, especially a team in the big leagues, team managers would quickly haul him in from centerfield and proudly place him on the pitching mound," the *Birmingham World* wrote on May 12. Mays didn't want to be a pitcher, but he would do whatever he needed to.

"The big question on the club right now is can the Black Barons keep the youthful Willie Mays all summer?" the *World* wrote on May 30. "He is just out of high school and has been starring both in the field and with the willow. It is known that several scouts have been turning their bifocals on Mays most of this season and debating in their minds whether he is of big league caliber or not."

She was taking them to a big league ballpark today, to the Polo Grounds in Harlem, where the Black Barons would play Alex Pompez's New York Cubans in a Sunday double-header. The Polo Grounds didn't scare Mays. He had played there in 1949 and perhaps hoped he might be seen now that he was making his first jump with the Black Barons after graduation. He had two brand-new outfits in his suitcase, sporty attire for somebody who might have a job interview. He also had no contract binding him to the Black Barons. He had been signed to a standard Negro American League contract in 1948, and if he didn't have one on file in 1949, he played under the pretense that he belonged to the Black Barons until he was sold after his graduation. Piper Davis told him that under no circumstances should he sign a contract with the 1950 Black Barons. "I knew if he did, he wouldn't get as much money from white folks' ball," Piper said.

Mays was coming to the Polo Grounds two weeks after graduation with no obligations binding him to the Black Barons. It would be as easy as plucking an apple off a tree. It never occurred to him that Alex Pompez and Tom Hayes had worked together at the Negro American League meetings in March to ensure that Willie's first trip after graduation would be to the Polo Grounds. As the bus rolled toward the Holland Tunnel, he was too worried about his future to fully comprehend that Pompez was waiting for him with New York Giants scouting czar Carl Hubbell.

She coughed again when she rolled into the Holland Tunnel, and some of the players smelled smoke. At first they ignored it, but it didn't take long for them to realize that their beloved bus was on fire. "We smelled something coming from the back of the bus," Bill Greason said. "Then we looked up and saw the smoke."

When Rudd saw the smoke, he knew he wasn't going to be able to save her this time. He began nursing her to the side of the road, realizing the inevitable as she wheezed and struggled to pull her boys to safety one last time. Rudd managed to pull her over. The guys who couldn't run suddenly had moves. The players grabbed only what they had brought with them on board that morning. Rudd nudged her to a stop and yanked the doors open. "We all piled out," Greason said. "We didn't get all the bags because the fire was back by the gas tank and we were looking for her to blow."

But in death she did them one last favor. The players ran a safe distance away, watching the windows shatter out of her frame, watching the seats and tires melt until the fire gradually crawled onto her back. But she never exploded. She just couldn't do that to her boys. They stood on the side of the road and watched her die. The fire department didn't show up until all her beauty was gone. That bus had been their home, the one safe haven they knew was always theirs. And like the league, she was a memory now, and it saddened the Black Barons to see a friend suffer. "That was a sad day for us," Greason said. "She just burned real slowly," he said. She was saying good-bye. "There were a lot of memories on that bus, a lot of singing and caring about one another, a lot of good times." And when she was finished, Piper turned and walked away, and called taxicabs to take her boys to the ballpark.

The Black Barons finally arrived at the Polo Grounds a few hours later than expected, wearing only the clothes on their backs and clinging to the money in their pockets. Mays had lost his suitcase and his brand-new clothes. By the time the Black Barons talked their way into the ballpark and walked to the locker room entrance in the outfield, they were stranded travelers, discarded baseball vagabonds with no spikes, gloves, or bats. The *Amsterdam News* reported that the team lost $3,000 worth of possessions, but the players called surviving their ordeal the miracle in Harlem. Pompez lent the Black Barons his team's road grays. They turned the jerseys inside out. That meant that nobody on the Black Barons had a name or number on their back.

Pompez was relieved. The 1950 season had, for once, started according to his designs when on May 7 opening day wasn't rained out for the first time in six years. He considered sunshine an illuminating omen as the Cubans drew a lusty crowd of 7,000 fans, plus a few thousand extra neighborhood kids for whom Pompez had purchased tickets. Pompez had emerged as a folk hero in Harlem, the former numbers operator who had defied the Dutchman, though his ambition to expand into white baseball was far beyond what most white teams expected of a Negro League owner.

"Pompez has an abiding faith in his people and in the destiny of Negro baseball," *New York Age* columnist Dan Burley wrote. "That is why he has willingly lost a fortune trying to keep the game alive." Burley praised Pompez as "the foxy Cuban boss man" and the "Noblest Roman of them all."

Pompez had made a handshake deal with Hubbell to make the Cubans a de facto "farm team" of the Giants in 1949, after he sold them

Alex Pompez (with glasses, front table, far right) was the mastermind of the New York Giants' connections in the Negro League and was responsible for making the Giants aware of Willie Mays. Seated to his right is Chick Genovese, who teamed with Pompez to later discover Juan Marichal and Orlando Cepeda. Scout George Genovese (second from the bottom left) signed players who combined to hit nearly 4,000 major league home runs. Two to Pompez's left is talent czar Carl Hubbell and to Hubbell's right, secretary Jack Schwarz.

Ray Dandridge and Dave Barnhill. He still had aspirations of legitimizing the Cubans as a black minor league team in white folks' ball, but the National Association, white organized baseball's minor league government, wasn't interested. Pompez was convinced affiliation was the only way Negro baseball would survive. He drew inspiration from the founder of the original Negro League. "If Rube Foster can do it," Pompez said, "I can too."

But if he couldn't became a storefront, then he would find a way to join the business. That's why Mays was so important to Pompez, who recognized that attaching himself to the young ballplayer was the surest way to enter white folks' ball. He would then be protected from the outside social and economic factors that were crushing Negro baseball. In turn, Hubbell knew he needed Pompez if he wanted Mays. To seal

Hubbell's trust, Pompez made sure Mays's name wasn't mentioned in the *Age*'s advance notices about the Black Barons visiting the Cubans, despite the fact that Mays's popularity was surging past Piper Davis's. Pompez moved carefully and covered his tracks. The Yankees and Dodgers had no idea Mays and the Black Barons were in town again.

Because of that secrecy, the box scores from the Black Barons–Cubans double-header that Sunday weren't published in any newspaper, as they normally were. The line scores and game recaps made it out, but nothing expressly about Mays did. Hubbell, in the ballpark where he was a star pitcher and now star official, could roam where he wanted. "You can see some things from the grandstand, but not enough," he said. "Get out there on the field with them and you see a whole lot more."

What Hubbell saw impressed him, reflected in his evaluation of Mays as a rookie in 1951. "He makes everything look easy," he said. "He is chiefly a straightaway hitter but he can pull and he can hit to right field with power. He hits very few high fly balls. Almost everything is on a line."

Black Barons first baseman Alonzo Perry, however, loved to hit home runs that were like his personality, both grandiose and extravagantly overdone, performed for effect and memory. Perry's power was unquestionable when he hit three home runs in the double-header, including one that "hit the 485-marker in deep centerfield on one bounce," the *Amsterdam News* reported. But Perry was a black ballplayer white baseball wasn't ready for, described later as a man with "diamond rings on his fingers, a gold chain around his neck and a Cadillac in the garage." He was known for his off-the-field habits. "Perry always had a reputation of messing around, foolin' with that dope," catcher Frazier Robinson said. "He was a guy who always seemed to be one step ahead of the law." Without question, Perry possessed major league ability. Scout George Genovese likened him to Hall of Fame slugger Willie McCovey.

This is when Perry unwittingly found himself at the intersection of black and white baseball history. Hubbell would need a black minor league roommate for Mays. Knowing that he would have to assign scouts to tail Mays to Birmingham where he could be purchased from Tom Hayes, he also wanted a cover story. Perry's home run display provided such a diversion. Mays was simply too important of a player not to take precautions. Though Hubbell's minor league system was stacked with capable first basemen at nearly every level, the cover player had to be talented enough so that other scouts wouldn't suspect that the reason for the Giants' sudden interest in the Black Barons was actually Mays.

And because Mays was wearing a borrowed jersey, his No. 8 having disintegrated in the Holland Tunnel, Hubbell sought confirmations. When he approached Perry, the first baseman thought his time had come. Instead, Hubbell had another question. "He asked me who the kid we had in centerfield was," Perry said. "I told him Willie Mays."

The shifty eyes of Alonzo Perry saw much living after the Giants used him as a decoy to conduct their scouting and signing of Willie Mays in 1950.

When the Black Barons saw Hubbell talking to Perry, not one of them believed he was really interested in him. "The scouts used Perry to keep Mays undercover," Bill Greason said. Hubbell was following Pompez's directions not to speak to Mays before he spoke to Hayes. Once Hubbell got his confirmation, he set in motion a trick worthy of a magician and baseball history was soon obscured by the Lie Heard Round the World.

Hubbell dispatched two scouts to follow the Black Barons when they left New York, touring back to Birmingham through the Carolinas with Pompez's New York Cubans. Because the Black Barons had lost their bus, the obvious solution was for the teams to travel closely together, which allowed Pompez to keep careful tabs on Mays. His primary role would be as the liaison between the Giants and the Black Barons when the teams arrived in Birmingham the following weekend. Hubbell's men, Bill Harris and Ed Montague, were assigned to Mays. Neither man had ever signed a black player. Hubbell had a closer relationship with Harris, like himself a former pitcher in the Giants organization. Hubbell had hired him as a minor league manager when jobs were scarce in the war years and retained him as a scout. Harris lived in South Carolina, where he was able to first see the Black Barons. "I remember everything about blacks, things in history that nobody gave the blacks credit for," Mays said. His own signing story would not be immune to segregated history.

Montague covered the South, but had never heard of Willie Mays. His story, however, implied that the Giants had no previous knowledge of Mays before he alone saw him and notified the Giants from Birmingham. "The reason I went into Birmingham was that, while at my home in Jacksonville, Florida, I received a call from our farm director, Jack Schwarz, to scout a player with the Birmingham Black Barons named Alonzo Perry," Montague wrote to *Look* magazine in his official account in 1954. "This fellow had a pretty good day in the Polo Grounds on the preceding Sunday and some of our scouts saw him and recommended him. I was told to scout Perry and see if he could help one of our Class A clubs. Willie Mays may have played in the Polo Grounds also, but no report was made on him."

Montague claimed sole discovery of Mays because there were no reports, but failed to mention that his boss, Hubbell, had seen him twice before he did. Hubbell didn't need permission to pursue a player he wanted, nor did he have to follow formalities. "Hubbell's word went a long way in that organization," said George Genovese, who scouted for the Giants for thirty years and reported to Hubbell. Furthermore, the Giants had no more use for Perry than the Red Sox had for Piper Davis. Perry was supposedly being scouted for Class A Sioux City, where the Giants had first baseman Allan Maul, who played in 148 games and batted .265 with 17 home runs. So as the Black Barons hustled through Mays's last week in the Negro Leagues, through minuscule towns on the way to the weekend, through tiny crowds that led Piper to believe that he played his best baseball in front of nobody who could help him, Eddie Montague needed a road map. "One of our scouts picked the club up there and followed them into Birmingham," he wrote.

Actually, there were two scouts, Harris and Pompez, working independently of each other. When Montague arrived at Rickwood Field, he claimed he "arrived in Birmingham for the Sunday double-header." He said he had "no inkling of Willie Mays" when he "discovered, found and signed a real gem."

There were several problems with Montague's claim. He actually arrived in Birmingham on Friday night, when several other scouts from major league teams were assembled for a white high school all-star game at Rickwood Field. There he was snapped in a photograph that appeared in the Saturday, June 17, edition of the *Birmingham News*. Montague was definitely not the only scout in Birmingham as Mays came home. Sitting around Eddie Glennon's table were Red Sox scouts Hugh East and Mace Brown, Cincinnati Reds scout Paul Florence, and Pittsburgh Pirates scout Shaky Kain, all respected veterans. And seated next to Montague, wearing a bow tie and a sour look, was Boston Braves scout Bill Maughn, who at the very least had come to Birmingham to see Willie Mays's last game as a Negro League star.

There was one other guest in Birmingham that weekend, who would never otherwise bother to show up for a high school all-star game. It was Dick Butler, Commissioner Chandler's legal enforcer, who had conducted the investigations surrounding the $15,000 Artie Wilson and $100,000 Paul Pettit bonus transactions. He could only have been sent by Chandler himself to avoid yet another controversial Negro or amateur signing. Though Pompez's skin color prevented him from sitting at the same table, his presence could not be excluded. Butler's involvement was a clear show of force from Chandler, who most likely sent Butler at Stoneham's insistence. That meant Hubbell, which meant Pompez.

The Giants recognized the gravity of Mays as a historically significant young player. They did not wish to lose him in a contractual squabble as the Indians had lost Artie Wilson. "Butler has done this kind of work for me for about five years," Chandler said. Chandler was also caving to some of the pressure Burley applied in the *New York Age* when he wrote, "It is actually a slave jungle since the raiders are signing Negro players while Chandler looks the other way. Jackie cost Rickey nothing, on the other hand, they're paying as high as $100,000 for some obscure teenage white rookie."

Around baseball, there was a growing sense that something momentous was about to occur. In Oakland, Artie Wilson tried one last-ditch effort to convince Oaks owner Brick Laws to bring Willie Mays to the West Coast. "I told them again, 'Y'all better get Mays because somebody is gonna get him.' But they messed around."

On Saturday, June 17, the New York Cubans played the Birmingham Black Barons at Rickwood Field in Willie Mays's last game. Mays had a proper good-bye and Birmingham prevailed, 7–1. "Centerfielder Willie Mays drove in four runs with a double and a single," the *World* reported. With Alex Pompez and Tom Hayes and scouts Montague and Harris in attendance, the time had come.

"The Giants wanted Pompez in Birmingham to buy Mays from the Black Barons so there would be no confusion at all," Genovese said. "Mr. Stoneham felt bad because the Cubans ball club was his living and his business. Stoneham felt that he owed Pompez something, so he brought him in after they got Mays."

Pompez had done what no Negro League owner had done or would do again. He had won the trust of a major league owner. Now Ed Montague sought to win Mays's trust. He went into the Rickwood Field locker room to claim his prize. "He had just gotten out of the shower and I saw a well-built young fellow," Montague wrote, prompting Bobby Veale to ask, "Was he looking at his upper physique or his lower physique?" Montague spoke words that Bill Maughn and John Donaldson desperately wanted to say, but never had the chance: "Would you like to play professional baseball?"

Mays was perhaps the last person in Birmingham to learn that he had been bought by the Giants. That was a nice fit, because Montague was not the first scout to learn about Mays, as he claimed for the rest of his life. He was the last. He said that he saw Mays play the following day, but Greason said Mays was gone on Sunday. "We looked up and he was gone," he said. "We said, 'Where's Mays?' They said, 'He's been bought by the Giants.' And we just went out and played like we weren't there, either." The Black Barons, distracted and flat, lost both games that day.

The deal was designed around Hayes's demands and insecurities. Hayes wanted $10,000 for himself and $5,000 for Mays, similar to the deal the Indians gave him for Wilson. He wanted all of his money at once, not if Mays only stayed with the Giants organization after a certain date. Pompez related the terms to Montague, who told Hubbell, who put Hayes in contact with farm director Jack Schwarz, Stoneham's clever and efficient secretary. Montague conducted the home visit with Mays and his aunt, and signed Mays. Stoneham agreed to Hayes's terms without argument. Mays said he received only $4,000 instead of the $5,000 Montague said was coming. What happened to the extra $1,000 is unknown, but the best guess is Alex Pompez skimmed a commission.

On the following Wednesday, Hayes spoke with Schwarz to confirm the agreement. When Hayes agreed to sell Mays, he took bittersweet pride in sending Mays to the Giants, because he knew his own involvement in baseball was nearing an end. Schwarz, with Stoneham's blessing, immediately wired Hayes to confirm the deal:

1950 JUNE 21 9:53 A.M.

NEW YORK, NY

TOM HAYES

PRESIDENT AND OWNER BIRMINGHAM BARONS

THIS WILL CONFIRM TELEPHONE CONVERSATION TODAY WITH OUR
MR. SCHWARZ IN WHICH HE OFFERED TEN THOUSAND DOLLARS
FOR THE ASSIGNMENT OF CONTRACT OF PLAYER WILLIE H. MAYS JR.
AND YOU AGREE TO ASSIGN HIS CONTRACT TO THE MINNEAPOLIS
BALL CLUB FOR THAT AMOUNT.

HORACE C. STONEHAM

In pencil, Hayes scribbled the words that sent Willie Mays to the
New York Giants: "Accept your offer of $10,000 for Willie H. Mays."
Later that day, Schwarz typed a letter to Hayes on bright orange-and-black
New York Giants Baseball Club stationery. Tom Hayes finally had what
he had wanted all along: respect from one businessman to another:

June 21, 1950

Dear Sir:

Enclosed please find two copies of an agreement to cover the
assignment of the contract of player Willie H. Mays Jr. by
the Birmingham Black Barons Baseball Club to the Minneapolis
Baseball Club. Will you please sign one copy of the agreement
and send it to Mr. W.D. Ryan, GM, Minneapolis Baseball Club,
3048 Nicollet Avenue, Minneapolis, Minnesota. Mr. Ryan will
send you the check for $10,000 upon receipt of the signed
contract from you.

Sincerely yours,
Horace C. Stoneham
President, New York Giants Baseball Club

When the news was official on June 22, the *Birmingham News* ran a
short article titled "Mays, Black Barons Star, Is Going Up," accompanied

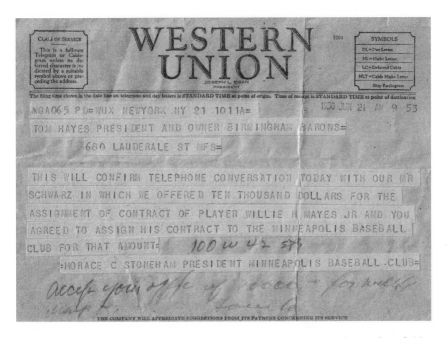

The Western Union wire confirming the New York Giants' purchase of outfielder Willie Mays from the Birmingham Black Barons, June 21, 1950.

by a new photo of Mays holding his bat over his shoulder. It was believed to be the first time the *News* had run a photograph of a black athlete from Birmingham. "They couldn't put no pictures of blacks in the paper, no sir," Greason said.

Greason chuckled when he saw the paper. He suspected it was a subtle form of social protest from *News* staffer Alf Van Hoosen, who in 1949 had promised Greason and Piper he would write stories about them if his newspaper would ever allow it. Van Hoosen stayed true to his word, and in 1979 finally gave Piper and Greason their due in print.

Pompez even appeared in the *News* when the Cubans left town; his name was mentioned in a non-bylined story about the Black Barons being swept on Sunday, a day after Mays signed. Pompez's name was above one about Birmingham's steel industry, and the *News* proudly wrote, "Our bread and butter, Birmingham makes steel and steel makes Birmingham." The New York Giants scouts left town with the city's other great contribution to America—Mays, steel proudly stolen with Pompez's help, a player for whom black and white people shared mutual admiration in the dark and bloody years ahead.

"Birmingham fans know the history of most of the players in organized Negro baseball," the *World* wrote. "They've followed them out of the coal mines, ore mines and steel plants." Willie was the last and the best. Birmingham knew he was destined for more than it could offer. And so he left the storm brewing behind him. Bombmakers stole wire and fertilizer. The Supreme Court questioned separate but equal. Bull Connor insisted segregation would never end in Birmingham. A few weeks later, when the Chicago American Giants came to Rickwood Field with three white players added to the team to help increase interest, they were threatened with arrest if they took the field with their black counterparts. The three players watched the game from the Coal Bin. Mays had escaped at the right moment. "Mays has nine or ten good years ahead of him," the *World* predicted. He had more than that.

In the race to win Mays, no scout benefited more than Pompez, though the Giants never thought of him as a talent evaluator. The Giants didn't care to publicize Pompez's contributions to signing Mays because of his underworld background, instead deferring to the more heroic version of Montague's discovery story. Pompez, however, wisely obliged his new bosses, though he did place a slight congratulatory note in the *New York Age* when it reported, "It was on the Birmingham Black Barons' last trip to town that the New York Giants picked up Willie Mays, the 19-year-old outfield sensation."

Pompez had brought players from Cuba and around Latin America for years. Now he would bring them to the Giants. A few years later, Jack Schwarz paired Chick Genovese with Pompez. Together, they discovered players such as Juan Marichal and Orlando Cepeda. Pompez helped the Giants find another star in Alabama in 1954, when his bird dog, Jesse Thomas, the brother of his former New York Cubans' first baseman Dan "Showboat" Thomas, saw Willie McCovey. Pompez got McCovey a tryout, where he was nearly cut. "I was scared to death," McCovey said. "Hubbell, Pompez, Schwarz, they were all there. They'd

NEWEST GIANT KILLER!—
The New York Giants are
looking forward to Willie
Mays Jr. to become one of
the brightest prospects in
their chain system in the near
future. The 19-year-old
youngster is now performing
with Trenton in the Inter-
State League.—Keystone
Photo.

When the Giants signed Willie
Mays in 1950 and assigned him to
Class B Trenton, they proclaimed
him to be an accidental discovery,
when in fact they had knowledge
of him in 1949 and possibly as far
back as 1948, his first year with the
Black Barons.

send for the boys who didn't look good. Alex Pompez was the one to
tell the Negroes. When Pompez came back to me with a sad look,
I thought it was over. My heart pounded."

But Pompez talked Hubbell into keeping McCovey, who hit 521
career home runs. When McCovey came to the Giants in 1959, Mays
took him under his wing, as Piper had done for him. Alabama baseball
blood ran thick. "Mays told me what to do and built up my confidence," McCovey said. "He let me make plays he could have made."

Pompez was always good at getting attention, even in death. He
died in 1974 and was elected to the Hall of Fame in 2006, where

his plaque described him as a "shrewd talent evaluator." But that is an inaccurate description of his greatest talent. He was a master of numbers and of rounding up numerous players hoping to win the lottery. It was Lyman Bostock, Tommy Sampson, and Winfield Welch from the 1948 New York Cubans, all former Black Barons, who led Pompez to the player who allowed him to unearth all the others.

"Pompez and my brother were an excellent team," George Genovese said. "But Pompez was not like the rest of us who could go out and look at talent and know what he was talking about. He'd sit in meetings but never comment on players. Pompez's bird dogs would round up the kids, Chick would say, 'This guy, this guy, and this guy,' and Pomp would spiff the bird dog if we signed the kid. My brother loved Pompez, but I always used to tell him, 'When a player makes good, he gets all the credit. When one of his guys gets released, you get all the blame.'"

Mays gradually became aware of Pompez's efforts to help him escape the hot box, and he did Pompez a favor in 1956 when he agreed to be the star attraction for Pompez's winter barnstorming team. He had willfully not told owner Horace Stoneham that he was playing for Pompez, and in turn, Pompez bought a special bus for the tour. Willie had never forgotten his games against the Jackie Robinson All-Stars in 1948 and 1949. Now the Willie Mays All-Stars, joined by Hank Aaron and Frank Robinson in what might have been the best outfield ever to play together, toured through Rickwood Field. The Black Barons were still in business, but just barely. Tom Hayes had sold his team and every player from the 1948 club was gone. Birmingham outfielder Jessie Mitchell remembered telling Mays that he still couldn't use the showers. Before the game, Mays took his brothers and sisters shopping at a downtown Birmingham department store. When he opened his wallet, two plainclothes city detectives descended and demanded to know how a black man had so much green. Mays took his siblings and spent his money elsewhere, but he never forgot his reminder of the segregation he had left behind.

The fans loved watching Mays hit and run and throw, but there was one skill they always asked for. It was a real moneymaker, so

Mays agreed. When he found himself on third base, he would break to steal home, but take just an ounce off his momentum. The pigtail would catch the ball and chase him back to third, even though he knew he could never catch Mays. "He permitted himself to be caught in rundowns between third and home," the *Sporting News* reported. "He befuddled his pursuers to emerge from the traps." Pompez laughed and Willie winked. You couldn't keep that boy in the hot box forever.

17

TAKE THAT GLOVE TO THE BIG LEAGUES

When Artie Wilson learned that the Giants had signed Willie Mays, he knew the Oakland Oaks would regret not listening to him. "I told them, 'You'll read about him,'" Wilson said. "He's a good ballplayer and he's gonna make it." When time passed and it became clear how special Mays was, Oaks owner Brick Laws lamented his lack of faith. "He said, 'I just let a million dollars run through my hands.' I said, 'I told you that.' Mays turned out to be one of the greatest ballplayers in history."

When Ed Montague signed Mays, he suggested to the Giants that he begin his career at Class B. It was not Montague's decision to make, but it wasn't a bad idea, and the Giants were thinking the same way. The contract called for Mays to be optioned to Triple-A Minneapolis, but if he was he would become the third black player on the team, joining Ray Dandridge and Dave Barnhill. Three black players on one minor league team was one too many, so the Giants sent Mays to Class B Trenton with a colored roommate, not Alonzo Perry, the Black Barons first baseman whom Montague dismissed with a crude assessment of "not a major league prospect, but OK for Class A."

Instead of Perry, it was Jose Fernandez Jr., the son of Alex Pompez's longtime player-manager for the Cubans. Fernandez had only played one year of low-level minor league baseball, and players who batted .100 in the East Texas League did not work out in major league uniforms with major league players in a major league stadium, as Fernandez had with the 1950 Giants, unless somebody was owed a favor.

So the Giants sent Mays to Trenton, where he could be mentored and protected by manager Chick Genovese. "They wanted my brother to take Mays because he was a hell of a center fielder and they wanted Mays to work with him," George Genovese said. When Mays met Chick, he was struck by the energy and the passion of a man he called "a little old guy," who he affectionately remembered "had a big mouth."

Chick had heard about Mays, but he was speechless when he saw him play for the first time. All of the amazing raw talents Mays had

A rookie minor leaguer in white folks' ball: Mays went 0-for-5 in his organized baseball debut in Trenton, then quickly found himself.

displayed in Negro baseball transferred effortlessly to white folks' ball. The pitching didn't intimidate him any more than it had Dandridge, who said black pitchers threw harder than white pitchers, and white pitchers threw "cute curves." The curveballs in Class B didn't faze Mays for very long. He was as advanced beyond the white players as he had been beyond the black players. Chick called George, who was playing for the Pacific Coast League's Hollywood Stars. George never forgot the breathless enthusiasm in Chick's voice. "He said, 'George, I've got the greatest ballplayer I've ever seen in my life. He makes plays you can't believe.'" George was skeptical. The instincts of a scout who signed players who combined to hit nearly 4,000 major league home runs were sharpening. "You mean to tell me you would rate him over DiMaggio?" George asked.

"He's better than DiMaggio," Chick said. George knew he wasn't lying by the profound seriousness in his voice. For the Genovese brothers, the sons of immigrant Ernest Genovese from Naples, Italy, there was no higher praise.

Chick also sang Mays's praises to Giants owner Horace Stoneham, who, although he had approved the purchase, didn't fully grasp Mays's significance to his team's future. Chick was bold enough to tell Stoneham that he thought Mays was better than DiMaggio. It seemed incomprehensible that a black man could be the best center fielder in New York City.

"Chick," Stoneham replied, wondering if Chick was in the whiskey, "have you forgotten we have Bobby Thomson playing center field?" Chick didn't miss a beat. "Bobby Thomson is going to have to move to left," he said.

Mays walked onto the field in Hagerstown, Maryland, on June 24 to play the Hagerstown Braves in his debut. "They call you all kinds of names," Mays remembered, "nigger this and nigger that." He remembered his lessons with Piper Davis aboard Charlie Rudd's bus. He ignored the insults and, starting slow offensively as he so often did, went 0-for-5 in his debut. But it didn't take Mays long to catch up.

Mays thought he had hit his way out of Trenton in about three weeks. He batted .353 in 81 games, while Chick looked after Mays like Piper had. "My brother took care of him," George Genovese said. "He sat with Mays when they made him eat in the kitchen instead of in the restaurants with the rest of the team." Fernandez quickly exhausted his usefulness, batting .211 in the 16 games Chick found creative ways to get him into, and was released at the end of the season.

Dandridge was scheduled to be Mays's roommate at Triple-A Minneapolis to begin the 1951 season, where the Millers would have three black players for the first time. Mays hit from the start. Dandridge, batting behind him in the lineup, was often the recipient of retaliation pitches aimed for his head. "Every time Willie would come up and bang one, they got to knock me down," Dandridge said. "I told [manager Tommy Heath], 'If you don't move me out of there, you're going to get me killed.'"

Mays murdered American Association pitching. He turned twenty in Triple-A, ravaging the league's pitching at an age when most boys were solving Class A. He stayed with Minneapolis for 35 memorable games in which he batted .477 and hit eight home runs.

When Mays came to the Giants, his path was cleared for him one last time by one of Willie's Boys. Mays would have been the fifth black player on the Giants roster, joining Hank Thompson, Monte Irvin, Ray Noble . . . and Artie Wilson. Artie had only four hits in his 22 major league at-bats, but his legacy should not be judged by a .182 major league batting average. The Underground Railroad's last stop was in Harlem. Artie saw no point in blocking Mays's path while he played once a week.

Artie had been purchased from the Oaks in a seven-player, $125,000 deal before the start of the 1951 season. Though Artie was with the Giants, he wasn't happy sitting on the bench behind shortstop Alvin Dark and second baseman Eddie Stanky. Giants manager Leo Durocher liked Artie and wanted to keep him with the Giants as a utility player. "A fellow who can field and hit the way he can is going to take somebody's job away," Durocher said.

But Artie knew Mays was ready. Artie did not see remaining in the majors as a bench player as a better career option than playing every day in the Pacific Coast League. "If you still think you can play, you want to play every day," said George Genovese, who in 1950 stayed with the Washington Senators for one month and had exactly one major league at-bat before asking to be released so he could rejoin the Coast League. "The money could be better than in the big leagues. A lot of us lived out here and made $10,000 a year. We did not look at it as any great advantage to stay in the big leagues to make less money and sit on our ass."

Artie saw it coming. When he checked the statistics in the *Sporting News* and saw Mays destroying Triple-A pitching, he said he went to Durocher and asked, "Why don't you let me go and bring Willie Mays up? I've known him my whole life."

There was symbolism to what Artie was trying to do, but also practicality. Durocher thought he was doing Artie a favor when he told him he would stay, bring up Mays, and send out Noble. Artie said no. Artie was no more a catcher than Mays was. "I told him, 'Let me go instead of Noble, because if [starter Wes] Westrum gets hurt, you won't have a catcher.'"

Durocher, as always, was painfully stubborn. He didn't like it when players told him what to do, but Artie wouldn't go away. "Wasn't doing me no good up there," Artie said. "Let him come on up and make some money. Let me go down and make me some of my own."

Finally, enticed by Mays's batting average and the uncommonly high praise of the minor league staff, Durocher relented. "So I went to Minneapolis," Artie said, "and they brought up Mays." Out went one former 1948 Birmingham Black Baron and in came another. Mays's gifts could no longer be ignored. The Giants brought him to the major leagues nineteen days after his twentieth birthday, debuting on May 25, the start of a career in which his totals became canon in baseball theology: 660 home runs, 3,283 hits, 1,903 runs batted in, a .302 lifetime average, and 24 all-star games for No. 24.

Mays went on to greatness, but countless great black ballplayers were left to continue the struggle in the minor leagues, including the great Dandridge, who said Stoneham refused to bring him up to the Giants because he was worth too much to the Minneapolis club. "They never really did give me a good explanation," Dandridge said, though the real explanation was that the quota system was in full effect. "Some say they already had too many blacks on the team."

Dandridge was right. There were too many blacks and not enough jobs. After the 1950 season ended, Tom Hayes had sold Piper Davis to the Houston Eagles, which was a favor. Shortly thereafter, Piper finally signed with a team from white folks' ball—Carl Hubbell's New York Giants. Perhaps Alex Pompez made certain that he received his commission for helping run his winning number to the majors. Piper began the 1951 season on loan from the Giants to the Oakland Oaks, where, of course, Artie had told them all about him. Artie played briefly in Minneapolis and then Ottawa, which traded him back to Oakland. Before the 1952 season began, Artie got his wish to play the rest of his career in the Pacific Coast League. He was sold to Seattle, where he racked up more than 200 hits for three consecutive years before finishing his career in Portland. After he retired from baseball he used his celebrity to help him sell automobiles when he could no longer run like one.

When Mays came up, Artie and Piper were essentially traded for each other. The Oaks owed the Giants a player in return for Artie in 1951, so Piper finished the season in Ottawa before he was returned to Oakland, where Piper finally found peace in white folks' ball. He batted .306 in 1952, and in 1953 he had 198 hits and hit 13 home runs, skillfully playing a different position every day, and earning the nickname "Lipper" because he killed high fastballs. Winning teams and profound respect followed Piper, who played on three minor league championship teams. He was a fan favorite, and in the final game of the 1952 Oaks season he played all nine positions in the same game. When racism occasionally appeared, Piper showed his teeth. In 1952, San Francisco Seals pitcher Bill Boemler applied what Piper felt was a dirty tag at home plate, so Piper came up punching. The brawl made national news. At the next game, plainclothes cops were in the stands because a letter signed by "The Gang of Nineteen" had threatened Piper's life if he played. Piper not only played, he got four hits.

A generation of young black players in Oakland, including Curt Flood, Willie Stargell, Vada Pinson, Frank Robinson, and Pumpsie

Green grew up admiring him. When Green became the first black to play in the majors with the Red Sox, he sent Piper a thank-you note, even though he didn't know him. What Piper did for Mays, he did for others, and his compassion was not confined by color. Jim Marshall, a young first baseman finding his way, fondly remembered long nights when Piper would sit with him, smoking his pipe like a baseball wise man, and teaching him. "He was a natural," Marshall said. "But I never remember him teaching me anything about hitting. He went deeper. His approach was very gentle and direct and his theories about the game were as modern then as they are now. He must have been a very good player-manager in the Negro Leagues, yet I never remember him saying he managed Willie Mays. And I want to say this. At no time did Piper Davis ever complain about the way he was treated. He was just too good of a man for that."

Piper never lost his sense of humor. Once, while catching for the Oaks against the Los Angeles Angels in 1955 with Gene Mauch batting, Piper called for three consecutive fastballs. Stunned because he was expecting a two-strike curveball, Mauch struck out, his bat dragging embarrassingly behind. Mauch later won 1,902 games as a major league manager, but this time Piper had outwitted him. Later that season, when Piper was sold to the Angels, Mauch was thrilled to see him join the team. He told him he was sure Piper would help them win, then asked Piper why he had dared have his pitcher throw him three successive fastballs. It defied baseball logic on a majestic scale. With his booming and proud voice, Piper bellowed, "Element of surprise, my dear brother!" A few weeks later, Mauch was summoned to the Boston Red Sox to play second base. Piper handed him his infielder's mitt and told Mauch to wear it and think of him when he played at Fenway Park. "Take that glove with you," Piper said. "That's the only way it's getting to the big leagues."

Bill Greason never gave up his quest to pitch in the majors, but during the 1950 season he mournfully remembered his mother, Lizzie, calling him to say that there was a letter from the president of the United

States. Greason knew what it meant. The U.S. Marines had recalled him for the Korean War, so he came to the ballpark in his street clothes and told Piper he had to leave.

Greason got lucky when a general found out he was a baseball player. He put him on his team, where Greason struck out twenty batters in a sixteen-inning game, winning Greason more fame than he ever attained in the Negro Leagues. After he was discharged, he was sold to owner Jimmy Humphries of Oklahoma City. In 1952, Greason's first year in white folks' ball, he went 9–1. Humphries set the asking price at $50,000. "Cool at all times, he's going to be a great major league pitcher," he said. In 1953, Greason won 16 games at Oklahoma City. The Yankees and the Red Sox showed interest, but said they were scared off by the price, not by the color. Finally, in 1954, the St. Louis Cardinals needed a roommate for first baseman Tom Alston, so they purchased Greason and sent him to Triple-A Columbus. Greason had a bad feeling that he was nothing but a goose shooter.

When Greason went to minor league spring training with the Cardinals in 1954 at Albany, Georgia, he was handed the Cardinals camp manual, which laid out in plain language the Cardinals' segregation policies for meals, transportation, and living:

> While you are in camp, you will receive a meal allowance of $3.50. All colored players will get their meals at Albany State College for Colored. They have a good cafeteria. If you are a white player, you should go to the Lee Hotel. On the other hand, if you are a colored player, you should take a taxicab to Gibson Hall, Albany State College for Colored, where you will be housed for the night and indeed for the entire time you are in training camp. A colored player will come directly from Albany State College in a special bus. All white players will be roomed in private homes while colored players will be housed in Gibson Hall, Albany State College for Colored.

Greason found his way to the big leagues that year, where he became the Cardinals' first black pitcher. The segregation and discrimination ate away at him, and his inner Piper flared when he was summoned to the Cardinals from the minor leagues, only to learn that the team made him take a pay cut. "When I left Columbus, I was making $1,200 a month," Greason said. "When I got to the Cardinals, they gave me a contract for $900 a month. I wasn't a preacher then, so I used a bad word. I said, 'What the hell is this?'"

Greason indelibly remembered this one-sided negotiation. "They told me, 'You got to prove yourself.' I said, 'You called me up, I must have proven something.' The Cardinals told me, 'Take it or leave it.' So what am I going to do? I took it. It made me feel bad. When they offered that contract, it just killed my spirit. For two weeks, I didn't touch a baseball. I just went running. I thought, 'This is the majors, I'm supposed to get more here than I did in the minors.' The league minimum was $1,250 per month and they gave me a contract for $900. I tried to get there for years, and then when I got there, I didn't want to stay."

Greason spent two miserable, lonely weeks with the Cardinals. He pitched only four innings. In his two starts, he was yanked out of the games faster than his Alabama-reared manager Eddie Stanky could spew tobacco juice from his front teeth. Greason never did get a chance. He was thrilled to return to the minors, where he bounced around until 1959.

The minor leagues weren't always an easy place, either. When Greason pitched at Triple-A Rochester in 1959, his catcher was Charles Staniland, a white player from California who grew up in the Cardinals organization. "There were a lot more players than Mays ready to play in the big leagues and white players took offense to that," Staniland said. "They used the n-word like drinking water. I played in Oklahoma in 1953 and 1954 when we had two black players. The players killed those guys in the locker room. The fans killed them during the game. It was horrible and I saw that happen to a lot of young black players. Old timers would bitch that black players ruined the game: 'They aren't paying us nothing and they'll play for less.'"

White players should have been angry with their owners for paying black players less than they were worth, driving their own salaries down, a practice that endured for decades and oppressed both whites and blacks. While Mays was the darling of the Polo Grounds and the Giants took sole credit for discovering and developing him, every-day black players suffered beneath him, men like his boys, the 1948 Birmingham Black Barons, playing careers that had few happy endings. Musty memories sustained the pride white folks' ball had stripped away with cheap contracts and segregation. Greason, however, found peace. He has led his own congregation for more than three decades after becoming one of the few former Negro League players to graduate college. "There came a point," he said, "when I had to let it go."

On the same jump to Harlem in 1950 when Charlie Rudd's bus burned, she wasn't the only one who didn't make it home to Birmingham. Pitcher Jimmy Newberry fled to Canada's Manitoba-Dakota League, where he signed with the Winnipeg Buffaloes and won 13 games in two years. Newberry made enough connections so the rest of the 1948 Black Barons could follow him north, and soon Willie's Boys were scattered across North America. Pepper Bassett, Johnny Britton, Sammy Williams, Bobby Robinson, and Ed Steele played in Canada. Herman Bell played the rest of his years for wherever cash could be found in Alabama. Later, Newberry and Britton became two of the first black players to be sold to play in Japan's major league. Steele had a brief, unsuccessful stint with the Hollywood Stars in the Pacific Coast League before he finished his career with the ragtag Detroit Stars and eventually came home to Birmingham. Years later, when he answered a questionnaire, he seemed shocked that someone remembered him. Like many Negro League ballplayers, his personal history was washed out like a faded photograph. "I will send some photos when I find my scrapbook. They moved it around when I was in the hospital," Steele wrote. "I have a glove and a bat with my name on it if you want it."

Newberry wanted to pitch. He bounced around the minors for most of the 1950s, the bottle his constant companion. Three times, teams exasperated with his antics traded him. His final stop was in Big Springs, Texas, in the Longhorn League, which folded after Newberry pitched for them for a few weeks late in the 1955 season. Newberry had a tryout with the Brooklyn Dodgers at Ebbets Field in 1950, but scout Elwood Parsons wired: "NEWBERRY LACKED ACCEPTABLE FASTBALL." Whatever fastball he once had was mostly gone in 1955, when another 1948 Black Barons outcast, Jimmy Zapp, was traded to Big Springs, where for a few short weeks they were reunited. "He was still partying," Zapp said. Newberry, though, didn't care that he had jumped the Black Barons. In his eyes, there was nothing to go back to.

No former Black Baron achieved more without ever playing in the majors than Alonzo Perry. For a time, he too followed Newberry to Canada, but he won his greatest fame as a flamboyant mercenary, playing summers in Mexico and winters in the Dominican Republic. In 1956, he won the Mexican League Triple Crown when he batted .392 with 28 home runs and 118 runs batted in. "I broke all of Josh Gibson's and Cool Papa Bell's records in Mexico," he said. In the Dominican Republic, where dictator Rafael Trujillo once told manager Chick Genovese, "If you don't win, you don't get off the island," Perry flashed his gold teeth and charmed Trujillo. Trujillo paid him a king's salary of $1,500 a month and housed him in a twelve-room mansion, where Perry undoubtedly sired some of the twenty-three children he claimed to be his own. "Whenever the Trujillo kids wanted to have a party, they held it at my house," Perry said. No party was louder than in 1951 when Perry hit a grand slam in the Dominican League championship game and drove in 10 runs in the series to lead the legendary Licey Tigres to the first of fifteen championships. From then on, Perry was called Su Majested, "His Majesty."

After realizing the Giants really had no interest in him, Perry turned his back on white folks' ball and counted his cash. Leo Durocher tried to sign him for the Giants in 1952, but the money was an insult. The Pirates made an offer a few years later, but Perry wasn't about to trade the good life to go sit in Triple-A and wait for a limited chance. Jimmy Zapp, who was Perry's closest friend and roommate on the 1948 Black Barons, said that though Perry didn't regret taking less money when he was younger, he saddened as he aged because he knew he could have done majestic things in the majors. "Deep down, he felt deprived," Zapp said.

"You wouldn't have missed his power," George Genovese said.

Bobby Veale shook his head. "That goes to show you when a player is repressed."

Bobby Veale. His was a name that Kansas City Monarchs owner Tom Baird became very familiar with in 1954, when with his franchise dying and local players turning their backs on him, he reached into Birmingham for the first time to recruit a local boy from Alabama's rich coal mine country. But Bobby Veale, like his father before him, had observed for years what they believed to be the false idolatry of the Monarchs. "Baird didn't chip no ice with me," Veale said.

Bobby had finally made his way into a Black Barons team photo in 1950, a right he earned with years of hustling for foul balls, carrying luggage for a coin, and honing his arm strength by throwing hours upon hours of batting practice. He knelt in the front row, a stern look on his face, without the heavy black glasses that would later frame his face. Willie Mays knelt also, with a glowing smile that indicated the photograph was snapped while Willie was laughing. Veale's passion complemented Mays's playfulness. Veale had longed to pitch to Mays in a real game, and though it would take him a few years and a journey of more than a few miles away from Birmingham to fulfill that goal, he was ready. He believed his fastball could overmatch any opponent, including discrimination. Buck O'Neil had seen that powerful left arm when Veale unofficially pitched for the Black Barons, and Tom Baird began writing letters:

November 24, 1954

Dear Mr. Veale:

If you want your boy to start with a team that sends more young players to the big leagues than any other team in the country, we think the Kansas City Monarchs can give your boy the chance to go to the big leagues.

The ice didn't chip:

June 10, 1955

Manager John O'Neil advised me that he talked to you and your son when the Monarchs played at Birmingham May 1. He was informed . . . that your boy wanted to join the Monarchs. . . . But you had changed your mind and your boy was going to school under some scholar set up, I heard was in Atchinson [*sic*], Kansas.

Veale said he never agreed to sign with the Monarchs. He and his father resented that Baird tried to coerce him into signing. "I could have played professional baseball when I was fourteen, I could throw just that hard," Bobby said. "But I wasn't going to sign." Veale ignored Baird and went to Benedictine College. Baird hated being snubbed by Birmingham blacks.

I am sure you know what you are doing. . . . I want to help not hurt your career. . . . I am sure you will find out that if you play organized baseball, it will be with or through the Kansas City Monarchs.

"Buck O'Neil and all those guys," Veale said, "were demagogues. They were out for their own personal gain, one way or another, for financial and prestigious gain, or whatever they were seeking at the expense of others. I didn't think it was too businesslike and I didn't think it was too compassionate. My daddy said, 'If you got what it takes, everything will work out.' That was some good advice from my daddy."

Veale found his way. After college, when a scout asked him how old he was and Veale said twenty-two, the scout sniped back, "You want to add six more years to that?" Veale glared at him. "What are you trying to make of that?" he said. "That I was born in 1929? I was born in 1935. All my stats are documented on my birth certificate. I'll be here five or ten years after you are gone."

Veale outlasted Cardinals scout Runt Marr by many more years. Marr gave Veale a workout with white pitcher Ray Sadecki and gave

Sadecki a brand-new major league uniform. Veale had to borrow spikes. His birthplace was Birmingham, so he made an art form out of correcting those in white folks' ball who assumed he was illiterate. "A lot of black athletes didn't have the education or the ability to speak like Piper," he said. "The major league owners were afraid to take a chance on some players because illiteracy was quite a problem. Most of them left home to work in the pipe shop or the wire mill or the foundry. That is why Mays was so lucky to get out, because they put him in that category, which he did not deserve. You had a guy like Greason, who was articulate and he could play, and he had a damn hard time. The guys who came from Alabama, Mays and Aaron, guys you could see from afar that they would be dominating major league players, they still had it harder."

Veale made it because he threw harder than almost any left-hander in the 1960s. Bobby Veale grew up to be known as Bob Veale, the fearsome six-foot-six pitcher for the Pittsburgh Pirates who, in his day, averaged one strikeout an inning and one nasty glare per batter. He struck out more than 200 batters in four years and led the National League with 250 strikeouts in 1964. It took Veale until he was twenty-six to get to the majors and he still pitched for thirteen years and compiled a 120–95 major league record. He pitched in relief for the world champion Pirates in 1971, participating in the first major league game composed entirely of minority players, including his longtime friend and teammate right fielder Roberto Clemente, of whom Veale said, "When you watched Mays and you watched Roberto, pick one, because they were the same player."

Veale made two all-star teams, in 1965 and 1966, and each time, Willie Mays played center field and batted leadoff. Veale didn't have to shag balls anymore, but, like Mays, he considered his time with Piper Davis and the 1948 Black Barons to be a silent part of his baseball identity. When he was done playing, he became a pitching coach and a scout, and he believes eleven of the sixteen players from a Piper kind of team could have played in the majors if they had been born at the right moment, just as he had barely been. If you counted Bobby Veale, always called Bobby in Birmingham, but only Bob outside of the trees and time, then it would actually be an even dozen who could have played or did reach the majors from the 1948 Negro American League champion Birmingham Black Barons. But if you ask him if he ever wore their uniform, Veale will only wink, and find it amusing that his real name cannot be found in the Black Barons box scores, not now, nor will it ever be.

On June 20, 1950, the day the Giants signed Mays, Tom Baird offered the New York Yankees another ballplayer. "I signed Ernest Banks, 19-year-old shortstop, and he looks like he will make a hell of a good ballplayer, have been hearing about him for three years." Just as the Yankees ignored Mays, they passed on Ernie Banks. Later, Baird bragged, "O'Neil said he has everything a ballplayer should have. You better get your information from Dizzy, for anything I say will look like a high-powered sales talk."

When Baird heard that Tom Hayes had sold Mays to the Giants, he was infuriated and envious. Mays's escape from Birmingham prodded every element of Baird's bigotry. Had he learned that Hayes had received a letter from Horace Stoneham, a white owner writing a letter to a black owner, he would have boiled. Not even the great Tom Baird of the great Kansas City Monarchs ever became privy to such a courtesy. Alex Pompez would have enjoyed Baird's angst.

Baird had been close to selling his best young player, Elston Howard, to the Chicago Cubs. But when Mays became a Giant, Baird decided that Howard must become a Yankee instead. "The Cubs wanted Elston Howard, but I wouldn't sell him, we may need him to replace DiMaggio," he wrote, knowing DiMaggio, who had collected his two thousandth career hit the day Mays signed and kissed the ball like it was Marilyn's lips, was breaking down as swiftly as the Negro Leagues.

There was no "we" between the Yankees and the Monarchs, even though Baird boasted imaginatively, "I feel like I am part of the Yankee organization." When Cubs farm director Jack Sheehan read in the newspaper that Baird had sold Howard to the Yankees instead of the Cubs, he wrote, "My disappointment is not in failing to get the player, but because you did not keep your promise to me."

Baird didn't care. Howard had to be sold to the Yankees immediately. Baird could not stand the thought of Birmingham becoming a greater source of players than Kansas City. He was petty and his letters to the Yankees reflected his prideful and boisterous gloating. "Jack Sheehan of the Cubs was sore as a wet hound [on] account I didn't give him a chance to deal for Howard. Some of the big league organizations seem to think they should get any player they scout or talk to me about with them. The other fellow is always wrong. I know you run into plenty of that kind of horse trading."

Baird might have started to grasp that he was dealing with the glue factory when he formed a friendship with Wid Matthews and, through him, sold Banks to the Cubs. Matthews wrote that the gleeful shortstop "hit the first ball pitched to him . . . into the left field bleachers" when he reported to the Cubs in 1953, the first of 512 career home runs. Baird was involved in virtually every major transaction involving black players in the 1950s. He bragged that he blocked the Giants from acquiring Henry Aaron in 1952, when the Giants called the Morrison Hotel in Chicago looking for Indianapolis owner Syd Pollack. Baird smelled Pompez, who knew about Aaron from Jesse Thomas, the same Mobile bird-dog scout who two years later sent him Willie McCovey. Baird detested the idea of Aaron and Mays in the same lineup. He made sure that the Clowns called the Milwaukee Braves to formalize their handshake agreement. The Braves were still fuming that they had missed Mays. Baird bragged, "Hank Aaron would have been with the New York Giants if it hadn't been for the help I gave."

Baird helped Buck O'Neil get a scouting job with the Cubs, though Buck owed much of his success to Cool Papa Bell, who, because he was in the lower levels of Negro baseball despite being ten times the player O'Neil was, knew about prospects long before Buck did. Cool was a generous soul, who once turned down the St. Louis Browns because he was too old and felt he would be blocking somebody younger. Cool wasn't a climber like Buck was. He was the purest Monarch. Baird failed to mention that it was Cool Papa Bell who sent Banks to Buck O'Neil, who in turn sent him to Baird.

Buck O'Neil (third from left) went from managing the Kansas City Monarchs to becoming one of the first full-time black scouts in baseball, following in the footsteps of former Monarchs pitcher John Donaldson, who became the first full-time black scout with the Chicago White Sox in 1949.

Bell did, however, take pride in knowing that he told Baird about Mays in 1948. When Bell was elected to the Hall of Fame, he posed with a large Adirondack baseball bat, which had been a gift from a center fielder from another time. Bell widely grinned and turned the barrel so the signature on the bat faced the cameras. It read: Willie Mays.

Baird finally got a small measure of respect from the Yankees when they got him a scouting job for the Kansas City Athletics in 1961, a year before his death, and six years after he sold the Monarchs in 1955, lamenting, "I am crazy about the Negro American League, but the baseball fans don't seem to give a damn about it." Though Baird would have hated it, the Kansas Klansman is forever linked with the Harlem Hustler and the Memphis Mortician and Willie Mays. Hayes sold the Black Barons in 1951 and occasionally clipped newspaper stories about his most famous player, but Baird refused to accept that the best all-around player from the Negro Leagues to the major leagues hadn't been a Kansas City Monarch, but a Birmingham Black Baron. In twenty-four boxes of personal material Baird left behind, only once does he mention Willie Mays. A few years before he died, he found himself in a pensive mood like the one his old rivals Tom Hayes and Abe Saperstein had also been in a few years before they passed away. "They were rough, tough days, but we were young, and could take most anything," Saperstein wrote to Hayes. Baird, sensing the end, typed out an all-star team comprised of former Negro Leaguers. In place of his own great center fielder, Willard Brown, Baird misspelled, "Willie Mayes."

The animosity between the Black Barons and the Monarchs continued well into death. Buck O'Neil died in 2006, a few months after he was denied election to the Hall of Fame by the same special committee that elected Alex Pompez. Two years later, a statue of O'Neil was erected at the entrance of the Hall of Fame gallery, where it is not far from the plaque honoring Willie Mays. But to see Mays, you must walk past the statue of the former manager of the Kansas City Monarchs, whose back is eternally turned to the Birmingham Black Barons.

Bill Maughn was never the same after the Boston Braves turned their back on him in 1949 and refused to heed his call to go after Mays. The official story was that the Braves didn't need another center fielder because they had spent $100,000 to purchase Sam Jethroe from the Brooklyn Dodgers a year after Branch Rickey's Dodgers bought him from the Cleveland Buckeyes for only $5,000. The Braves had cash flow problems, having dropped from a league-leading 1.45 million fans in 1948 to 944,391 in 1950, when they finished seventh in attendance, the only statistic baseball owners truly care about. But Maughn's dogged persistence finally convinced the Braves to dispatch a scout to cross-check Mays. The scout, Hugh wise, told Maughn the Braves were not interested in signing Mays. Maughn couldn't understand how any scout could reject Mays, but deep down he knew exactly why his hands were tied. "For some reason unknown to me then or now, he passed Mays up," Maughn said.

Maughn was too much of a gentleman to admit that the Braves wouldn't sign Mays because he was black. Braves farm director Harry Jenkins was following mandates from ownership, the descendants of whom can be found in baseball today. At Triple-A Milwaukee in 1950, the Braves had two black players, Negro League veterans Buster Clarkson and Lenny Pearson. There was no room for Mays there. At Double-A were former Negro Leaguers George Crowe and Stanley Glenn. Two Negroes per team were enough for the Boston Braves. In 1951, Crowe joined Clarkson and Pearson in Milwaukee, making it three. Jenkins turned down Tom Baird's overtures to sell pitcher Jim LaMarque there, writing, "The truth is we have three colored boys at Milwaukee. And if we take another, I am fearful the club will get top heavy."

Top-heavy was the reason Willie Mays never played for the Braves. Bill Maughn always felt he should have been the guy to sign Mays, but when he knew he wasn't, he told Eddie Montague about him. Montague denied until his death that Maughn ever mentioned Mays to him, writing, "I believe he should correct his statement and say that he spoke about a young ballplayer around Birmingham with a great arm, but I do not recall Maughn even mentioning the name of Willie Mays."

Maughn resented Montague for his condescending tone. Al LaMacchia said he dined with Montague and Maughn in June 1950 in Montgomery, where Montague stopped on the road to Birmingham. "The three of us were having dinner," LaMacchia said. "Eddie Montague said, 'I'm down here to see Alonzo Perry.' Bill Maughn said, 'You should see Willie Mays.'"

"I did not go into Birmingham to see Willie Mays because Bill Maughn talked about him," Montague wrote. In that case, Montague was going to unusually extreme lengths to acquire a lowly minor league first base-man. Scout Bob Zuk, who signed Hall of Famers Willie Stargell, Reggie Jackson, and Gary Carter, believed a scout never forgot the behind-the-scenes circumstances that led him to his claim to fame. "If you are not lying to other scouts, you're not scouting," Zuk said. "But your lies should never take credit for the work other people did."

Al LaMacchia, who became a legendary scout, just shook his head. "Ed Montague didn't consider himself the luckiest scout in the world," he said. "But he should have."

Maughn drove to Birmingham in 1965 to give an interview to the *Birmingham News*. There was urgency in his voice as he told his story. A year later, he died of cancer. "The only thing I want to get straightened out," Maughn said, "is the fact that I was not out hustled."

There are three transactions that changed both America and baseball: the sale of Babe Ruth to the Yankees from the Red Sox, the Brooklyn Dodgers' signing of Jackie Robinson, and the New York Giants' signing of Willie Mays. Mays's signing was also the reason the Braves wanted Henry Aaron so badly two years later. Nobody in the National League wanted Mays and Aaron, Alabama's best, together. Mays's deal shaped so many deals around him that it belongs, like him, in a class by itself, one that changed the major league landscape and influenced almost every major move many teams made. What if Mays and Aaron had played together? What if Mays and Ted Williams had played together? Would the Red Sox have won a World Series? Would the Yankees have been forced to integrate sooner? Who would be the home run champion? If Mays hadn't been a Giant, would young Bobby Bonds have signed with the San Francisco Giants because he wanted to play with Mays and because his girlfriend was pregnant with the baby who became Mays's godson?

John Donaldson also wished his employers had listened to him. He had signed Bob Boyd and Connie Johnson, but the Chicago White Sox wouldn't let him sign Mays. When Donaldson lost Ernie Banks to the Cubs, he was finished. He quit, and the greatest left-handed pitcher nobody has ever heard of went on with a quiet life. There was a dignity about him, one that transcended the callousness that had transpired on Willie Mays's rocky ride aboard the Underground Railroad out of Birmingham and into the big leagues. When he heard Mays was gone, Donaldson wrote to Tom Hayes.

June 26, 1950

Dear Sir:

I've boasted highly of William Greason to Mr. Lane, General Manager of the White Sox. I have a letter asking me if I could get Greason to come up for a workout at Comiskey Park. I told him I would write you concerning the matter. Let me know if you can arrange it. I'll see that the fare and expenses will be taken care of.

Respectfully your friend,
John W. Donaldson

PS—Glad you sold Mays. I wish him the best of luck.

"HE WAS THIRTEEN AGAIN"

The curse of the gifted baseball player is that what he is best at ends early in life. Age caught Willie's Boys one at a time, until 2006 when only four were left. At the Professional Baseball Scouts Foundation banquet, Mays was asked to choose who should receive the inaugural award named after him. He donated his appearance fee and called Grease, Squeaky, Zapp, and Sammy C. On the event floor, Mays was an old man, tired of the same celebrity routine, worn out from signing a zillion autographs and fielding a million "Do you remember that time?" moments. He sought that which could be not be duplicated. He found his boys inside the lobby of the Beverly Hills Hotel, but the moment the five survivors converged, the five-star hotel with glass walls and marble floors became Bob's Savoy on Negro Avenue, and of course, they went upstairs. Inside the hotel room, Charlie Rudd's bus rode again. It could have been Kansas City or Birmingham. Mays was a little boy again and the only child of a great big happy baseball family, where nothing else mattered but winning, playing hard, and having fun.

An event organizer saw something she never forgot. There was seventy-five-year old Willie Mays, happy as a teenager sitting Indian-style in a 1948 team photograph, with a hat too large on his head. He wasn't Willie Mays. He was Buck Duck. "When I saw him," she said, "he was thirteen again."

"These guys mean so much to me," Mays said. "We had some good times together."

Mays gave the microphone to Bill Greason, who is as comfortable on a pulpit as he was on the pitcher's mound. He didn't tell stories about how great Mays had been. He didn't share stories of discrimination, or of something called the hot box. It was the last time the survivors were going to be together and they knew it. Just like Greason took the ball in the championship game and beat the Monarchs, he knew it wasn't about Mays. It was about survival, compassion, and consideration. Most of all, none of them were thinking about Mays. They thought of the teammate they missed most. "Let me tell you about our manager," Greason told the audience, "Piper Davis."

Willie's Boys returned to their hotel rooms after dinner. Willie stood and hugged each man. Then, just like the night in Chattanooga in 1948 when Piper brought Willie to the world, he thanked each man and prepared for the rest of his life. One by one they left, until Willie was finally alone, a senior citizen and baseball legend. Willie, who represented youth to millions, watched as his 1948 Black Barons went home. To him, they represented *his* youth. But he had never been alone. When the world watched Mays play baseball, they never knew they were watching the souls of the men he carried with him from the 1948 Birmingham Black Barons.

When they saw his physical gifts, they saw Mays alone, the born ballplayer who only knew that he had been chosen, but never knew why. When the world watched Willie, they didn't know they were also seeing Artie Wilson's beaming smile. When they saw Willie's daring, they saw Ed Steele grinning after a good throw. When they heard about

Willie hitting the town, it was really Jimmy Newberry, Alonzo Perry, and Jehosie Heard having one last blast. When they saw him become a veteran player, grumpy as his body broke, they saw Pepper Bassett desperate for a good night's sleep on a bus ride that never ended. When they saw him age and seek perspective in moments like this, they saw Bill Powell's calm, Bobby Veale's wit, and Bill Greason's perspective.

More than anyone else, when the world saw Willie, it saw a Piper kind of player. When they saw Mays angry, they saw Piper. When they saw him proud and defiant, they saw Piper. When they saw him laugh and joke, they most certainly saw Piper. When they saw him struggle at the end of his career, they saw Piper, who warned him how difficult it would be to walk away. When they saw him become a hero instead of a target, they also saw Piper, who taught him he could not be touched. Over the years, Mays's skills deserted him, his body softened, and his arm became an arm. One deal after another came and went, and he followed the money, but even when the cash occasionally blurred his vision, the world still saw Piper, because Mays would always try to set things right.

When you saw Willie Mays, you saw baseball, you saw what you wanted it to be, and it did not matter what color it was. Somewhere Piper was proud when he looked down on that stage, and perhaps he was standing behind Mays. Willie's roots burrowed deep into America and wound around those black and white, good and bad, rich and poor, honest and dishonest, racist and unbiased, secure and insecure. Willie Mays, the product of an imperfect America, stemmed from a long-ago place on a long-gone map, pure iron ore, the protégé of a man called Piper.

Mays was seated in front of a large video monitor in the ballroom that played black-and-white footage of his baseball career. The image of him making his famous over-the-shoulder catch in the 1954 World Series flickered over his shoulder. Mays had made better catches, but only four men that night would have believed it. As surely as the image of the ball rocketed out of the frame, the fans never realized that the throw was better than the catch, an inkling of what he really could do in Birmingham, when he was playing for love. The film clip played all night, long after the tables were empty.

NOTES

You can't have a baseball story without statistics, especially about the Negro Leagues, where most players didn't care as much about their batting average as about where they were going to eat and sleep. Because Negro League history lacks reliable statistical records, the research for *Willie's Boys* was based on a concerted, disciplined, time-consuming survey of period newspapers from around the country, complemented by the existing literature and firsthand accounts, and finished off with my own personal interviews with thirty-two different sources. All told, the research for *Willie's Boys* combed about two hundred different sources. In the interest of space I must omit itemized footnotes, but these notes will be useful for those wishing to hop the bus and immerse themselves in this long-gone world.

I consulted twenty period newspapers in the research, the most important of which were the black-owned and black-produced *Birmingham World, Kansas City Call, New York Age, Chicago Defender,* and *Pittsburgh Courier.* Other newspapers that helped illuminate uncharted narrative territory were the *Sporting News, New York Times, New York Amsterdam News, New York Newsday, Los Angeles Times, Jefferson City (MO) Post Tribune, Joplin (MS) Globe, Oakland Tribune, Minneapolis Star Tribune, Huntsville (AL) Times, Cullman (AL) Banner, Cullman Democrat, Cleveland Call and Post,* and *Baltimore Afro-American.*

There is a core of reference books that serves as the backbone for any Negro league effort. These canons are *The Biographical Encyclopedia of the Negro Baseball Leagues* by James A. Riley (New York: Carroll & Graf, 1994) and *The Negro Leagues Book,* edited by Dick Clark and Larry Lester (Cleveland: Society for American Baseball Research, 1994). *The Encyclopedia of Minor League Baseball,* 2nd ed., edited by Lloyd Johnson and Miles Wolff (Durham, NC: Baseball America, 1997), provides the road map for the vast minor league system of the postwar era, and *The Sporting News Baseball Guides* from 1948 to 1950 serve as valuable references.

Among the rich oral histories of former Negro League players, Brent Kelly's trilogy was read from beginning to end: *Voices from the Negro Leagues: Conversations with 52 Baseball Standouts* (Jefferson, NC: McFarland, 1998), *The Negro Leagues Revisited: Conversations with 66 More Baseball Heroes* (Jefferson, NC: McFarland, 2000), and *I Will Never Forget: Interviews with 39 Former Negro League Players* (Jefferson, NC: McFarland, 2003). Also, *Black Diamonds: Life in the Negro Leagues from the Men Who Lived It* by John B. Holway (New York: Stadium Books, 1991) provided further commentary from players from the 1948–1950 era.

Generally speaking, I feel that *Great Negro Baseball Stars and How They Made the Major Leagues* by A. S. "Doc" Young (New York: A. S. Barnes, 1953) was the period's best account of baseball integration. Doc Young was a bold man to call out Branch Rickey on his quota policy. More recently, *Baseball's Great Experiment: Jackie Robinson and His Legacy* by Jules Tygiel (New York: Vintage, 1983) is the grandfather to *Willie's Boys*.

Among Willie Mays literature, I most frequently consulted *Say Hey: The Autobiography of Willie Mays* by Willie Mays and Lou Sahadi (New York: Simon & Schuster, 1988), *Willie Mays* by Arnold Hano (New York: Tempo, 1966), *The Willie Mays Story* by Ken Smith (New York: Greenburg, 1954), and *Willie Mays: My Life In and Out of Baseball* by Willie Mays and Charles Einstein (New York: Dutton, 1966). A carefully chosen number of one-liners from the *Interview with Willie Mays* (Washington, DC: Academy of Achievement: A Museum of Living History, 1996) was useful, especially in the 1949 and 1950 years, as were Mays's comments at his Hall of Fame induction speech from 1982.

The personal papers of Birmingham Black Barons owner Tom Hayes and Kansas City Monarchs owner Tom Baird greatly enhanced the story of the rivals. Hayes's papers are housed at the T. H. Hayes Collection, Memphis and Shelby County Room, Memphis Public Library and Information Center. Baird's papers are located inside the T. Y. Baird Collection, Kansas Collection, Spencer Research Library, University of Kansas Libraries. Scouting reports were procured from the Branch Rickey Papers, Collections of the Manuscript Division, Library of Congress.

Among databases compiled by the Society of American Baseball Research, the Minor League Player Database saved me many times. Rod Nelson's scouts database helped me track the ivory hunters and the Ballparks Database helped me confirm sites. Along online databases, www.retrosheet.org and baseball-reference.com were invaluable.

Several newspaper clip files from the Baseball Hall of Fame were consulted, including files for Pepper Bassett, Joe Scott, Piper Davis, Artie Wilson, Johnny Britton, Ed Steele, Norman Robinson, Willie Mays, Jimmy Zapp, Jimmy Newberry, Bill Greason, Jehosie Heard, Alonzo Perry, Buck O'Neil, Hank Thompson, Willard Brown, Bob Thurman, Luke Easter, Alex Pompez, Winfield Welch, Carl Hubbell,

Paul Pettit, Wid Matthews, Jack Fournier, Dan Bankhead, George Genovese, and Chick Genovese. Also, the clip files housed at the Birmingham Public Library were utilized with great success.

Piper Davis's strong voice is ever present throughout *Willie's Boys*. Piper did many interviews in his lifetime, three of which comprise the majority of his comments in this narrative: oral histories conducted by Chris Fullerton, Sam Fischer, and Theodore Rosengarten, whose definitive 1977 interview published as "Reading the Hops: Recollections of Lorenzo 'Piper' Davis and the Negro Baseball League" (*Southern Exposure*, Summer/Fall 1977) is the gold standard. Fullerton's interview can be found in the archives of the Birmingham Public Library and Fisher's interview is on file at the Baseball Hall of Fame. Jules Tygiel also conducted an interview with Piper, and it is on file at the Baseball Hall of Fame. Artie Wilson's personal interviews are supplemented by his interview with Tygiel and a roundtable conducted at the Negro League Baseball Museum, also on file at the Baseball Hall of Fame.

Chapter 1. Trapped in the Hot Box

Describing Piper Davis's early years was best achieved with the help of Rosengarten's and Fullerton's interviews. Those were supported by John Holway's interview "Piper Davis" (*Baseball History* 4, January 1991), his Mule Suttles interview in *Blackball Stars: Negro League Pioneers* by John B. Holway (New York: Carroll & Graf, 1988), and his "Historically Speaking: Harry Salmon, Black Diamond of the Coal Mines" (*Black Sports Magazine*, November 1974). The Birmingham Black Barons clip files, ACIPCO News, Jefferson County period road maps, additional Black Barons oral history tapes, and Piper Davis's funeral program at the Birmingham Public Library were all vital to recreating Piper's Alabama. Descriptions of Willie Foster were aided by Buck O'Neil's scouting report in the Baseball Hall of Fame clip files and a personal interview with Tommy Butler. The *Birmingham World* and *Chicago Defender* newspapers assisted, as did Piper's daughter, Faye Davis.

Chapter 2. Negro Avenue

Every Other Sunday: The Story of the Birmingham Black Barons by Christopher D. Fullerton (Birmingham, AL: R. Boozer Press, 1999) is the best starting point for reconstructing black Birmingham and the role of its baseball team. "Caste in Steele: Jim Crow Careers in Birmingham, Alabama" by Robert J. Norrell (*Journal of American History*, Volume 73, December 1986) provides an idea of the tough life of the mill worker. *Ted "Double Duty" Radcliffe: 36 Years of Pitching & Catching in Baseball's Negro Leagues* by Kyle P. McNary (Minneapolis: McNary Publishing, 1994) is a fine oral history of one of the many all-stars who played in Birmingham. Tommy Sampson's interview with Brent Kelly and Piper's recollection of recruiting Artie Wilson were vital and also described by Holway. The Hall of Fame clip files of Jack

Fournier, Winfield Welch, and Buck O'Neil were consulted, as were the *Birmingham World*, *Chicago Defender*, *New York Times*, and *Los Angeles Times*.

Chapter 3. A Piper Kind of Team

Birmingham General Ordinance, Section 859, Separation of the Races, is on file at the Birmingham Public Library. Also at Birmingham are the oral history tales with 1948 Black Barons Wiley Griggs and Bill Powell. Personal interviews with Bill Greason, Jimmy Zapp, Bobby Veale, and Bob Scranton were used, as were the clip files of the 1948 Black Barons at the Baseball Hall of Fame. Buck O'Neil's scouting reports on Monarchs Willard Brown and Hilton Smith are also at the Hall of Fame. The *Birmingham World*, *Chicago Defender*, and *New York Times* were consulted, as were the books *Black Writers/Black Baseball: An Anthology of Articles from Black Sportswriters Who Covered the Negro Leagues* by Jim Reisler (Jefferson, NC: McFarland, 1994), *20 Years Too Soon: Prelude to Major-League Integrated Baseball* by Quincy Trouppe (St. Louis: Missouri Historical Society Press, 1977, 1995), and *Press Box Red* by Irwin Silber (Philadelphia: Temple University Press, 2003).

Chapter 4. The Defenders of Rickwood Field

Personal interviews conducted with Bob Scranton, Bobby Veale, and Al LaMacchia played vital roles in recreating Rickwood Field. *Good Wood: A Fan's History of Rickwood Field* by Ben Cook (Birmingham, AL: R. Boozer Press, 2005) is Rickwood's definitive history. The *Birmingham World*, *Kansas City Call*, and the *Sporting News* were consulted. Oral histories from pitcher Bill Powell and infielder Wiley Griggs from the Birmingham Public Library were used, as was an interview with pitcher Sammy C. Williams published by Brent Kelly. Jackie Robinson's infamous Fenway Park tryout with the Boston Red Sox in 1945 is precisely described in Glenn Stout's article "Tryout and Fallout: Race, Jackie Robinson and the Red Sox" (*Massachusetts Historical Review* 6, 2004). Scouting reports of players Willard Brown and Hilton Smith written by Buck O'Neil and can be found on O'Neil's clip file at the Baseball Hall of Fame. Personal interviews with Bill Greason and Jimmy Zapp were also consulted, as was "Slidin' and Ridin': At Home and on the Road with the 1948 Birmingham Black Barons" by Tim Cary (*Alabama Heritage*, Fall 1986).

Chapter 5. "The Best Little Boy Anybody Ever Seen"

Jimmy Zapp and Bill Greason also helped describe the moment when Piper Davis inserted Willie Mays into the starting lineup. Piper's account of how Willie spoke to him about joining the Black Barons is a vital part of his folklore, and is a story he told verbatim to many people and was recounted by Mays in his books. Mays's original 1948 contract can be viewed in the T. H. Hayes Collection, Memphis and Shelby County Room, Memphis Public Library and Information Center. In describing young Mays, *Birmingham World* reporter Ellis Jones was paying attention. The personal observations of Artie Wilson and Bobby Veale are crucial, as are Bill Powell's recorded memories, on file at the Birmingham Public Library.

Chapter 6. Readin' the Hops

Personal interviews with Faye Davis, Bobby Veale, Bill Greason, and Jimmy Zapp were vital to this chapter. Quincy Trouppe described how he tried to sign Mays in *20 Years Too Soon: Prelude to Major-League Integrated Baseball* (St. Louis: Missouri Historical Society Press, 1977, 1995), and Cool Papa Bell described his efforts in a 1970 oral history belonging to the Western Historical Manuscript Collection at the University of Missouri–St. Louis. *The Book of Negro Folklore*, edited by Langston Hughes and Arna Bontemps (New York: Dodd & Mead, 1958) verified Charlie Rudd's story about the slaves in the graveyard. Chris Fullerton's original thesis, Buck O'Neil's scouting reports, and *Coming Through the Fire: Surviving Race and Place in America* by C. Eric Lincoln (Durham, NC: Duke University Press, 1996) helped put the reader on those long road jumps. The *Birmingham World* allowed me to retrace the Black Barons.

Chapter 7. Whammy Alabama

The *Kansas City Call* covered the Monarchs with enough detail to recreate the Black Barons–Monarchs series in Kansas City in August, verifying the smaller accounts in the *Birmingham World*. Bill Greason and Jimmy Zapp, who played in those games, complemented their work with personal interviews, and the first reference from Tom Baird's papers helped describe the Monarchs players. *The Kansas City Monarchs: Champions of Black Baseball* by Janet Bruce (Lawrence: University of Kansas Press, 1985) helped polish my profile of the Monarchs.

Chapter 8. "A Player Who Shouldn't Have Been There"

The *Chicago Defender* and *Birmingham World* were most useful in recapping the last days of the summer of 1948, which allowed for the reconstruction of the events in which Mays first started to be noticed by white teams. Lyman Bostock Jr.'s memories of his father appeared in the *Los Angeles Times*. The oral history with Benjamin Givens was conducted by Ben Cook and belongs to the Birmingham Public Library. Winfield Welch's clip file at the Baseball Hall of Fame was consulted, and conversations with Bobby Veale helped shape the landscape.

Chapter 9. "A Horseshit Scout"

Al LaMacchia's colorful opinion, in his personal interview, of what kind of scout would miss Willie Mays serves as a perfect chapter title, and his descriptions of seventeen-year-old Willie Mays were vivid. The memories of baseball men Lenny Merullo, Bill Wight, and Jerry Stephenson, whose father played for the 1948 white

Barons, helped relive the atmosphere through personal interviews, which were also graciously granted by Lou Johnson. Newspapers consulted were the *New York Times*, *Chicago Defender*, *Birmingham World*, *Baltimore Afro-American*, and *Kansas City Call*. Willard Brown's clip file at the Hall of Fame was useful. Baird's papers were consulted in the discussion of Buck O'Neil and Dizzy Dismukes.

Chapter 10. "Come On, Willie!"
The 1948 Negro American League playoff series between the Monarchs and the Black Barons was carefully reconstructed through the box scores, line scores, game summaries, and full-game stories and commentaries published mostly in the *Kansas City Call*, supplemented by the *Birmingham World* and the *Chicago Defender*. Personal interviews from this series include Artie Wilson, Bill Greason, Jimmy Zapp, and Willie Mays. Wiley Griggs's oral history interview, Baird's comments in his personal letters, and Jim LaMarque's comments to Brent Kelly were useful. *Buck O'Neil: A Baseball Legend* by Sean D. Whitlock (Mattituck, NY: Amereon House, 1994), *I Was Right on Time: My Journey from the Negro Leagues to the Majors* by Buck O'Neil with Steve Wulf and David Conrads (New York: Simon & Schuster, 1996), and *Innings Ago: Recollections by Kansas City Ballplayers of Their Days in the Game* by Jack Etkin (Kansas City: Normandy Square Publications, 1987) were helpful. Piper's "Come on, Willie!" anecdote was quoted in the *San Francisco Chronicle* in 1994.

Chapter 11. "Josh Gibson Is Dead and We Still Can't Beat These Guys"
Four books were valuable for shedding light on the 1948 Negro League World Series between the Black Barons and Homestead Grays: *Buck Leonard: The Black Lou Gehrig; The Hall of Famer's Story in His Own Words* by Buck Leonard with James A. Riley (New York: Carroll & Graf, 1995); *My Life in the Negro Leagues* by Wilmer Fields (Westport, CT: Meckler, 1992); *Catching Dreams: My Life in the Negro Baseball Leagues* by Frazier "Slow" Robinson with Paul Bauer (Syracuse, NY: Syracuse University Press, 1999), and *Beyond the Shadow of the Senators: The Untold Story of the Homestead Grays and the Integration of Baseball* by Brad Snyder (New York: McGraw-Hill, 2003). The *Chicago Defender*, *Kansas City Call*, and *Birmingham World* covered the series in varying degrees of detail. The Hall of Fame's clip files of Grays players Luke Easter and Bob Thurman were helpful. Personal interviews with Greason, Zapp, Sammy C. Williams, and Artie Wilson, as well as Rosengarten's Piper Davis interview, spoke for the Black Barons.

Chapter 12. Somebody Is Always Watching
Scout George Digby's magnificent memory and talent evaluation skill collected in his personal interview were priceless, and were supported by personal interviews with Al LaMacchia, Bob Scranton, Bobby Veale, and Jimmy Zapp. Bill Maughn's professional background was assembled through the *Sporting News* and the *Cullman*

(AL) Democrat and *Cullman Banner*. His quotes originate from his 1965 interview with the *Birmingham News*. The *New York Age* helped support Maughn's assertions about the racial policies of the 1949 Boston Braves. Historian Peter Gorton's collection of newspaper clips relating to former pitcher and scout John Donaldson are culled from several newspapers, and most notably from the *Chicago Defender*. *Time* magazine's 1954 description of Willie Mays missing the bus is the best contemporary account of the incident, but placing it in 1949 was achieved through careful screening of the *Birmingham World*.

Chapter 13. The Goose Shooter

The compilation of one of this book's most research-intensive chapters called upon all forms of sources. Personal interviews with George Genovese, a former Giants scout who managed for Branch Rickey, illuminated the goose shooter method. The Ray Dandridge quotes originated in 1987 in the *Minneapolis Star Tribune*. Willie Mays's quotes are from his 1996 interview with the American Academy of Achievement. The New York Yankees scouting reports from Joe Press were cited in the late 1990s by the *New York Times* and repeated in full in *Pride of October: What It Was to Be Young and a Yankee* by Bill Madden (New York: Warner Books, 2003). The anonymous Yankee scouting report can be read in the files of the Baseball Hall of Fame, where the clip files of Carl Hubbell and Alex Pompez were consulted. The Piper Davis quotes come from his interviews with Rosengarten, Fischer, and Fullerton. The letter confirming the purchase of Piper by the Red Sox belongs to the T. H. Hayes Collection, Memphis and Shelby County Room, Memphis Public Library and Information Center. *What's the Matter with the Red Sox* by Al Hirshberg (New York: Dodd, Mead & Company, 1973) demonstrated Boston's company line. The background of Dick Butler was assembled with the aid of the *Sporting News*, historian John Paul Hill, and numerous national stories about pitcher Paul Pettit as seen in "Deal of the Century" by John Klima in *Best American Sports Writing 2007*, edited by David Maraniss and Glenn Stout (Boston: Houghton Mifflin, 2007). *Ain't Nobody Better Than You: An Autobiography of Joe Black* (Scottsdale, AZ: Ironwood Lithographers, 1983) describes Black's duels with Piper and Bill Greason and his early memories of Mays. Black's former catcher, Roy Campanella, remembered his first look at Mays in 1949 in his *It's Good to Be Alive* (Boston: Signet, 1959). In creating the scene for the 1949 East-West All-Star Game at Chicago's Comiskey Park, the *Chicago Defender* and *Pittsburgh Courier* were vital. The *New York Age*'s box score provided proof that Mays played in the Polo Grounds in 1949 against the New York Cubans and Ray Dandridge, who was purchased after the game in a high-level transaction that indicates key Giant front office personnel scouted Mays a year before they signed him. As always, the *Birmingham World* allowed me to retrace Mays's steps in the crucial summer of 1949, with help from the *Montgomery*

Advertiser. Letters from Tom Hayes and Tom Baird added commentary about different players.

Chapter 14. "Wait until You See Mays"

Artie Wilson's comments are from personal interviews, the *Oakland Tribune*, and oral histories filed at the Baseball Hall of Fame. The portrait of scout Tom Greenwade is drawn from the *Country Gentleman*, July 1942, personal interviews with Al LaMacchia, and the *New York Times* and *New York Daily News*. Tom Hayes's Ku Klux Klan background came to light as a result of Tim Rives's diligent work in "Tom Baird: A Challenge to the Modern Memory of the Kansas City Monarchs," from *Satchel Paige and Company: Essays on the Kansas City Monarchs, Their Greatest Star and the Negro Leagues*, edited by Leslie A. Heaphy (Jefferson, NC: McFarland, 2007). Tom Hayes's papers and Tom Baird's papers were both rigorously consulted. Newspapers consulted to reconstruct Artie Wilson's deal with the Indians were the *Pittsburgh Courier* and the *Sporting News*. Wilson's Hall of Fame clip file was most useful. The *Chicago Defender*, *Birmingham World*, and *Kansas City Call* contributed.

Chapter 15. The Boston Gold Sox

The *Birmingham News* disclosed Joe Cronin's visit to Birmingham a week before Mays's high school graduation, which was determined in the *Birmingham World*. Cronin's visit was confirmed by personal interviews with Bob Scranton. *The Boston Red Sox* edited by Tom Meany (New York: A. S. Barnes and Company, 1956) was consulted. Personal interviews with George Genovese, Paul Pettit, Lenny Yochim, and especially Faye Davis were most useful.

Chapter 16. Miracle in Harlem

Scout George Genovese was a valuable resource in discovering the tactics the Giants front office used. The personal papers of Tom Hayes included the key transaction documents between the Giants and the Black Barons. Alonzo Perry's quotes that appear in this and the next chapter, including the comment that confirmed that Carl Hubbell saw Mays before Ed Montague did, can be found in the *Birmingham News*. Montague's account of Mays's signing was originally written to *Look* magazine and was published in *Willie Mays: My Life In and Out of Baseball* by Willie Mays and Charles Einstein (New York: Dutton, 1966). Montague's claim that he "discovered, found and signed" Mays was quoted in an undated interview Montague recorded for Gerald Tomlinson, property of the Society of American Baseball Research. Background and quotes from Carl Hubbell originate from his clip file at the Baseball Hall of Fame. Writer Arnold Hano's personal notes from his interview with Willie McCovey showed Alex Pompez's Mobile, Alabama, scout to be Jesse Thomas. Tom Baird's letters were again useful. The *Birmingham World*,

New York Amsterdam News, New York Age, New York Times, Chicago Defender, and the *Sporting News* contributed, as did personal interviews with Bobby Veale, Bill Greason, and Jessie Mitchell.

Chapter 17. Take That Glove to the Big Leagues

Artie Wilson's story about how he convinced Leo Durocher to send him to the minors so Mays could come to the majors was first discovered in Jules Tygiel's interview housed at the Baseball Hall of Fame. Other parts of Wilson's quotes were culled from his other oral history on file at the Hall of Fame and subsequently confirmed in personal interviews. Piper Davis told the story about striking out Gene Mauch to Chris Fullerton and the story about giving his glove to Mauch to John Holway. Former Cardinals minor leaguer Ron Smiley wisely saved his spring training manual. Personal interviews with Charles Staniland, Bob Zuk, Bobby Veale, Jim Marshall, George Genovese, and Bill Greason, as well as Tom Baird's letters to Veale, were crucial. Bill Maughn's quotes are from the *Birmingham News* and the *Sporting News.* Other newspapers consulted were the *Birmingham World, New York Age,* and *Chicago Defender.* Baird's letter about Hank Aaron supplemented *Some Are Called Clowns: A Season with the Last of the Great Barnstorming Baseball Teams* by Bill Heward with Dmitri V. Gat (New York: Thomas Y. Crowell Company, 1974) and *I Had a Hammer: The Hank Aaron Story* by Hank Aaron with Lonnie Wheeler (New York: HarperCollins, 1991). The Boston Braves party line was set by *The Braves: The Pick and the Shovel* by Al Hirshberg (Boston: Waverly House, 1948). The Ray Dandridge quotes appeared in the *Minneapolis Star Tribune.*

INDEX

NOTE: Page references in *italics* refer to photos.